PERSEPHONE'S QUEST

Persephone Gathering Wild Flowers
Wall painting from Stabiæ. Naples, Museo Nazionale.

PERSEPHONE'S QUEST:
Entheogens and the Origins of Religion

R. Gordon Wasson, Stella Kramrisch,
Jonathan Ott, and Carl A. P. Ruck

YALE UNIVERSITY PRESS
New Haven and London

This book originally appeared in a privately printed edition
in a larger format.

Printed in the United States of America.

Library of Congress catalog card number: 87-51547
International standard book number: 0-300-03877-1 (cloth)
0-300-05266-9 (pbk.)

A catalogue record for this book is available from the British Library.

The paper in this book meets the guidelines for permanence and durability of the Committee on Production Guidelines for Book Longevity of the Council on Library Resources.

6 8 10 9 7 5

'*We have no knowledge . . . but what has been built up by pleasure, and exists in us by pleasure alone . . . The knowledge both of the Poet and the Man of Science is pleasure.*' Wordsworth's insistence in the 1802 preface to the *Lyrical Ballads* on the inseparable association of knowledge and pleasure takes us straight to a profound conjunction in the work of scientist and creative writer . . . The 'happy ending' of successful theorizing, satisfactory experiment, achieved work of art, creates pleasure. And so does the process, or story, of discovery.

Gillian Beer, TLS, *2 Nov. 1984, p. 1255*

TABLE OF CONTENTS

PART ONE

Entheogens and the Origins of Religion

Page

Prelude 16

CHAPTER 1

Persephone's Quest *by R. Gordon Wasson* 17

Interlude 30

Our discoveries: 1. Soma and the Vedic Culture 32. 2. The Mystery of Eleusis 33. 3. Our first *Velada* 33. 4. The *Grecas* 38. 5. The New World and the Thunderbolt 45. 6. The Meaning of *Kakuljá Huracan* 47. 7. A Glimpse of the Domestic Use of Soma 54. 8. The Chinese and the Nivkhi 57. 9. Greece and Soma 60. 10. Soma among the Mediaeval 'Monsters' 63. 11. The Chukotka 68. 12. The Fool's Mushroom 68. 13. 'Happiness Mushroom' 72. 14. The British and the 'Nameless Mushroom' 73. 15. The Vikings and Soma 74. 16. The Tree of the Knowledge of Good and Evil 74.

Epilogue: the Age of the Entheogens 78

Unfinished Business 81

CHAPTER 2

Lightningbolt and Mushrooms *by R. Gordon Wasson* 83

CHAPTER 3

The Mahāvīra Vessel and the Plant Pūtika *by Stella Kramrisch* 95

The Secret of the cut-off Heads 95

The Elixir of Life: Soma and Pūtika 102

Putka and the Santal of Eastern Bihar 106

The Mahāvīra Vessel 109

The later and separate Lives of Mahāvīra and Pūtika 112

CHAPTER 4

The Last Meal of the Buddha *by R. Gordon Wasson* 117

What was *Sūkara-Maddava*? 117

The Santal and the *Putka* 123

The Buddha's Last Meal 132
The Indus Valley and Kashmir 134
Memorandum by Walpola Rāhula on the early Sources for the Meaning of Sūkaramaddava 137
Epilogue 138

CHAPTER 5

Carved 'Disembodied Eyes' of Teotihuacan *by Jonathan Ott* 141

PART TWO

Poets, Philosophers, Priests: Entheogens in the Formation of the Classical Tradition

by Carl A. P. Ruck

CHAPTER 6

Mushrooms and Philosophers 151
Shade-foots 151
The Scene of Necromancy 152
Peisander and the Affair of the Profanations 153
The Swamp of Dionysus 156
Tongue-in-Bellies and Revealers 157
Socrates as Profaner of the Mysteries 159
Mushrooms 160
Aja Ekapād 165
Prometheus as Shade-foot and the Theft of Fire 169
Philosophers 176

CHAPTER 7

The Wild and the Cultivated: Wine in Euripides' *Bacchae* 179
The Discovery of Wine 180
The Reconciliation with Primitivism 191
The Making of Wine 194
The mad Ring and the God 198
Double Birth and the God's Surrogate 200
The first Birth 202
The second Birth 209
The Paradigm of Actaeon 210

The Regression of Cadmean Thebes 212
From Pollution to Fertility 216
Toward an Understanding of Tragedy 219

Chapter 8

The Offerings from the Hyperboreans 225
Introduction 225
The Route for the Offerings 226
Hyperboreans 227
The Garden of Apollo 230
Lycians 233
Apollo 236
Sacrifice 238
Thargelia 240
Soma 248
Daphnephoria 249
The Secret Offering 250

Notes on the Essays in this Book 257

LIST OF ILLUSTRATIONS

CHAPTER ONE

Page

Wall Painting from Stabiae. Naples, Museo Nazionale. Frontispiece

Fig. 1 Aurelio Carreras, *Sabio*, and his son Mauro, 5 July 1955. 34

Fig. 2 Archaic Greek amphora, found at Eleusis. 38

Fig. 3 Copper swastikas, found in Hopewell mounds of Ohio, *ca* AD 500. 39

Fig. 4 A bee goddess with animals, birds, and swastikas, found in Boeotia, dating from *ca* BC 700. Gimbutas: 'Old Europe'. 40

Fig. 5 'Old Europe': Marija Gimbutas. Map of Old Europe; with '*grecas*' or frets, found there that date from BC 5000 to BC 3500. 42/43

Fig. 6 A farmer's cottage in Orissa, India, in Santal country. 44

Fig. 7 Aristeo Matías, *Sabio*, center; Roberto Weitlaner, right; interpreter, left. 45

Fig. 8 *Terra cotta* figurines suggestive of Soma, *ca* AD 100, from Mexico, discovered by Peter T. Furst. 51

Fig. 9 The Black Tezcatlipoca, in aspect of Huitzilopochtli: he is uniped, '*hurakan*'. 52

Fig. 10 Iambe-Baubo Figures, *Terra cotta*, Priene, Asia Minor. V century BC. 63

Fig. 11 'Monsters' representing Soma, frequently reproduced in manuscripts and early printed books of western Europe. a. Single-footed man b. Cyclopes c. 'Tongue-in-Belly' d. Drawing of group with other 'Monsters'. e. Scenes from mediaeval manuscript of Marco Polo's travels f. Reproduction of the 'Folk with but One Foot' from *The Travels of Sir John Mandeville, Kt.* 65/67

Fig. 12 Map of the Chukotka region and chart of mushroom shapes. 69

Fig. 13 N. N. Dikov, copying petroglyphs and view of mushroom carvings. 70

Fig. 14 One-sided man, or 'unilateral figure', or 'halfling'. 80

CHAPTER FIVE

Fig. 1 'Predella' from Zacuala, Teotihuacan, repainted by the late Abel Mendoza. 141

Fig. 2 Drops of entheogenic potion with appended 'disembodied eyes' from Teotihuacan murals. 141

Fig. 3 and 4. Drops of entheogenic potion and appended 'disembodied eyes' issuing from entheogenic flowers. 142

Fig. 5 Gold ring of Isopata near Knossos, greatly enlarged. Scene depicts epiphany of goddess (presumably Artemis) on the right, and four worshippers, all represented as anthropomorphic bees. 142

Fig. 6 Looking north at Teotihuacan, with Pyramid of the Moon at right and Palace of Quetzalpapálotl at left in foreground. 143

Fig. 7 Entrance to Palace of Quetzalpapálotl at Teotihuacan. 144

Fig. 8 Column showing Quetzalpapálotl chimera and 'disembodied eyes'. 144

Fig. 9 Closeup of 'disembodied eye' from column. 145

Fig. 10 Closeup of 'disembodied eyes'. 145

Fig. 11 West column with frontal view of avian creature and 'disembodied eyes'. 145

Fig. 12 West side of courtyard, showing columns surmounted by painted lintel and carved stone 'combs'. 146

PART ONE

Entheogens and the Origins of Religion

Prelude

In the opening chapter of my SOMA *I said that there always hovered in my mind's eye the admonitory finger of Tristram Shandy's warning against the occupational hazard of those who advance hypotheses:*

> It is in the nature of a hypothesis when once a man has conceived it, that it assimilates everything to itself, as proper nourishment, and from the first moment of your begetting it, it generally grows stronger by everything you see, hear or understand.

I was reasonably sure of my ground but also I knew how fallible I was, and I added Laurence Sterne's danger sign, in case I had committed a blunder. Nevertheless now it turns out that I was right the first time, and I present this book with the proofs from various angles corroborating each other. We are well beyond the stage of hypotheses.

R. G. W

CHAPTER ONE

PERSEPHONE'S QUEST

by R. Gordon Wasson

As I am nearing the end of my days, I will draw up an account of our mushroom quest, Valentina Pavlovna my late Russian wife's and mine, followed by the highlights of our discoveries as I see them.

THE QUEST

Back in 1921 I fell in love with a Russian girl, Valentina Pavlovna, in London, where she was studying medicine. We got married at the end of 1926 in England and came to America where she requalified as a physician. I was a newspaper man covering the Wall Street bank-run for the old *Herald Tribune*. We took our delayed honeymoon late in August 1927 in Big Indian, the Catskills, in a chalet lent to us by Adam Dingwall, a publisher. On our first day, after lunch, we went for a walk, down a path that led by a pond and then a clearing on the right, and, on the left, the upward slope of a forested mountain. We were hand in hand and a picture of bliss. Suddenly, before I knew it, my bride threw down my hand roughly and ran up into the forest, with cries of ecstasy. She had seen toadstools growing, many kinds of toadstools. She had not seen the like since Russia, since 1917. She was in a delirium of excitement and began gathering them right and left in her skirt. From the path I called to her, admonished her not to gather them: they were toadstools, I said, they were poisonous. 'Come back, come back to me!', I pleaded. She laughed the merrier and continued picking, as it seemed to me indiscriminately. To make a long story short, we had our first marital crisis. During our five year engagement mushrooms had never come up between us and here she was possessed by the mushrooms! Our walk ended then and there, she with her skirt full of mushrooms of various kinds. Some she put into the soup when she prepared our supper, others with the steak, others she strung together carefully by the stipes and hung out to dry in the sun, for use in winter, she said. I was beside myself. I acted the perfect Anglo-Saxon oaf confronting a wood nymph I had never before laid eyes on. I would eat nothing with mushrooms in it. Later she said I had predicted I should wake up the next day a widower, but I have always denied this allegation.

We checked the attitude to mushrooms with our respective friends, – mine Anglo-Saxon mycophobes, hers Russian mycophiles. Then we looked at the vocabularies: the English use three working words, – first and foremost the 'toadstool' (with no translation in Russian), then a Latin quasi-scientific term, 'fungus', and third the uncertainly defined 'mushroom' borrowed from the French *mousseron*. The Russian vocabulary was endless.

Well, we were off. Our primary preoccupation was with our careers, hers in medicine; mine in Wall Street. Our secondary avocation was mushrooms, gathering notes of all kinds, in various languages, stopping on our travels to talk, preferably with professors or unlettered peasants. Then, late in the 1930's, we held a fateful meeting to decide our course of action, either to launch a systematic and massive assault on many fronts, or abandon the quest entirely. At that meeting we made a discovery to our mutual surprise. Each of us had harbored a nascent thought that we had been too shy to express even to each other: religion possibly underlay the myco–philia/phobia contrast that marked the peoples of Europe. This religious twist struck us as absurd, yet we agreed that the evidence pointed in that direction. If religion it was, it had to date back to prehistory, and as for us, we had to try and write a book.

A little thing, some of my readers will say, this difference in emotional attitude toward wild mushrooms. Yet my wife and I did not think so, and we devoted a part of our leisure hours for more than thirty years to dissecting it, defining it, and tracing it to its origin. Such discoveries as we have made, including our documentation of the religious role of the entheogenic mushrooms by the Algonkian nation in North America[1] and the Maya in Mesoamerica,[2] by the identification of the sacred Soma of the Aryans as *Amanita muscaria*, and the religious use of the same species of mushroom by the most ancient tribes in the northern wastes of Siberia, in short the religious use of *A. muscaria* around the globe, can be laid to our preoccupation with that cultural rift between my wife and me, between our respective peoples, between the mycophilia and mycophobia (words that we devised for the two attitudes) that divide the Indo-European peoples into two camps. Moreover this religious role of *A. muscaria* is accompanied by a startling identity of vocabulary, of religious observances, that bespeak a trait going back for tens of thousands of years, when the virtue of the sacred fungus was first discovered, somewhere in Eurasia.

1. Keewaydinoquay: *Puhpohwee for the People: A narrative account of Some Uses of Fungi among the Anishinaubeg*, Botanical Museum of Harvard University, Cambridge, Mass., Feb. 1978. Ethnomycological Studies No. 5; R. Gordon Wasson: 'Traditional Use in North America of *Amanita muscaria* for Divinatory Purposes', *J. of Psychedelic Drugs*, v. 11 (1-2) Jan-June 1979.

2. *Infra*, p 47 *et seq.*

If this hypothesis of ours be wrong, then it must have been a singular false hypothesis to have produced the results that it has. But it is not wrong. Thanks to the immense strides made in the study of the human psyche in this century, we are now all aware that deep-seated emotional attitudes acquired in early life are of profound importance. I suggest that when such traits betoken the attitudes of whole tribes or peoples, and when those traits have remained unaltered throughout recorded history, and especially when they differ from one people to another neighboring people, then you are face to face with a phenomenon of profound cultural importance, whose primal cause is to be discovered only in the well-springs of cultural history.

The next event, momentous for the success of our fungal enterprise, was our encounter with Roman Jakobson, Russian refugee lately arrived on our shores, prodigious scholar, breath-taking lecturer, bon vivant. We met him in the early '40's and disclosed to him our feeling about the religious role played by mushrooms in the prehistoric background of the European peoples. His response bowled us over. The thought had never occurred to him, but his instinct told him we were right. He could not contain his enthusiasm for our idea. We became fast friends: he and his wife often dined with us and we with them. A Russian friend of ours, Katya Ladyzhinskaya, a colleague of my wife's, became tired of hearing us praise Roman's qualities so highly and we challenged her to attend a lecture of his, any lecture. She did so one afternoon on Morningside Heights. Before entering the lecture room, Katya looked at the announcement on the bulletin board. The lecture, to last a double period, one hour and forty minutes, was to be 'On the third person singular of the Russian verb'. 'Goody, goody', Katya said to herself in Russian, 'I've won my case. No one could make that subject interesting, let alone for a double period.' She entered the lecture hall just before Roman arrived. He launched into his theme immediately. She quickly found herself sitting on the edge of her chair, spellbound by his lecture and by his command of the classic Russian language, and so she remained till the end of the double period. He was incomparable. She telephoned us later that she had to come to dine with us and surrender. . . . Such was Roman.

So long as they were in New York we saw much of the Jakobsons. He moved to Harvard, later to M.I.T. This took us to Cambridge often, and he would stop sometimes with us when he came to New York. He fed us ideas about mushrooms continually, citations in books, proper names in Russian derived from the mushrooms, rare and archaic mushroom names in Russian with their etymologies. With Roman spurring us on, we never more considered dropping our mushroomic theme.

Full of years, Roman died on 18 July 1982, and at his funeral friends, admirers, scholars, from all over the country – California, Texas, *etc* – gathered in the Russian Orthodox Church in Boston to do him honor.

*

In the 1940's we felt increasingly the need of a mycologist to be our guide in the arduous discipline of mycology. I had been reading the *Revue de Mycologie*, drawn to it by its surprising interest in aspects of mushrooms of a nature that goes far beyond the usual preoccupation of the professional mycologist. The editor of the *Revue* was Roger Heim, *directeur* of the *Laboratoire de Cryptogamie, membre de l'Académie des Sciences*, destined to be chosen *Directeur* of the *Muséum National d'Histoire Naturelle* in 1951 and to be elected for a term *Président* of the *Académie des Sciences* in 1963. In the spring of 1949 I was in Paris and I decided to invite Heim to be our guide in mycology. As I climbed the steps to enter his *Laboratoire* I asked myself what my reception would be. A colleague of his whom I had just met that day had volunteered to 'phone him and say that I would call. When I was announced, he came out of his laboratory to the elevator door and welcomed me. We hit it off immediately. I outlined to him what Tina and I were doing and what we needed: a mycologist to consult on themes both simple and remote. I added that I wished to illustrate our forthcoming book with the mushroom watercolors of the late Henri Fabre and asked how I could win permission to do so. It turned out that they were now owned by the French state and lay under Heim's jurisdiction in Fabre's *harmas*, in Sérignan, four kilometers from Avignon! (*Harmas* means in Provençal any arid little property. Fabre had bought an *harmas* but under his loving care the arid little property had become a luxurious tropical garden, but still called 'Fabre's *harmas*.) We arranged that I would come back shortly with Tina and our daughter Masha and we would all drive south together, to the *harmas* of Henri Fabre. This plan we put into effect soon thereafter, stopping on the way south in Vienne, on the Rhone, to have dinner *chez Point*, already sporting three stars in the Michelin. We chose our illustrations in the working laboratory of Fabre.

On 19 September 1952 I received an envelope from Robert Graves in Majorca with a clipping of the house organ of Ciba's U. S. subsidiary making known that one Richard Evans Schultes, Professor of Botany at Harvard and shortly to become Director of the Botanical Museum there, had published two papers containing the startling news that a mushroom cult had been reported by the sixteenth century friars in Mexico and also that Schultes had brought back from Mexico specimens of the entheogenic mushrooms! On the same day, Friday 19 September, I 'phoned Schultes and though he knew as little about me as I knew about him, we talked for a long time. He had been alerted by Blas Pablo Reko to the survival of the cult in a remote village in the State of Oaxaca, and he invited Reko to go with him to the Indian village, Huautla de Jiménez, in 1937. Schultes returned to Huautla again in 1938 and also in 1939. He published two papers on his discoveries, one a Harvard *Botanical Museum Leaflet* in 1939, the other an article in the *American Anthropologist* in 1940. Tina and I resolved to visit the village in the rainy season of 1953 with our daughter Masha. I naturally cultivated the acquaintance of Schultes and we became friends. Until the following June Tina and I were reading the narratives of the sixteenth century friars who accompanied the Conquerors in Mexico, giving their observations on the native way of life. In Mexico we leaned on Roberto Weitlaner and his daughter Irmgard, veterans in knowing how to behave with the natives. (Reko, after writing me one most helpful letter, had died that spring.)

Over the years Professor Schultes has done well by me, arranging for the President and Fellows of Harvard College to appoint me to an honorary post on the faculty of the Botanical Museum in 1960 and renewed through the years, a post that I still hold. This has given me the privilege of contributing to the Harvard *Botanical Museum Leaflets*, and helped me much when I spent years in the Far East in the 1960's. He has conferred on me a room in the Botanical Museum to house my books, slides, files, and collection of valuable mushroom artifacts, designated as 'The Tina and Gordon Wasson Ethnomycological Collection'.

And so we made the first of ten annual visits to Mexico, exploring the villages of Oaxaca and of the other states thereabouts, where many native tribal languages were living tongues. On our pressing invitation Roger Heim came over and joined us in 1956, 1959, and 1961. We made notable visits to the Chatino country, to the Mixe where we were lavishly entertained by the notorious *cacique* don Luis Rodríguez but where we learned that he penalized any native (no laughing matter!) who would take the entheogenic mushrooms, and of course repeatedly to Huautla de Jiménez (and there discovered the *Sabia* María Sabina), destined to become the Mecca of entheogenic mushroom hunters.

Meanwhile a terrible tragedy was taking place. In 1956 Tina's health began to fail. We precipitated work on our book: it was to include our first reports on our Mexican findings. The work, *Mushrooms Russia & History*, was brought out on May 13, 1957, – 512 copies in two large octavo volumes stunningly illustrated and printed by Giovanni Mardersteig in Verona, on the finest paper, boxed, at $125. It was published by Kurt and Helen Wolff. Simultaneously *Life* in the issue of May 13 featured an adventure story that I wrote on our discoveries. (Harry Luce gave orders that not a word of my text was to be altered.) The price of our books rose slowly in the auction market and among antiquarian bookdealers until, years later, a high of $2,600 was established. The price is now (December 1983) down: an antiquarian bookdealer in Los Angeles is offering a set at $1,750. My wife's health grew worse and she died of cancer on the last day of 1958 in the evening. Heim and I had been working hard on a book to be published by the *Muséum*, also a large octavo handsomely illustrated, *Les Champignons hallucinogènes du Mexique*. It was dated 1958 but appeared early in 1959. Without telling me, Heim had dedicated the volume to the memory of Valentina Pavlovna and signed the dedication with his initials and mine. Heim's *Préface*, five pages long, was a warm tribute to us both.

In 1963 Heim flew to New Guinea, he from Paris, and I by freighter from San Pedro, Cal., to look into the 'mushroom madness' of the Kumá people, on which we reported in a paper, 'La Folie des Kumá', published in French in the *Cahiers du Pacifique*, and also in English in the Harvard *Botanical Museum Leaflets*, Vol. XXI, No. 1, June 11, 1965. In 1968, again on my invitation, Heim from Paris and I from New York took planes to Calcutta, where we met on the Dum Dum airport landing field. This time we were to visit the Santal villages in Orissa and the Santal Parganas in Bihar. We were seeking an answer to the strange fact that a mushroom, one single species, the *putka*, was 'animate' in their language, was 'endowed with a soul', like all animals and human beings, but unlike all other vegetation, which is construed grammatically as 'inanimate', as 'without a soul'. Heim identified scientifically the *putka* but no one could tell us why it alone in the plant world enjoyed its enviable distinction. It was not entheogenic. Our prize informant in the Santal Parganas, Ludgi Marndi, gave us a hint on our last day in Dumka, shortly before we left. We had solicited the talk and we covered the same ground as before. We were getting nowhere. Suddenly our informant leaned over the table and said in a whisper to Mrs Strønstad, the wife of the missionary who served as our translator, 'I will tell you why I think the *putka* has a soul'. We too leaned over the table. She went on, 'You must eat the mushrooms quickly, for if you don't they will stink like a cadaver'. We knew not what this meant, but I wrote it down in my notebook. We published a paper on this anomalous situation in the *Cahiers du Pacifique*, 'Les *Putka* des Santals champignons doués d'une âme', No. 14, September 1970. The mystery baffled us for several years, until one day we received a telephone call from Professor Stella Kramrisch, the famous Indologist and authority on Indian art, who had come upon our French article, read it, and perceived at once that the *putka* was derived from the Sanskrit *pūtika*, the name of a plant never theretofore identified that the Aryans had used as the first surrogate for Soma. What a powerful argument this was for our candidate for Soma, that its surrogate turned out to be another mushroom! Furthermore this other mushroom, the *pūtika*, gave off a bad odor just as the *putka* of the Santal does, after a matter of hours, thus clinching its identity! (*Pūtika* is the same word as our 'putrid'.) Its bad odor served a purpose in the Pravargya sacrifice, when the clay of the Mahāvīra pot was mixed with the mushrooms and then was fired and the smell burned away! It was a mushroom whose identity had been lost for three millennia! Our trip half-way around the world to the Santal country thus proved in the end richly rewarding.

On all our trips Roger Heim was the best of traveling companions, whether to remote places or in big cities. He entertained me when I was in Paris and I played the host when he was in New York. On our journeys to far parts, each of us paid his own way.

There was another great scholar that I must dwell on, who led us to make our Santal trip. I had told Roman I intended to visit Afghanistan after I retired in 1963 and specifically Nuristan and the Hindu Kush. He said I had to meet Professor Georg Morgenstierne of Oslo University. I went to Oslo, was charmed by his graciousness and by his lively interest in my search for the identity of Soma, and discovered that he would like to go to Afghanistan in the spring and summer of 1964. He specialized in the five languages spoken in the Hindu Kush that he said split off from the root stock of common Indo-European even before Sanskrit. He knew those languages better than any other scholar, but he knew well the whole medley of languages spoken in Afghanistan, and the Dardic group in west Pakistan, also Sanskrit with its prolific progeny. He was such a winning person and knew so much about languages! It was he who had told me, since I was specially interested in mushrooms, about the *putka* of the Santal, and got me a copy of Bodding's five hefty volume dictionary of the Santal language where I could read about the *putka*. He was able to tell me about Faroese and Frisian and Tadzhikistan! He gave me a key passage in the Avesta that strengthened my case for my identification of Soma. Traveling with him in Nuristan, to Kamdesh and Bagramatal, was one of the richest experiences of my life.

*

And so we completed ten trips in the rainy season to parts of Mexico that were among the most interesting, parts never visited by tourists or trippers. On our tenth trip, in 1962, I was accompanied by Albert Hofmann, the Swiss chemist, specialist in the alkaloids of ergot of rye, the discoverer of LSD, and his wife Anita. He had analysed our *Psilocybe* mushrooms and I also had sent him from Mexico the seeds of the two species of entheogenic morning-glories. He was amazed to discover that these phanerogams produced chemicals of the same family as our Mexican mushrooms, as well as ergot, and when he presented a paper setting forth that fact to an assembly of chemists in Australia, they had been plainly incredulous! Mushrooms are of a lower order of plant life and their chemistry had been considered of necessity distinct. On our Mexican excursion in 1962 we visited the Mazatec country, entering the area on 30 September with animals from Jalapa de Díaz, spending that night in La Providencia, reaching Ayautla on 1 October. We stayed in the inn of doña Donata, who served us her delicious rural Mexican fare, going on to San Miguel on 5 October, and then the next day passing down to San José Tenango. Finally we backtracked and climbed up to Huautla de Jiménez where we stayed until the 13th, the Hofmanns coming to know the *Sabia* María Sabina. They formally presented her with a bottle of synthetic psilocybin pills and she performed for them a *velada* where she took the pills rather than the mushrooms!

I have one more publication to report in the Mexican field. In 1958 I taped a complete ceremony of María Sabina's *velada*, as we have come to call the customary night-time session. A boy about 17 years old had contracted a serious illness when working down in the hot country: something was gravely wrong with his liver or kidney. María Sabina would devote her healing *velada* to asking the mushrooms whether the boy would live or die, and if he was to live, what he should do to recover. The verdict however was that the boy had to die: within weeks he was dead. It took us some fifteen years to publish the *velada*, in Mazatec, in Spanish, and in English, the English and Spanish texts being translated from the Mazatec directly by George and Florence Cowan, experts in the Mazatec language, and printed in parallel columns with numbered lines. They proof-read the Mazatec and added notes, and an essay on the Mazatec language with its oddities. We invoked the help of Willard Rhodes, Professor emeritus of Music at Columbia University and Director emeritus of the Center for Studies in Ethnomusicology. He wrote out the entire musical score and was in charge of its printing. I described the setting for the rite. We gave over the left hand page to the Mazatec text and printed the text in English and Spanish on the right hand page in parallel columns. Rhodes prepared sections of comment on the work, and many others contributed notes for relevant texts. We ran Allan Richardson's photographs assembled in sequence.

So far as I am aware, no one has paid the slightest attention to *María Sabina and her Mazatec Mushroom Velada,* but I am prouder of it than of anything else I have done. I think it was the first time a shamanic performance had been fully taped and published in the native language with musical score and editorial comments.

⋆

Just as the '50's were devoted to our studies of the entheogens of Mexico, the '60's were dedicated to Soma, a plant that the Aryans when they moved into the Indus Valley in the second millennium BC, were worshipping as a god. They elaborated an extraordinary culture, their society divided into castes, and the Brahmans, the superior caste of priests, were the custodians of the secrets of Soma. Over centuries and in different centers they composed a collection of 1028 hymns in their Sanskrit language and as they had no method of writing, of course they learned to sing them by heart. The collection was called the *Rig Veda* and the *Rig Veda* was permeated by Soma. From the hymns it was clear that the Soma was pressed, then mixed with other ordinary potable fluids such as milk but *not* alcohol, and drunk by the Brahmans and perhaps a few others, who thereupon passed some hours in what we now call the bliss of an entheogenic experience. The late Louis Renou, a great Vedist, one of the foremost that the world has produced, once wrote that the whole of the *Rig Veda* was summed up *in nuce* in Soma. But its identity was never explicitly disclosed, and *no Sanskrit scholar had sought its identity.*

I recalled in the course of my inquiries concerning the Aryans that my father, who had studied Sanskrit briefly in the 1880's, had told me about the mystery of Soma. In the light of our Mexican discoveries, I was now asking myself whether Soma could have been a mushroom. I said to myself that inevitably the poets would introduce into their hymns innumerable hints for the identification of the celebrated Soma, not of course to help us, millennia later and thousands of miles away, but as their poetic inspiration freely dictated.

However, I felt the need of a Sanskrit student versed in the *Rig Veda* to consult at every step. I reported to Roman Jakobson on my need and he introduced me to Daniel H. H. Ingalls, Wales Professor of Sanskrit in Harvard. Ingalls wrote me that there was one student of his, a doctoral candidate, who would be ideal but she was much too deeply involved in living and would never accept. There was another student whom he would approach, if I wished. I asked him why he declined on behalf of the ideal student, not allowing her to decline: why make up her mind for her? He asked her and she accepted instantly and with enthusiasm.

Wendy Doniger was outstanding in many ways. She was young, stunningly beautiful, smartly dressed, gracious; conversant with Latin, Greek, German, French, Russian to come, and of course at home in Sanskrit. She was an extraordinarily speedy worker, prompt in replying to letters, single-spacing her typewritten replies on postcards, filling the available postcard space to the final fraction of an inch, where her final sentence seemed always to finish with a graceful flourish. (Her typewriter permitted her to type to the very bottom line!) Our friendship was chiefly by correspondence, New York⟷Harvard, later New York⟷Oxford. When I was with her she seized my questions before I had finished asking them. She took her doctor's degrees at Harvard and Oxford, then went for a year to Russia where she made cordial friendships with the Toporovs, he a leading Indo-European scholar and she the outstanding Vedic scholar in Russia – and Wendy learned a substantial amount of Russian. After teaching a few years in the London School of Oriental and African Studies, and after that in the University of California, she is now at the University of Chicago Divinity School where she is professor of the History of Religion and of Indian Studies.

I asked Wendy to write the history of Soma from the time when it was abandoned down to date. Strangely, this had never been done. For my reading only, she prepared such a survey quickly. I then suggested that, using her paper as a draft, she write Part II of *SOMA: Divine Mushroom of Immortality*, 'The Post-Vedic History of the Soma Plant'.

Here I must mention the one setback that I have had in our Soma researches: the death, premature and tragic, of Louis Renou. I visited him twice in Paris, where on a later occasion Professor Heim and I had dinner with him and Mme Renou, and they were my hosts for a weekend at their Normandy retreat. He was obviously one of the supreme Vedists of our time: there is no one left in France to compare with him. In his correspondence with Daniel H. H. Ingalls, he was so open to new ideas. He is greatly missed. All of my exchanges with him were years before our *SOMA* appeared.

At the end of 1968 or the beginning of 1969 our *SOMA* finally appeared, Wendy Doniger O'Flaherty writing Part II and I the rest. I supervised the translations that finish the book. We both made endless suggestions to each other, all of them received gratefully and considered, and some even incorporated! The Sanskrit faculties of the world were not ready for a book identifying Soma: they had never heard of anyone who had even thought of tackling this. Most of them were unprepared by training or instinct for botanical arguments and they had, each of them, their own exegetical problems on their desks. What would they do when letters came asking their opinion about *SOMA*? I know that many of them simply referred the inquirer to thirty pages of congested type of a review article in the *Bulletin* of the London School of Oriental and African Studies, Vol. 34, Part 2, 1971, and espoused the writer's views. Written by John Brough, Professor of Sanskrit to the University of Cambridge, an outstanding exegete of Sanskrit and kindred tongues, his views were unfavorable. He had never heard of me, nor had he ever tried to identify Soma. Vedic scholars who were shocked by our *SOMA* rallied behind the eminent Brough: even though few if any read him, they endorsed him unread. I did read him, every page of his congested type, and found it weak, unworthy of this eminent authority.

Brough decided to cross the Atlantic with Mrs Brough after his critique had appeared, ostensibly to visit his brother in Tarrytown; he wrote me that they would like to call on me in Danbury. I invited them to lunch with me on Sunday, 8 August 1971. The weather was at its best and we had a lovely lunch together on my garden porch. At the end of lunch he presented me with an offprint of his review, 'With compliments'. Though I knew it was coming and the tenor of its argument, I had not seen it. In 1972 I published my *Rejoinder*.

Early in 1984 in his home town of Bishop's Stortford Dr. Brough was struck by a car and instantly killed. This was a blow to me. That he had crossed the ocean with his wife really to present his review article to me had impressed me greatly, and his geniality capped his visit mightily. I was convinced that in the end I would convert him, and in this book we have mobilized evidence that sums up to proof. Our progress has gone far beyond our initial hopes, discovering as we have done a whole chapter in prehistory never before suspected to exist. Our subject turned out to be the entheogens, primarily but not solely the fungal entheogens: the phanerogams were important also. But Soma turned out to have had the longest and most widespread human history. Ergot, growing millennia later on certain cultivated grains, seems to have coincided in its arrival on the human stage with the discovery by Man of agriculture. Our remote unlettered ancestors, characterized by us as 'savages' from the lofty eminence of our own conceit, knew how to cope with these miraculous entheogens, not talking noisily and ignorantly about them as some of us do, until I virtually despair of our technicians ever being able to explore thoroughly their possibilities. Competent teams fear to be linked unjustly to the 'Drug' abuse.

Three of us have written another book, this time a small one for a change: *The Road to Eleusis: Unveiling the Secret of the Mysteries*, by R. G. W., Albert Hofmann, and Carl A. P. Ruck, Professor of Greek in Boston University. It came about thus.

One day in July 1975 I asked my house guest, Albert Hofmann, when we were visiting together on my studio porch, whether Early Man in Ancient Greece could have derived an entheogen from the ergot that would have given him an experience comparable to LSD or psilocybin. He said he would reflect on my question and when he had thought it through, he would send me his reply.

As Albert well knew, my thought was to arrive at the active agent in the potion drunk at Eleusis, and that gave to Eleusis immense prestige over the whole of the known world in antiquity. About two years later he wrote me that, yes, Early Man in Ancient Greece could have worked out a potion with the desired effect from the ergot of wheat or barley cultivated on the famous Rarian plain adjacent to Eleusis; or indeed from the ergot of a grass, called *Paspalum distichum*, that grows around the Mediterranean. If the Greek herbalists had the intelligence and resourcefulness of their Mesoamerican counterparts, they would have had no difficulty in preparing an entheogenic potion: so said Albert Hofmann and he explained why. Just as I received that answer from Albert, I came to know Carl A. P. Ruck, and I invoked his indispensable help in writing our book. This was a providential encounter for me. He was a brilliant Greek scholar and specialized in the role played by botany in ancient Greek life and he proved a marvelous partner in our enterprise. Our volume came out in 1978, published by Harcourt Brace Jovanovich as a Helen and Kurt Wolff book, written by the three of us. Dr. Danny Staples composed for us a new translation of the *Homeric Hymn to Demeter*. So far as we could see our new book had no impact. The Greek departments both in American and British Universities seem intellectually inert. (Ruck was certainly not 'intellectually inert'! He was the exception.) One well known English professor of Greek burst out in anger at our saying that a potent potion was drunk at Eleusis: we had touched him at a sensitive spot. He seemed to wish to join the class of those pastors in our Bible Belt who, when Prohibition was flying high, seriously pretended that Jesus served grape juice, not wine, at his Last Supper! Why do he and many colleagues of his feed such patent pabulum to their students? Greek studies would be far more exciting if the students were taught Greek history as it was. It is astonishing that no students rebel against their teachers on an issue such as this. Today we know much more than we did previously about the mighty entheogen and the role it played in prehistory, and also for a millennium and more in Early Greek History.

I cannot refrain from citing, if but briefly, two other Sanskrit scholars who have meant much to me, not only for their help but for the spirit behind that help.

Sir Harold W. Bailey, who is about my age, has been encouraging from the start. I have sought his aid when I needed guidance, by letter and when I called on him repeatedly in Cambridge. Until his retirement he was the Professor of Sanskrit to the University of Cambridge. When he came to New York to deliver some lectures a few years ago, I had the privilege of entertaining him over a weekend. His knowledge has always seemed to me fabulous.

One day in the middle '60's I found myself in Poona, and I put up for the night in the American Institute of Indian Studies. There was only one other guest. In India I did not normally discuss my mission with strangers. But this scholar, Henry von Stietencron, was so engaging and obviously knew so much about India that I broke my rule. He was fascinated by my interest in Soma and asked me endless questions. His University connection was at Heidelberg, to be changed in a couple of years when he was appointed successor to the famous Paul Thieme who had graced for many years the Sanskrit Chair in Tübingen University, in the heart of idyllic Swabia. Henry and his lovely family have made me welcome in Heidelberg and later in Tübingen.

Let me add, before I end this initial stretch of my essay, that my practice, almost invariable, was not to ask whether, even after my *SOMA* appeared, Sanskrit scholars were for or against my thesis. I knew what it would cost them, or some of them, in principle, being only human, to admit to me that I was pursuing the right track: they were almost compelled to withhold assent, though perhaps not to reject my case outright. I did not learn Wendy O'Flaherty's attitude until I read her note to 'The Last Meal of the Buddha' in the *Journal of the American Oriental Society* and also in this book! (p 138)

We were in a peculiar position: not scholars, my wife and I had chosen to pursue the entheogens, a project that no one else had tackled. When we started, before we knew anything of the field, it seemed a formidable task. During the first thirty years we were educating ourselves. With limited time at our disposal, we nevertheless made major progress. We gained field experience in Mexico. Rather quickly we laid out the dimensions of the subject and saw clearly that

Soma could be only *Amanita muscaria*. Shortly after the death of Valentina Pavlovna, I retired from my bank and was free to study and travel. Soma – as I will call it hereafter – was common everywhere in the woodlands of the temperate zone. All in all, Soma was the entheogen of choice, until grains came to be cultivated in prehistory and then ergot emerged as a major alternative, also thoroughly safe to those who knew how to use it. No genuine entheogen is, so far as I know, an addictive under any circumstances. All entheogens inspire awe and reverence and possess power for good.

INTERLUDE

I will take advantage of the Interlude to explain a word that I have already used: 'entheogen'.

In Antiquity people spoke of the Mystery of Eleusis, of the Orphic Mysteries, and of many others. These all concealed a secret, a 'Mystery'. But we can no longer use 'Mystery', which has latched on to itself other meanings, and we all know the uses and misuses of this word today. Moreover, we need a word that applies to the potions taken in the antique Mysteries, now that at last we are learning what they were. 'Hallucinogen' and 'psychedelic' have circulated comfortably among the Tim Learys and their ilk, and uncomfortably among others including me for want of a suitable word: 'hallucinogen' is patently a misnomer, as a lie is of the essence of 'hallucinogen', and 'psychedelic' is a barbarous formation. No one who respects the ancient Mystery of Eleusis, the Soma of the Aryans, and the fungal and other potions of the American natives, no one who respects the English language, would consent to apply 'hallucinogen' to those plant substances. Antiquity remained silent on these plant substances, for they were never mentioned, except perhaps person to person in a low voice, by the light of a candle at night.

It is natural that a new discipline, as it works out its course, should find occasion to coin words for new meanings, creating neologisms. Some of us formed a committee under the Chairmanship of Carl Ruck to devise a new word for the potions that held Antiquity in awe. After trying out a number of words he came up with *entheogen*, 'god generated within', which his committee unanimously adopted, not to replace the 'Mystery' of the ancients, but to designate those plant substances that were and are at the very core of the Mysteries.

A distinguished English scholar, sensitive to the language that he used, was unable to find a word when speaking of the sacred plant substances in Mesoamerica, and took refuge in 'narcotics', sleep-producers, an absurd term, for the potion keeps you awake so long as its influence lasts. That English scholar surely never ingested our mushrooms and he took liberties assuming they were opiates! Again, hashish has been used for millennia as a recreational drug like alcohol and it is not entitled, I think, to be called 'entheogen', any more than alcohol is an entheogen.

We must break down the 'Drugs' of popular parlance according to their properties and overcome our ignorance, which in this field is still monumental. 'Entheogen' is a step in that direction.

*

At this point I will dwell on certain unusual circumstances that have marked our pursuit of the cult of the entheogenic mushrooms. The West had tidings of such a cult in Siberia since near the start of the eighteenth century, where it surprised the travelers, was described briefly, and generally dismissed as unworthy of serious study.

In India, Soma was not to be the subject of botanical inquiry and identified, an attitude hardly surprising since Soma was at the heart of their religion. Three millennia ago Soma was known to the Brahmans, who composed many hymns exalting it. The hymns to Soma are still being sung, yet no one, not even among the Brahmans, knows what it was. Nowadays Soma grows in a mystical garden forbidden to all mankind. I understand and sympathize with the Brahmans. But I have been surprised to find a school of Western scholars who felt I was doing something untoward, improper, even to the point that in one country I have been shunned, formally ostracised, for pursuing the identity of the Sacred Plant! They have even warned off their interested publishers from my books.

In sixteenth century Mexico distinguished Spaniards wrote about the entheogenic mushrooms of that land, ably though briefly: Francisco Hernández the King's physician, friar Diego Durán O. P., the Franciscan friar Bernardino Sahagún, the first two from families of converted Jews and the third probably so. At first there were many other references to our mushrooms but the flow quickly dried up. From 1727 for two centuries I have found one mention of them and that one trifling, and one famous Mesoamerican scholar even forgot that they had ever existed![1]

1. *The Wondrous Mushroom*, pp 212-214.

Reko backed up by Schultes was on the point of calling attention to the Mexican entheogenic mushrooms when the cataclysm of the Second World War broke out and engulfed us all. Schultes was destined to go to the Amazon Valley where he remained for years, seeking to mobilize and increase the flow of rubber to the U.S.A. A full decade later Valentina Pavlovna and I came upon the Schultes papers and upon Schultes himself.

The Indian (or more precisely Amerindian!) communities that knew the sacred mushrooms continued to treat them with awe and reverence and to believe in their gift of second sight, – rightly so, as the reader will see when he reads our account of our first *velada*, pp 33-8. Traditionally they have taken the simple precaution not to speak about them openly, in public places, or in miscellaneous company, only with one or two whom they know well, and usually by night. White people seldom know the Indian languages and seldom live in Indian villages. And so, without planning, the Indian by instinct has built his own wall of immunity against rude interference from without.

OUR DISCOVERIES

1. *Soma and the Vedic Culture*

With the aid of Stella Kramrisch, Wendy O'Flaherty, and other scholars, we have identified the plant-god of the Aryans as *Amanita muscaria*, a mushroom, as I have said, that carries no name today in English, though it is one of the commonest and perhaps the most beautiful in our woodlands. It must have been the victim of a religious tabu. We have been accumulating proofs of its identity for more than half a century. It is the plant that pervades the *Rig Veda*, the plant that the Aryans were worshipping until shortly after BC 1000, the plant that the Hindus still venerate nostalgically, though it does not grow there commonly. It is the plant that the Maya worshipped in antiquity as they made clear in their pre-Conquest poem the *Popol Vuh*, the plant that the Nahua worshipped, and also the Algonkians in North America, the ancient Paleosiberian tribesmen in Siberia, and the Ob Ugrian and Samoyed, and some of the Finnic peoples, the Lapps too and probably many many other peoples whose traditions and languages we have lacked the opportunity to examine. In fact, among the entheogens, Soma seems to have been in prehistory the focus for the awe and reverence of our ancestors for countless millennia. It heightened their powers, physical and mental, and people referred to it with many evasive terms that would not be understood by the uninitiated, such as One-Leg, Single-Eye, Tongue-in-Belly. It stepped up the physical endurance of one who took it and also endowed him often with what the Scots call second sight.

Entheogens are extraordinarily rare in the Eurasian botanical world, and *Amanita muscaria* was *the* entheogen of the ancient world. The citations of Soma in the *Rig Veda* are all consistent with this reading, and some fit *A. muscaria* like a glove, *eg* Apālā with Indra, *Rig Veda* 8.91; infra p 54.

2. *The Mystery of Eleusis*

Carl A. P. Ruck, Albert Hofmann, and I have advanced a theory that explains the Mystery of Eleusis, a major focus of the religious life of the ancient Greeks: it was well within the capacity of the hierophants of Eleusis to prepare a water solution of the *Claviceps purpurea* (ergot) growing on their wheat and barley or the water solution of the powdered ergot of *Paspalum distichum*, a grass growing around the Mediterranean, both of which would give the worshippers an entheogenic experience with no danger of a deleterious effect.

3. *Our First* Velada

We have published the story of our first *velada* only once, in *Mushrooms Russia & History*. The account was lost in the two big volumes: just as we wanted it to be. A few readers commented on it personally to us but it drew no public attention. I had always had a horror of those who preached a kind of pseudo-religion of telepathy, who for me were unreliable people, and if our discoveries in Mexico, including our initial *velada*, were to be drawn to their attention we were in danger of being adopted by such undesirables. The story of the *velada* itself in *MR&H* was largely written by Roberto Weitlaner, an old hand at this sort of thing, but we three read over the script most carefully and what we printed in *MR&H* had the approval of the three of us. We here detach those details that are pertinent to our present purpose and add some comments. The *velada* was held on the night of Saturday, 15 August 1953 stretching into the early hours of the following day, in Huautla de Jiménez, Oaxaca.

We had already engaged animals for Sunday to return to Teotitlán and a car to go from there to Tehuacán. We were talking with one of our best informants in Huautla, don Aurelio Carreras, a one-eyed butcher. (He had lost an eye to a

Fig. 1. Aurelio Carreras and his son Mauro (Huautla de Jiménez, 5 July 1955).

bull many years before.) He had furnished us with entheogenic mushrooms of two species and clearly meant us well. We had had no success in finding a shaman: none of those who had been promised us had turned up. An inspiration seized Roberto. As we chatted with Aurelio, quite casually, don Roberto asked,

'And tell us, Aurelio, when you give treatments (*hace curaciones*), are they successful?'

'Always', he answered.

For days we had been talking to a $\check{c}o^{4}ta^{4}\check{c}i^{4}ne^{4}$ ('one-who-knows' in Mazatec, 'shaman') all unawares.

Don Roberto went right on. 'Will you help us this night?' Aurelio hesitated. He needed time to think the matter over. It turned out that his late wife's mother lay on the point of death in her house and there might be objections on the part of kin. But the kin advised him that we had come from afar, and he should help us. He asked us to make our way to his compound at nine o'clock.

Aurelio explained to us that his method of handling the *velada* differed from others'. The mushrooms spoke only in Mazatec and his son Demetrio would translate the Mazatec for us into Spanish. (In the early morning hours the mushroom began to speak either in Mazatec or Spanish.) He would take thirteen pair of mushrooms, the good-sized *derrumbe* (Sp. 'landslide') mushrooms (*Psilocybe caerulescens*), but as he lacked just one of the *derrumbes*, he would make up for it with three of the little ones (*P. mexicana*), figuring that they were equivalent to one *derrumbe*. He never sang nor did he recite any fixed text. He would speak only when the mushrooms spoke to him. Wrapped in his sarape, he sat on his stool or shifted to his chair. After having slowly eaten the thirteen pair of mushrooms, he smoked a big, black, strong cigar all night in a room lighted only by his draughts on his cigar, by embers in a receptacle on the floor, and from time to time by wax tapers. He sweated profusely.

Aurelio asked us what problem troubled us. We said we wished to have news of our son Peter, age 18, from whom we had not heard for many days. (Peter did not know our address.) This seemed a legitimate reason. He asked where Peter was. We said on the outskirts of Boston, a big city. (Peter was working for the summer in a plant near Boston making iron lungs.) A little later, Aurelio says he has trouble seeing Peter because he is so far away in a city big and strange. Finally, after a long interval, he says that Peter is alive but 'they' are reaching out for him to send him to war. Possibly 'they' won't 'get' (Sp. *agarrar*) him, but it is hard to say.

Then, after an hour's silence, loud and clear, Aurelio declares flatly that Peter is in his home in New York. (Demetrio was translating Aurelio's Mazatec.)

He says Peter's thoughts are on us to the point of tears (*hasta las lágrimas*). He is in turmoil, he is well but in a difficulty that he can hardly cope with, he is stumbling, he is not used to this difficulty where he finds himself and does not know how to go about writing to us to tell us about it. Then Aurelio suddenly says we may smoke and the room is illuminated with two more cigars, Roberto's and Demetrio's.

After another interval Aurelio suddenly declares that a relative of mine is destined to fall seriously ill within the year, and gravely fixes on me his single eye. It is now about 1.45 o'clock. Some time later he repeats that a relative of mine is destined to fall ill within the year. This information about my relative was volunteered by Aurelio: it was not solicited by me.

Here we should prefer to bring our story of Huautla to an end, but candor compels us to add a few more lines. Our attitude toward the divinatory performance and especially the oracular utterances had been one of kindly condescension. We said to ourselves it was cruel on our part to ask Aurelio, locked up in his unlettered Indian world, to enter understandingly into the problems of the Wassons of New York. His divinatory powers, put to this test, had seemed to us thin, but of course we had duly entered in our notes all that he had said. In brief, he had declared that Peter was not in Boston as we had said, but in our home in New York, that Peter was alive but in a deep emotional crisis and longing for our help, and finally that the army was reaching out for him and might get him. There was a hint of foreign military service – Germany was mentioned as a possibility. Later in the night Aurelio predicted ominously that a member of the Wasson family would be gravely ill within the year.

We reached home in the second week of September a month later. In the kitchen of our New York apartment we found the leavings of a party that during our absence Peter and his friends had held. The bills from the purveyors supplied the date: the weekend of 15-16 August! Peter easily confirmed this when we saw him. Laughingly we credited the sacred mushrooms and Aurelio Carreras with a hit, a palpable hit, and then gave the matter no more thought.

Aurelio's prediction about the army had seemed badly aimed. After all, Peter at the age of 17 had enlisted in the National Guard, and this exempted him from the draft. Soon after our return to New York, I left for Europe on a business trip, and late in the morning of Monday, 3 October, I arrived at the Hotel du Rhône in Geneva. There a cablegram from home awaited me with sensational news: Peter had just made known his settled determination to enlist in the regular army for a three year term. He had come to this decision after a prolonged emotional crisis involving a girl, and that crisis, we now learned, had been boiling while we were in Mexico. Would I please send a cablegram at once begging Peter to postpone his rash step? I sent the message but, before it reached Peter, he had signed up. The army, after all, had reached out and got hold of him! At the moment of the October crisis our thoughts were so far removed from Huautla that days passed before suddenly Aurelio's pronouncement came to mind. Another hit, a palpable one indeed!

A few months later, after the usual training period, the army sent Peter abroad for duty, but to Japan and Korea, not Germany.

There remained one final prediction: grave illness was to strike the Wasson family (not Tina's) within the twelvemonth. (In the Mazatec world the 'family' embraces all the kin.) This seemed on its face unlikely, for my family is unusually small. No one of the previous generation survived. I had only five first cousins and three first cousins once removed. In January one of my first cousins, in his 40's and abounding in vitality, suddenly died from heart failure.

Aurelio did not tell us that Peter was in distress over a girl who rejected him. Did Aurelio know it was a girl and did he withhold that fact so as not to add to our distress? We do not know. Peter, after some time in the Far East, was sent to Germany for years, then to Viet Nam for two tours of duty, a gunner in a helicopter.

In 1958, at the *velada* that we held for the sick boy Perfeto, María Sabina officiated with Aurelio Carreras. I observed that she treated him with marked deference, among other indications calling him *čo*^{4}*ta*^{4}*či*^{4}*ne*^{4} – *Sabio*, 'one-who-knows'. The intelligent villagers have known each other all their lives and appraise each other accurately.

No one in all of Mexico, least of all the Wassons, knew what Aurelio told us in the course of that *velada*. We did not question him about his utterances because we did not believe him. But all that he said turned out to be true. The entheogen, at least when taken by a wise shaman, also by the interested party, conveys information – but how?

We visitors had fallen into the rude habit of speaking among ourselves about the sacred mushrooms as the 'instant postoffice'. The natives told us of other wonders within the power of the mushroom: 1) if a young wife vanishes, the mushroom tells in a vision where she is; 2) if money has disappeared from a secret place, the mushroom reveals who has it and where it is; 3) if the *burro* has disappeared, the mushroom says whether he is stolen and toward what market he is being driven for sale, or else whether it has fallen into a *barranca* where he lies with a broken leg; 4) if a boy in the family has gone away into the world, perhaps to the States, the mushroom will bring news of him. The Indians are agreed on these matters.

4. *The* Grecas

As we delved into the Mexican past, we were startled and at first baffled to find *grecas*, 'greeks', playing a well known role in its pre-Conquest archaeology, yet no one else was surprised by this term, taking it for granted. *Grecas* are what we in English call 'frets', – abstract designs, angular or curvilinear,

Fig. 2. Archaic Greek amphora, found at Eleusis. Notice the 'frets' or 'fillers' or *grecas*, abstract designs embellishing the mythical scene.

serpentine, sinuous, often repeated in a band or a border, ornamentally pleasing. Such designs were characteristic of the archaic period in the painted pottery of ancient Greece, ending about BC 620; whence they are called in Spanish and Italian *grecas*. Today this word is a common noun in Spanish and Italian and no one (except me) thinks of its origin when it is used.

We reproduce a superb archaic amphora from Eleusis, *ca* BC 640, and draw attention to the numerous *grecas* or frets that grace its decoration. During the entheogenic experience there comes a time when one is apt to see visions, eyes closed or eyes open in a darkened room, of *grecas*. The frets usually are seen in the opening phase of the entheogenic experience. In the dark they are seen more clearly, eyes open or closed, than anything seen in this world. They impress the observer uncannily, as though they are components that come down from the Creation, from the Beginning, into the Night of our *velada*, our Entheogen. Once seen, they are not forgotten: they survive in stone carvings, in paintings on *terra cotta* pottery. (I can hardly believe that, of all people, it falls to me to draw attention to the inspiration for these frets, these *grecas*.) There have been many discussions about particular designs, whether they are of independent invention or borrowings. Whenever this issue comes up, the question to ask first is whether those who drew the designs knew the entheogens and the *grecas* that usually accompany them. Are not the *grecas* of Greek art, as elsewhere, an attempt to depict that special moment when the artist communed with the spirits of the sacred myths – or at least a stylized remembrance of such a tradition?

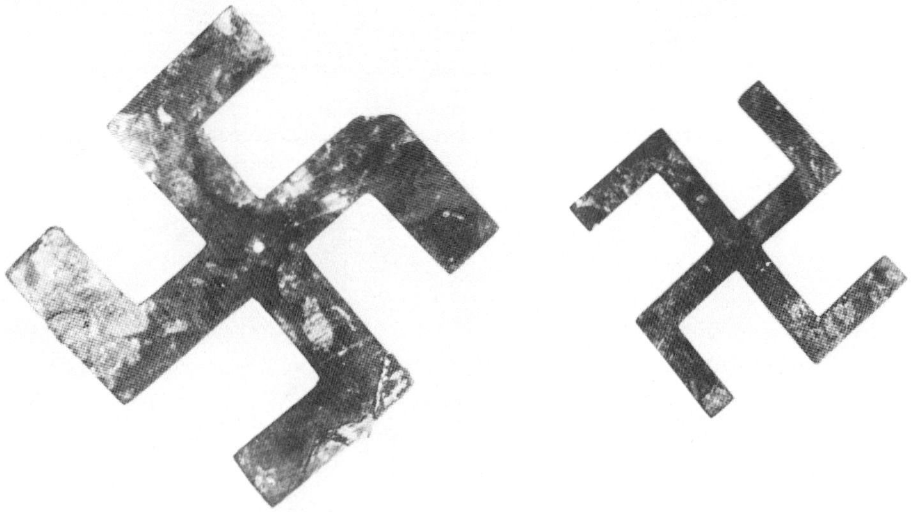

Fig. 3. Copper swastikas, found in Hopewell mounds of Ohio, *ca* AD 500.

The *Swastika.* Stanley A. Freed and Ruth S. Freed in the January 1980 issue of *Natural History* published an article on the widespread and early dissemination of the swastika. Among many others, they showed copper swastikas uncovered in the Hopewell mounds of Ohio, dating from about AD 500, now on exhibit in the Field Museum of Natural History in Chicago. 'Because of its isolated occurrence,' they say 'this find may be interpreted as a case of independent invention of a shape whose symbolism, if any, would have been unrelated to the swastika of the Old World.' The authors could not have known, since no one of our culture knew, the entheogenic experience. In Ohio, where I am assuming these swastikas were made, they could have been inspired by several fungal entheogens such as Soma, by the seeds of an entheogenic morning-glory, or, through trade with the Southwest, by the buttons of the *peyotl* cactus. It seems that the Old World swastikas, widely disseminated as they are, were a fret ('*greca*') inspired by entheogens, many of which we are now uncovering for the first time.

Fig. 4. A bee goddess with animals, birds, and swastikas, found in Boeotia, dating from *ca* BC 700. Gimbutas: *The Gods and Goddesses of Old Europe.* Such archaic and prehistoric swastikas have been found widely scattered, and we feel certain that they are among the visions produced by the entheogens.

Marija Gimbutas, the distinguished prehistorian holding a chair in the University of California L. A., published in 1974 her *Gods and Goddesses of Old Europe: 7000–3500 BC* (Univ. of California Press) and it marked a breakthrough for the English-speaking world, a fresh chapter in the history of the Balkans and adjacent lands. Her book deals with prehistory long before the Greeks and other Indo-European peoples had swept in from Asia and overrun the peoples who already lived there, whoever they were and whatever languages they were speaking. We are going to devote two pages to reproducing from the Gimbutas book (with her express and most gracious permission but without committing her to my conclusions, of which she is unaware) samples of her illustrations of artifacts made from BC 5000 to BC 3500. The ones that we have chosen are beautiful examples of the *grecas* one may see in the course of the entheogenic experience. Professor Gimbutas tells us that the 'Old Europeans' were cultivating wheat and barley: therefore I suspect their entheogen was ergot. These designs preceded by millennia Eleusis, and Greek civilization, and Greek archaic pottery. The Eleusinian ritual was originally performed in Thrace and it moved south to Eleusis early in the first millennium BC. *The Homeric Hymn to Demeter*, expressing the lovely myth of Demeter and Persephone was composed, it is believed, early in the first millennium.

Here is proof that '*grecas*' antedated Greek civilization by millennia, just as Mesoamerican civilization shows '*grecas*' flourishing in America long before the Conquest. In all three cases the same cause inspires the same art.

Plato's 'Ideas'. No one knows whether Plato had been an initiate at Eleusis; we have no knowledge either way. But as a well born young man in Athens, it would have been normal for him to go through the Lesser and then on to the Greater Mystery. The 'Forms' that he would see in the early phase of the effects of the potion at the Greater Mystery would be commanding in his mind and he could easily have transmuted them into his famous 'Ideas', a realm existing somewhere that harbored the archetypes of everything in our life on earth, *eg* the Chair, the Dog, the Stone. Plato's revelation of this would have violated the Athenian law, which set the severest penalties on disclosure of the secrets of Eleusis, but since he did not mention his source, the hierophants of Eleusis could not have brought charges against him without themselves giving away a portion of the secret of the Mystery. Many Greeks in Antiquity must have suspected where Plato's inspiration for his 'Ideas' lay, but I am the first in modern times to be familiar with his source for the '*grecas*'.

When I visited the Santal and Ho peoples in India in 1965 and 1967, on this second trip accompanied by Roger Heim, two good informants, Ludgi Marndi in Dumka as center of the Santal Parganas in Bihar, and Ganesh Ram Ho, Chief of the village of Nawana in the Simlipal Hills in Orissa, both volunteered to tell us that there was a common entheogenic mushroom and they led me to believe it was often consumed. During our fleeting visit their efforts to find specimens were unsuccessful. It grew in cattle dung, *never near* the dung, and was white rising to yellow at the peak of the rounded pileus when mature. This should be *Stropharia cubensis*. The Santal and Ho peoples are closely related to each

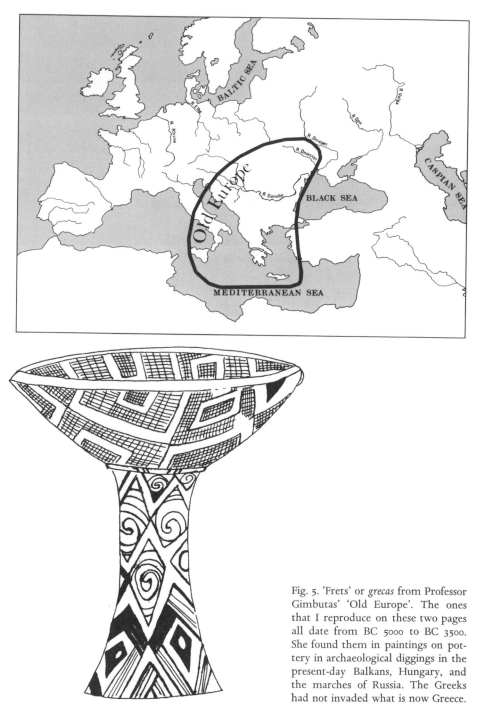

Fig. 5. 'Frets' or *grecas* from Professor Gimbutas' 'Old Europe'. The ones that I reproduce on these two pages all date from BC 5000 to BC 3500. She found them in paintings on pottery in archaeological diggings in the present-day Balkans, Hungary, and the marches of Russia. The Greeks had not invaded what is now Greece.

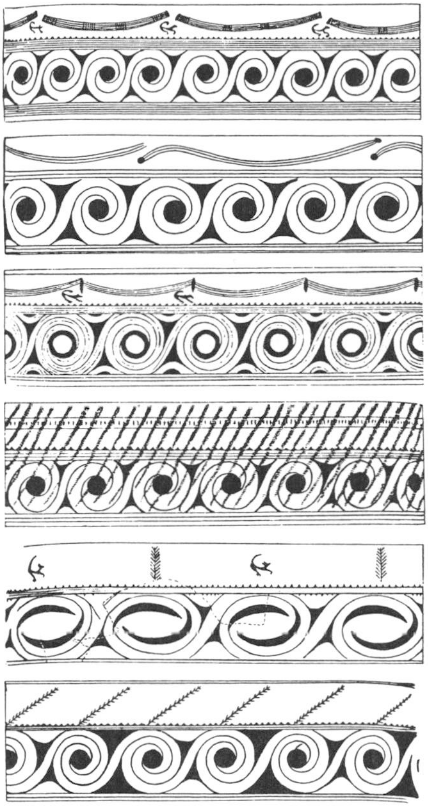

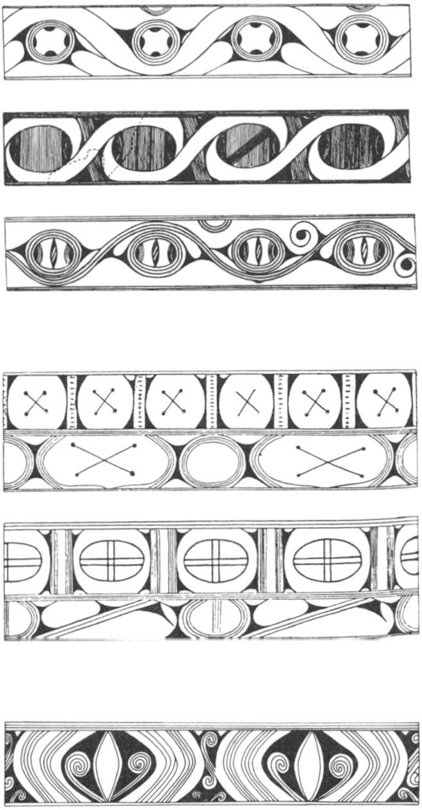

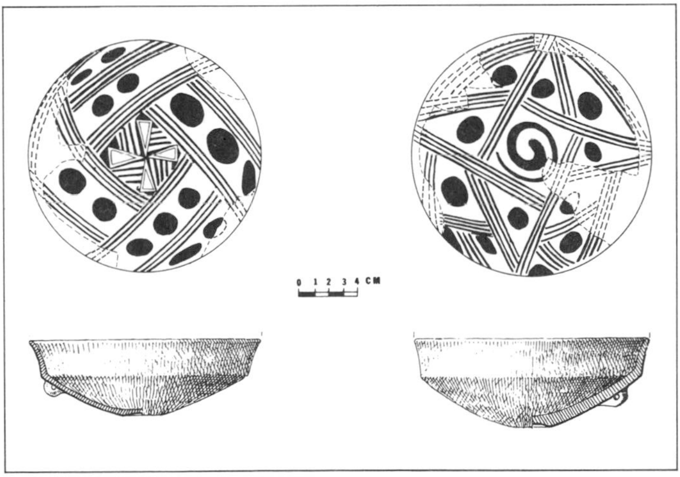
0 1 2 3 4 CM

Fig. 6. A farmer's cottage in Orissa, India, in Santal country. It is suggested that geometrical patterns painted on walls, such as we see here, were inspired by entheogenic mushrooms. In the Santal country of India such paintings are common on the houses, and the Santal people are also familiar with entheogens.

other and are not Hindus. We did not discover whether the Hindus ever eat these mushrooms: the three upper castes are forbidden by their religion to eat mushrooms but the fourth caste, the *'sudras*, are free to eat them and they are more numerous by far than all the other castes taken together. If the *'sudras* ate the mushrooms, might not the cows have gradually acquired the sanctity for which they are famous today? In historic times the cows were not always holy. Just as the lightningbolt was credited with planting the divine Soma in the rain-softened earth, so cows gave birth in their dung to the humbler but still marvelous entheogenic *chattra* (= mushroom).

The Santal often paint on the exterior of their homes geometric designs in color, thus adding to their attractiveness, their modest houses and farmyards being already models of neatness inside and out. We reproduce a photograph that we made in Orissa of a farm house showing such a painting in duplicate. We think the artist may have taken his inspiration from a vision of *grecas* seen in an entheogenic experience.

5. *The New World and the Thunderbolt*

In July 1955 Roberto J. Weitlaner and I were spending a few days in San Agustín Loxicha, a village of Zapotecs high in the mountains looking south over the Pacific, many miles away.[1] At that time Spanish was spoken by few of the inhabitants. The language of the village was one of the seven unwritten dialects, mutually unintelligible, of Zapotec, known to linguists as the dialect

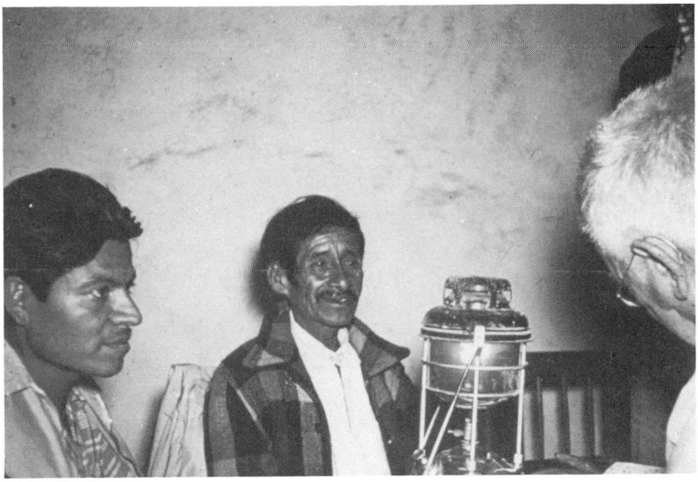

Fig. 7. Aristeo Matías, center; Roberto Weitlaner, right; interpreter, left.

of the Sierra Costera. We were successful in our main object, which was to attend a midnight *velada* wherein a *sabio* ('wiseman'), don Aristeo Matías, consumed some entheogenic mushrooms and, later after they had taken effect, chanted for us the traditional melodies. In the days before and after the *velada* we asked don Aristeo such questions as seemed to us pertinent for shedding light on this religious observance hitherto neglected by scholars. In the course of our questioning we asked don Aristeo whether any special observances marked the gathering of the mushrooms, and he startled us by telling us what follows, as translated into Spanish by our interpreters and into English by us:

1. To grasp fully the meaning of this Discovery, it is advisable for the reader to have read Chapter 2.

I make a practice, four days after gathering the mushrooms, of returning to the same spot, with candles and flowers, and I address a supplication for an increased yield the following year. My prayer is directed to [three] Beings:

1. the earth,
   God the Father Most Holy (a post-Conquest interpolation), the Trinity (a post-Conquest interpolation)
2. the Great Lightning Bolt that bred [*crió*] the *piule*[1] (*mdi'ndó' pse' bìul*), and
3. the Great Lightning Bolt that put blood into the *piule*[1] (*mdi'ndó' blò ren bìul*).
   In Spanish: *El gran rayo que le echó sangre al piule.*

Omitting the two post-Conquest interpolations, we are left with a pre-Conquest explanation of the generation, not of all mushrooms, but of the entheogenic species, and that explanation lies in the sexual union of the lightningbolt and the fecund mother earth. As Aristeo put it through our interpreters, *el rayo es la fuerza de la tierra*. Our interpreters made abundantly clear that the lightningbolt carried the sperm, the spunk, to the soft mother earth. The entheogenic mushrooms are the miraculous fruit of this coitus. Aristeo Matías was explicit in his explanation, which we had gathered elsewhere, notably in the *Rig Veda*, but only as a strong inference.

I propose the following: in this remote corner of the world the same belief prevails in a far earlier stage of evolution than we have found in Eurasia. In Europe it still survives as a moribund relict, a verbal fossil, repeated by half-literate peasants out of habit, but retaining with remarkable persistence the one requirement that the verbal fossil relates to a single kind of mushroom, though a different kind in each region. When the original belief in the entheogenic mushrooms – those mushrooms that take one to a miraculous haven for some hours – gave way to other religious beliefs, each region chose a substitute to replace the entheogen and the belief lived on without a *raison d'être*. In Asia the belief existed in a far earlier recension in the *Rig Veda*, where we find *Aja Ekapād*, 'not-born single-foot', not-born because not born from seed but miraculously from lightning, and single-foot because the mushroom has only a single 'foot' or stipe. In Mesoamerica the belief in the entheogen survives and Aristeo is ready to give Plutarch[2] the answer to his question why thunder makes a certain mushroom to grow: Aristeo speaks out of prehistory, a voice from the millennia before mankind devised the art of writing.

1. In Zapotec there are three tones: I have indicated high by ', low by `, and middle by no accent. In our spelling 'j' is as in 'judge'. The apostrophe represents a glottal stop. *Piule* is the word in the native languages for our 'entheogen', probably derived from *peyotl*.

2. p 84, *infra*.

6. *The Meaning of* Kakuljá Hurakan

From the village of San Agustín Loxicha, in Zapotec country, we will now visit the lands of the Maya, a few score miles due east as the bird flies, where the natives speak Tzeltal and Tzotzil, Mayan tongues in the Mexican State of Chiapas; and some score miles further, in the Guatemalan highlands where they speak Quiche and Tzutuhil. The Quiche were and are the most numerous of the Maya peoples. It is they who have left us as a legacy the *Popol Vuh*, a pre-Conquest poem almost 8600 lines long, which has inspired many translations into Spanish, English, French, German, and Russian, plus two translations from these languages into Italian and Japanese. Mushrooms are mentioned expressly once in the *Popol Vuh*, in what is a religious context.[1] The mushroom caps lie in deerskin and are carried to the top of the mountain, – doubtless a sanctuary. We are given no hint of their species nor what was done with them.

The mycologist Bernard Lowy, now retired from his chair in the State University of Louisiana, had decided many years ago to pursue my subject – ethnomycology – and early on chose the Maya region to see what discoveries awaited him in that ancient and storied land. In the last decade he has made a dramatic break-through, reenforcing mightily the trend of my findings, already strong. Knowing of my preoccupation with lightningbolts and mushrooms, when he went down in June of 1973 to Guatemala he felt the need to familiarize himself with the vocabulary for lightning in the Quiche language. To this end he consulted the professional linguists of the Proyecto Francisco Marroquín in Antigua and specifically Dr. William Norman, a specialist in Quiche. He learned that in Quiche *kakuljá* is the word for lightning.[2] But did it correspond with *rayo* in Spanish or simply with *relámpago*? *Rayo*, definitely. *Rayo* is the powerful word corresponding to *foudre* in French. *Rayo* provokes the tension of a nearby flash of a blinding lightningbolt and a deafening clap of thunder. *Relámpago* corresponds to *éclair* in French and, as he was told, to *xkoyopá* in Quiche. English is singularly weak in its thunderstorm vocabulary.

In July of that same year Prof. Lowy went on to Chichicastenango, in the heart of the Quiche country, and some kilometers north in the forest-covered mountains, where he gathered specimens of *Amanita muscaria* and *A. caesarea*. He

1. *The Book of Counsel: The* Popol Vuh *of the Quiche Maya of Guatemala*, tr. and ed. by Munro S. Edmonson, Publication 35, Middle American Research Institute, Tulane University, 1971; line 6266.

2. '*Amanita muscaria* and the Thunderbolt Legend in Guatemala and Mexico', by B. Lowy, *Mycologia* LXVI.1, Jan.-Feb. 1974.

brought his mushrooms down to the marketplace in the city and displayed them to the women mushroom vendors squatting on the sidewalk. They knew his mushrooms at once and he was admonished not to eat the *kakuljá*: it was *itzel ocox*, the 'evil or devilish mushroom'. So *kakuljá*, 'lightningbolt' in Quiche, really was the ordinary name of Soma! Originally it must have served as a most powerful metaphor, but now no one thinks of 'lightningbolt' when speaking of fungi. Lowy asked the women to pronounce the name slowly and carefully. It was the same as the word for the mighty lightningbolt, unmistakably.

The clergy in the Quiche country and, much later, the anthropologists and linguists when they arrived on the scene, were of West European stock and therefore probably mycophobes who ignored the toadstools of the country, until Prof. Lowy turned up in 1973 with his persistent questions. Scholars only now are, a few of them, learning of the importance of entheogenic mushrooms in prehistory, including our own Indo-European collateral ancestors, in the Indus Valley, who had not yet learned the art of writing.

Do all those among the Quiche who characterize the *kakuljá* as *itzel ocox* believe this, or may these short words serve as an amulet to free them from the disapproval of the authorities? Are there possibly Quiche or Tzutuhil who ingest the *kakuljá* according to age-old rites?

In the summer of 1978 Prof. Lowy spent some time in Santiago de Atitlán, where Tzutuhil is spoken. There he investigated the beliefs concerning the gods in which, it seems, they still believe. I shall give these beliefs as he recorded them, in a document, dictated to him by a foreign resident of the village. Here is what he wrote down:

> According to Tzutuhil legend as narrated to me by Martín Prechtel, a talented painter and linguist living in Santiago de Atitlán, there once were 12 sacred trees, each of them associated with a different species of mushroom. The Nahuales decided to select one of these trees to rule over men on earth. Each tree in turn was asked whether it would accept the heavy responsibility. Only one accepted, an unlikely, undersized candidate called *chipi* or Little Brother. He said he had a dream or vision in which he was directed to find a certain hill at the foot of the volcano San Lucas (still venerated by the Tzutuhil) where a tree called the *palo de pito* grew surrounded by numerous mushrooms. As the tree was approached, a strong south wind arose bringing with it a violent storm, and presently the tree was split by a thunderbolt. The tree was hollow, and within it *chipi* observed a vague countenance which he then proceeded to carve out of the soft wood. This effigy became the god Maximon. Each stroke of *chipi*'s knife was accompanied by a sacred word, and each stroke likewise gave origin to a musical note, tone, or *son*. The notes provided the musical basis for

> traditional songs. When Maximon was fully formed, each Nahual conferred upon the newly created god a special power. Then Maximon was commanded to stand, for he was to be tested to determine whether he was able to use the powers conferred upon him. A deaf mute from the village was brought before him and Maximon was directed to cure his infirmity. According to one version of the legend, a fragment of one of the mushrooms growing around the *palo de pito* was fed to the man, who thereupon became rejuvenated and his infirmity disappeared. The Nahuales were pleased, and Maximon has ever since presided over the Tzutuhil people. It is this divine mushroom which is known among the Quiche as *kakuljá*, only recently identified as *Amanita muscaria* and which takes its name from the Maya god whom it personifies. *Kakuljá* is one of a trinity of gods referred to in the Popol Vuh as *kakuljá huracan*, the others being *chipi kakuljá*, and *raxa kakuljá*.
>
> The first of these, *kakuljá huracan*, enigmatically refers to a single leg, *huracan*, that is, the single shaft of the thunderbolt. Where this shaft struck the earth the miraculous mushroom *Amanita muscaria* arose.

Martín Prechtel is married to a Tzutuhil woman. The *palo de pito* is a leguminous tree, *Erythrina rubrinervia*. Prof. Lowy's account of the Tzutuhil folk belief appeared for the first time in the spring of 1980, in the *Revista-Review Interamericana*, p 100, Vol 10 No 1, Copyright © 1981 Inter American University of Puerto Rico. Professor John Zebrowski is the Director-Editor of the *Revista* and he graciously granted us permission to quote from Prof. Lowy's article.

In Chiapas the vocabularies of both Tzeltal and Tzotzil also link Soma with the lightningbolt mushroom. Dr. Robert M. Laughlin, Curator of Anthropology of the Smithsonian, the authority on Tzotzil, tells us that Soma is called *tzajal yuy chauk*, meaning 'red thunderbolt's *yuyo*', *yuyo* being, it seems, a Quechua word. In San Cristóbal Lowy found that the fly-agaric is commonly still called by natives *yuyo de rayo*. These names raise the question whether Soma, when *yuyo* originally came to be used for the fly-agaric, was considered by the natives as edible: we hope this question will engage the attention of linguists, who should also be asked to explain the presence of a Quechua word in the native languages of Chiapas. Quechua is the dominant language of the Indians of Peru.

Dr. Laughlin gives us supporting evidence for the former currency of *kakuljá* in a *Vocabulario de Lengua Kiche* copied in 1787 from a now missing original by D. Fermín Joseph Tirado. On p 119 of vol. 2 it reveals *cakolha* in the last entry as an *hongo ponsoñoso*, 'poisonous mushroom'.

The famous 'mushroom stones' of the Mayan archeological world never resemble the numerous species of *Psilocybe* that are much sought after throughout Oaxaca and thereabouts, but they present, most of them, good profiles of Soma, and this adds support (as if support were needed!) to the linguistic evidence that the Maya people used Soma as their most holy entheogen.

From the *Popol Vuh* we learn that there were three kinds of *kakuljá* in traditional belief:

1.
kakuljá hurakan
Lightningbolt One-Leg

2.
chipi kakuljá
Dwarf Lightningbolt

3.
raxa kakuljá
Green Lightningbolt

There is no doubt about the priority of *kakuljá hurakan*. When the three are first mentioned in the *Popol Vuh* their ranking is made clear:

Quiche text		*Edmonson Translation*
R umal ri, u K'ux Kah	183	Through him who is the Heart of Heaven,
Hu r Aqan u bi	184	One-Leg by name.
Ka Kulaha Hu r Aqan nabe	185	One-Leg Lightningbolt is the first,
U kaab g'ut Ch'ipi Ka Kulaha,	186	And the second is Dwarf Lightningbolt
R ox chik Raxa Ka Kulaha	187	Third then is Green Lightningbolt,
Chi'e q'u oxib ri, u K'ux Kah.	188	So that the three of them are the Heart of Heaven.

Ka Kulaha Hu r Aqan	in the Preconquest *Popol Vuh* becomes
Kakuljá Hurakan	in contemporary Quiche and
Lighningbolt One-Leg	in English.

The three kinds of *kakuljá*, making up a trinity, are jointly cited eight times in the *Popol Vuh* but not repetitiously. Each citation is in a fresh context and is itself freshly composed. The eight citations in Edmonson are centered on lines 188, 235, 353, 1496, 1741, 2282, 4982, and 5187, each of these being several lines long. But special distinction is conferred on one of the three: *hurakan*, the 'one-leg' first member of the trinity, being cited alone five times, in lines 506, 712, 1512-1524, 4016, and 8198. Furthermore, in the eight joint citations, the 'dwarf' and the 'green' are in each instance linked to *kakuljá*, whereas *kakuljá* appears with *hurakan* only the first time, showing that *hurakan*, 'one-leg', is strong enough to stand alone when it means the sacred mushroom.

There can be no question that *hurakan*, the 'one-leg', loomed large in Quiche and Tzutuhil minds, larger than the other two.

Certain it is that these uses of *kakuljá* do not mean lightningbolt at all. They refer to entheogens, the secondary meaning. The 'one-leg lightningbolt' means Soma. The 'dwarf lightningbolt' means the various entheogenic *Psilocybe* species, normally much smaller than the fly-agaric, by comparison 'dwarfs'. The 'green lightningbolt' is the entheogenic morning-glories and any other phanerogamic entheogens. These are obvious interpretations for anyone who knows the entheogens.

Lowy's discovery of a secondary meaning for *kakuljá* is a major development in Quiche linguistics, a long step forward toward a grasp of the meaning of the *Popol Vuh*, a promising key to hitherto hidden (from us) meanings of other passages. It is certainly also a brilliant climax to Valentina Pavlovna's and my suspicion in the 1930's that mushrooms had played a major role in religion, a confirmation of Roman Jakobson's enthusiastic response to our presentation of our feelings. And what that religious role was! In India and among the Maya, not to speak of other peoples. It must be seldom that in these remote fields one achieves such success.

It is clear that Soma enjoyed a marked priority as the entheogen of choice, at least as late as when the *Popol Vuh* was written and perhaps as late as the Conquest, but the other Mesoamerican entheogens had gained a foothold among the Quiche. We must remember that the Algonkian nation were using Soma

Fig. 8. *Terra cotta* figurines suggestive of Soma, *ca* AD 100, from Mexico, discovered by Peter T. Furst.

Fig. 9. The Black Tezcatlipoca, in aspect of Huitzilopochtli. Note that he is Uniped, 'Hurakan'. Both pictures are from *Codex Fejérváry-Mayer*, Liverpool Museum.

until only yesterday, and there may still be use there among the Ojibway and Chippewa. In Nayarit and in the region of Guadalajara, Peter T. Furst has photographed *terra cotta* mushrooms that date from *ca* AD 100 and that suggest Soma. This Maya discovery of Bernard Lowy's quickens the significance of those artifacts.

The Spanish missionaries reached Quiche country and began proselytizing about 1540. An unidentified member of a noble Quiche family about ten years later began to write out the *Popol Vuh* in the Latin letters (with modifications to accommodate sounds that Latin lacked) that he had learned from the clergy, and he finished the task in less than five years. Apart from being of lofty lineage, his identity is unknown. Strangely, the manuscript seems to have enjoyed little circulation during the next century and a half. Then the Rev. Francisco Ximénez O. P., who had mastered well the Quiche language, shortly after the turn of the 18th century, was asked by his superiors to copy that Quiche manuscript. He did so and the original manuscript was shortly afterwards returned to its home. It has never been seen since. It must have been lost or deliberately destroyed. Or does it possibly still exist, hidden in some conventual cupboard or Quiche secret place?

It is idle to speculate on the age of the *Popol Vuh*. That it goes back, far back, long before the Conquest, is obvious. A link between Soma and lightningbolt existed among the Aryans, just as it does among the Quiche, the Zapotecs, the Algonkians, and countless others, just as it did until yesterday among the Paleosiberian tribes. The presence of the entheogen has hung over the soul of the tribes in each of these places. The entheogen has drawn no study from linguists or anthropologists. The Sanskritists, as I have said, made no effort to find the Soma until I came along and with the essential help of Wendy Doniger O'Flaherty and other friends identified it as *A. muscaria*. As for Mesoamerica, conventional scholars are still apt to call the entheogens 'narcotics' and ignore their place in the lives of the natives. How misleading and odd is this unnatural reticence of scholars, even some of the greatest of them!

For years I had been seeking a pre-Conquest divinity of the Nahua who would be charged with the entheogens. Thanks to the brilliant analysis of H. B. Nicholson in the *Handbook of the Middle American Indians*, Vol. 10, 1971, it seemed to me that Tezcatlipoca was the mighty god suitable for the role. When I discovered that in his aspect of Huitzilopochtli, he had only one sound leg, this was good evidence that here was One-Leg, Tezcatlipoca paralleling the role of the Quiche *hurakan*! Anthropologists had of course known this for a long time, but now we see Tezcatlipoca in the mighty personage of Soma. At about the same moment I learned of the twenty-seven line poem in the Tzotzil language discovered and revealed to us by Dr. Robert M. Laughlin, Curator of Mesoamerican Anthropology at the Smithsonian, and Professor Evon Z. Vogt of Harvard, ending with the lines:

> They saw that it was the same as, the same size as a hawk,
> Having to do with the father-mother (*Totilme'il*)
> 'One-Leg' as we call it.

I felt confident that here we have to do with the lightningbolt mushroom (Soma), though the various interpretations of the poem leave it still as obscure to me as it was when I first read it.

There has been discussion whether the Tzotzil borrowed this notion from the Quiche or from the Nahua of the Valley of Mexico. But did they not, all three of them, inherit it from far back? Did not the idea come with their ancestors from Asia? In the *Rig Veda*, *Aja Ekapād*, the 'Not-Born Single-Foot', is cited seven times and in 1972, in my *Rejoinder to Professor Brough*, I suggested that this meant Soma. There is a verse in the *Rig Veda* that says Parjanya, the god of Thunder, was the father of Soma and in the next hymn we learn that 'the gods, those fathers with a commanding glance, laid the Somic germ'. The *Rig Veda* hymns were composed, as I have mentioned, in the second millennium BC and this is a possible date for the composition of the *Popol Vuh*. How odd it would be if the Brahmans in the Indus Valley were composing their hymns invoking the Not-born Single-foot (*Aja Ekapād*) at the same time as the Mayan priesthood were paying obeisance to One-Leg Lightningbolt (*kakuljá hurakan*)!

7. *A Glimpse of the Domestic Use of Soma*

By rare chance we have caught a domestic practice, a peculiar way, in the consumption of Soma that is identical among the Koryak in the 19th century and among the Aryans, separated by 3,500 years and thousands of miles of most accidented terrain. It must have been a widespread custom, a noteworthy sharing of Soma with the women folk.

In 1903 J. Enderli published in *Petermanns Geographische Mitteilungen*, pp 183-4, an account of the Koryak, of which the following excerpt interests us:

> ... [the Koryak] have another substance with which they can produce narcotic intoxication. ... At the man's order, the woman dug into an old leather sack, in which all sorts of things were heaped one on top of another, and brought

> out a small package wrapped in dirty leather, from which she took a few old and dry fly-agarics. She then sat down next to the two men and began chewing the mushrooms thoroughly. After chewing, she took the mushrooms out of her mouth and rolled them between her hands to the shape of a little sausage. . . . When the mushroom sausage was ready, one of the men immediately swallowed it greedily by shoving it deep into his throat with his indescribably filthy fingers, for the Koryak never wash in all their lives.
>
> [My *SOMA*, pp 261-262]

This has been translated from the original German.

Vladimir Jochelson in his account of the Koryak confirms this account:

> As far as I could see, in the villages of Penshina Bay, the men, before eating it, first let the women chew it, and then swallow it.
>
> [My *SOMA*, p 266]

Vladimir Bogoraz[1] says the same thing:

> Among the Koryak, the woman chews the mushroom, and offers the ready quid to her husband to swallow.
>
> [My *SOMA*, p 273]

Traveling now back some three thousand five hundred years from the scenes in the Koryak country, and thousands of miles to the Indus Valley, we see a clinching detail of the continuum of Soma worship. We will quote three verses from a hymn of the *Rig Veda*, 8.91:

> 1. A maiden going for water found Soma by the way. She brought it home and said, '*I will press it for you*, Indra; I will press it for you, mighty one.
> 2. 'Dear man, you who go watchfully into house after house, drink this that *I have pressed with my teeth*, together with grain and gruel, cakes and praises.
> 3. 'We do not wish to understand you, and yet we do not misunderstand you. Slowly and gently, ever more gently, flow for Indra, O drop of Soma.'

This is the translation by Wendy Doniger O'Flaherty published in the Penguin Classics. Unlike most of the Hymns, it gives us a domestic scene, where we see (as I let my fancy free) a young lady, Apālā, going for water to the spring and returning home, one arm balancing the water vessel on her head, two or three Soma plants in her right hand held by the stipes [Sanskrit: *aṃśū*], full of joy as she planned her cakes, gruel, and grain for her most distinguished guest.

1. Bogoraz and Jochelson knew each other and I am uncertain whether this is independent testimony or whether it merely repeats Jochelson.

On arriving home her first duty was to dry the Soma plants, placing them near the fire where they would dry quickly but not so near that they would begin cooking. When Indra arrived home, all was ready, and her happiness knew no limit. Mighty Indra possessed her and naturally her affliction was healed.

Little did the nineteenth century actors in the Koryak country know the antiquity of what they were doing, and the foreign observers were ignorant. Here are two views of the same scene, one *en beau* and inviting, the other repulsive, but both scenes of the same informal manner of serving Soma at home. I think this way of consuming Soma was probably the common one, in the Aryans' homeland, whence they emigrated to south Asia, rather than the exalted sacrifice with a full complement of chanting priests.

I would not have my readers think that this episode of Apālā and the Koryak account three or four thousand years later offer us weighty evidence in favor of the fly-agaric as Soma. Here is corroborative evidence in favor of our case: in both instances the woman in the household masticates the Soma for her man. That is all and it is a good deal when we are discussing how the essential Element in a most ancient and truly universal religion is handled. In the Koryak case the quid is passed to the man after thorough mastication; presumably the woman has swallowed the juice. In the Aryan instance, the young lady conserves the juice in a container of some sort and presents it to Indra to drink. (The Sanskrit word is *piba*, from the root *pī*, cognate with English 'imbibe'.) This would call for skill on her part, and the drink would be a mixture of *pávamāna* (a Sanskrit word for the expressed and filtered juice of Soma) and her saliva. Was the poem composed in the Indus Valley where the Soma plant was notoriously scarce and was the poet unfamiliar with the details about the quid? Did Apālā swallow the quid? Or do we see an Aryan poet paying obeisance to an inaccurately remembered practice of the Aryans in the land whence they had emigrated generations earlier?

⋆

Soma is the only mushroom whose biography lends itself to being written up, but this must await some future scholar. It will be an absorbing theme, the life story of the supreme entheogen of all time, which survived (and survives!) prehistory only in spots and but briefly, the cult in disarray and pitiful, its practitioners in Siberia generally despised and downgraded by those Europeans who have been privileged to establish contact with them. The visitors exercised their power to impose their distilled liquor (vodka, whiskey, and gin) in place of the 'toadstool', smugly certain that they were doing the natives a favor. They disregarded the testimony of the natives, who said they preferred the mushroom: it left no hangover and the inebriation was superior. Among the visitors there were some competent observers, but culturally even these were so far removed in time from the people before them that they could not be expected to appraise adequately what they were witnessing.

8. *The Chinese and the Nivkhi*

In the lower valley of the Amur[1] there lives a people from time immemorial formerly known to the West as the Gilyaks but now as the Nivkhi. They are one of the Paleosiberian peoples, speaking a language related to no other. They number between 20,000 and 30,000. In my *SOMA* I did not cite them for at that time I had learned little about them. I now have learned that they practiced shamanism, at least until recently, with *Amanita muscaria* as their entheogen. Furthermore, it is said that they once had important cultural contacts with the Daoists of China.[2]

I will now quote from a Nivkhi myth, translated from their tongue into Russian and thence into English:

> Two titmice brothers, living under the shelter of a hummock, were at that time the only inhabitants of the earth. The titmice lived for a long time, not knowing what was to be found along the river beyond their hummock. Then they decided to go and look. The younger brother went up the river, the elder down the river. As he went up the river, the younger brother saw a larch, 'A thick larch rising to the very sky.' At the foot of the larch there was food, grown and placed there by the 'masters of the larch,' unknown to the brothers. The younger brother tasted the food and took some to give to the older one. The next day the titmice brothers proceeded together to the source of the food. There they met heavenly people, two little birds, a silver and a gold one, who had descended to the base of the larch and declared themselves the masters of the food.
>
> [*Studies in Siberian Shamanism*. edited by Henry N. Michael, Univ. of Toronto Press, published for the Arctic Institute of North America, 1963. A. F. Anisimov: 'Cosmological Concepts of the North', Chap 1, pp 169-170, 173-4]

1. See map, p 69; the Amur is at lower left.
2. To follow my argument the reader should refresh his memory of what I said in *SOMA*, pp 80-92. (In the first edition and early reprintings of *SOMA* I committed an error, unimportant but inexcusable: where I mention *Pleurotus ostreatus*, p 82, I should have said *Auricularia auricula-Judae*.)

The larch, a conifer with deciduous needles, is for the Nivkhi the Tree of Life, the Tree of the Knowledge of Good and Evil, and is revered accordingly by them. Why? Because there springs up under its boughs *A. muscaria*, the 'food' mentioned in the above myth. Throughout Siberia, indeed Asia, wherever grow the trees that serve as hosts to *A. muscaria*, – the birch, the pine, the cedar, the larch, others – that tree is revered as giving birth to the Marvelous Herb. The entheogen at the foot of the tree is the explanation of the reverence paid to the tree by the natives round about. How has the world overlooked for so long a time this key to the mystery of the Tree of Life?

With the reticence that we find everywhere in the world where the entheogens are encountered, the identity of the food found at the foot of the larch is not disclosed in the Nivkhi myth that I have quoted but it would be obvious to any Nivkh and, as the Nivkhi would think, to any stranger worth his salt. That the tree is revered goes without saying but it is not so holy as to be subject to the verbal tabu sheltering the miraculous plant at its base, a plant whose name is pronounced only in a whisper and only when two or three are gathered together, preferably at night. And even then when one examines that name, it is invariably a euphemism; *ie*

Sanskrit *Soma*:	'the pressed one'
Sanskrit *aja ekapād*:	'not-born single-foot'
Quiche Maya *kakuljá*:	'an overwhelming lightning strike'
Quiche Maya *hurakan*:	'the one-legged one'
Mazatec *ˀnti*^{1} *xi*^{3}*tho*^{3}:	'The Holy [Ones] that leap forth'

We do not know the Nivkhi name for the plant that grows at the foot of the larch but it would be noteworthy, indeed unique, if it were not another euphemism.

*

When I brought out my *SOMA* at the end of 1968, I failed to deal with China and the use of entheogens there because I felt inadequate. Since then I have learned much and will now give my views.

If indeed the Daoists in the early days were in touch with the Nivkhi, they must have shared with each other the knowledge of the mighty and holy entheogen. No one can say which had the knowledge first: it goes back so far that the origin is forever lost and unimportant. We shall see in Chap 2 (p 90) that the lightningbolt belief is securely grounded in the Chinese culture and vocabulary: proof as I see it that they shared with others in their high regard for the sacred entheogen. In the *Li Ji*, one of China's 'Thirteen Classics',[1] there is a significant statement that the *zhi* 芝 defined as an herb, 'a small plant that is not woody', was eaten by the Emperor as a ritual food. It was therefore edible and sacred. Nothing is said that others were prohibited from eating it. It would be natural for the hierarchs of the Daoists to share in it, and the Court circles, perhaps others, possibly many others. China was more wooded then than now but we do not know whether there was overharvesting, nor whether the Chinese knew how to harvest the mushrooms without breaking the tie with their mycelium. At any rate in the reign of the First Emperor Shihuang, before the Han, we hear for the first time that there are big troubles, the necromancers looking in vain for a sacred herb, and for the first time the *ling zhi*, 靈芝 as distinct from the simple *zhi*, is cited. Clearly there was a crisis in the supply that agitated the Court circles, as the *zhi* faded from view and the *ling zhi* became the official surrogate. The replacement took place only after the voluble élite circles of the Chinese made a furor that we can document in historical texts, in poetry, in paintings, and in carvings, and that lasted into the Later Han. In the reign of the unpopular Wudi there took place what would be called today a remarkable and successful 'public relations ploy', which the reader can learn about in *SOMA* (p 85) with unalloyed admiration, and which served to strongly consolidate the legitimacy of the changeling. Suffice it to say that the replacement of the *zhi* (*A. muscaria*) by *ling zhi* (*Ganoderma lucidum*), of the 'not woody herb' by the 'woody herb', stunning in its protean shapes and with its deep red lacquered finish, won the day. But the Chinese never let out the secret of the small 'not woody' herb.

This explanation meets all the peculiar circumstances of the event, including the character of the Chinese people. I am convinced that it is right.

The High Priests of the Daoists today wear vestments that are bespattered with the auspicious *ling zhi*, and they also wear emblems of the *ling zhi*. How much of this history – the adoption of the changeling to replace the 'not woody herb' – is known to them?

Far to the south of them the Brahmans of India faced an identical problem, when they had to make do with a changeling, the *Pūtika* replacing the Soma. But the different circumstances permitted them to be far more discreet and hide the identity of both plants until Professor Heim and I visited the Santal and learned the fungal identity of the substitute, the *Pūtika*.

1. The *Li Ji* was put together in the Early Han but from documents that date from the late Zhou, BC 700 to the third century BC.

9. *Greece and Soma*

Carl Ruck has discovered in ancient Greek an assemblage of rare words that can only apply to Soma, but we cannot be sure, in the light of the circumpolar field that we have found for the adoration of this plant, whether the Greeks derived their knowledge of it from the Indus Valley to the east, or from the north whence they had migrated, or both; or perhaps some Greeks had always known it as a part of traditional family lore. Ruck's exposition of this aspect of Greek culture is in the early pages of his first essay in this book, pp 151-178.

A traveller named Skylax early in the fifth century BC is mentioned in Herodotus as having visited the Indus Valley. Herodotus says little more and the book by Skylax has not survived but he is cited by various writers including Pliny and is reported to have said that the Indus Valley was the homeland of the 'Shade-foot' (Gr.: *Sciopodes*) people, who possessed a single powerful leg on which they leapt with astonishing vigor or else lay on their backs and shielded themselves from the sun with their single foot serving as a parasol. Another Greek name (though surviving only in Latin sources) for these creatures was 'One-legs' (Gr.: *Monocoli*), and a third term, used only by the seventh century poet Alcman, is 'Cover-foot' (Gr.: *Steganopodes*). If indeed Alcman in the seventh century BC wrote of the 'Cover-foots', here is proof that the Greeks possessed information about the marvelous entheogen before Herodotus, who also has told us (4.33 *et seq*) that Greece was in regular contact with the Hyperboreans, in the heart of Siberia, since long before his time, possibly since the Greek migrations. Another Greek, Ktesias, made a journey to India a century after Skylax, and his narrative survives in part. It is noteworthy that the Greeks knew about the entheogens down the centuries, but characteristically hardly mention them, so that Western scholars ignore them.

In Vedic Sanskrit we find the congener of these Greek words, *Aja Ekapād*, 'Not-born Single-foot', referring to Soma: 'not-born' because born without seed, but conceived miraculously, from the coitus of a lightningbolt with mother earth rendered soft by rains, and 'single-foot' because the divine Soma plant had only one leg, the stipe (or stem, *aṃśū*[1] in Sanskrit) of the mushroom. The

1. Another word for Soma, far less holy, is *aṃśū*. Those whose function it was to handle the plants every day – receiving them, drying them, storing them, producing them for the Offices – needed a word without the exalted attributes of 'Soma'. Some of the observers in Siberia have noted that the merchants string the plants together in threes, threading them together

word in Sanskrit for a mushroom, introduced in post-Vedic times, was *chattra*, whose primary meaning was 'parasol'. We will find the 'parasol' reappearing centuries later in the manuscripts written in the Middle Ages. The mushroom (= Soma) has gills (or *laminae*) suggestive of the struts of a parasol. This is as much as a Greek traveller could have learned in the Indus Valley about Soma. The use of Soma there had been abandoned centuries earlier and the Brahmans, who were the custodians of the secrets of Soma, were now intent on suppressing every memory of the marvelous herb. It was unlikely that a Greek would ever meet a Brahman, and if he did, the Brahman would not engage in a discussion of Soma with him.

The Arimaspians, a people allegedly possessing only a single eye, were placed near the Hyperboreans by Herodotus, though with naïve charm he expresses scepticism about their very existence (3.116). What he is talking about is the race of Cyclopes and we now understand them for the first time: they are of course the personification of Soma as a single eye. The Cyclops is originally Soma under an aspect different from the 'Cover-foots'. In *SOMA* I published, all unknowing, in Plate 10, a picture of Soma as a 'single-eye' and on pp 46-47 I published a list of the 'single-eye' citations that occur in the 9th mandala of the *Rig Veda*. The Cyclopes evolved far in Greek culture and their origin may well have been lost to view by most Greeks in the time of Aristophanes. The single eye and the single leg are combined in a 'one-sided man or woman' shown to us in *The Chukchee*, where V. G. Bogoraz says he represents the spirit of the estuary of the Anadyr River. Rodney Needham calls this creature a 'unilateral figure' in his *Reconnaissances*. Others have called it a 'halfling'.

Rudolf Wittkower in his classic 'Marvels of the East: A Study in the History of Monsters'[1] recognized that both Greeks and Indians possessed cyclopic races and he adds: 'they may have had a common mythical origin in times beyond our historical reach.' He divined what we have established, the common origin of the Indian and Greek Cyclopes, a common origin but *not* a mythical origin, a common origin in Soma the Divine Mushroom.

Our third 'monster' has no head but his face is in his torso, extending from his shoulders to his belly: he is called in Greek a 'Tongue-in-Belly' (Gr.: *Englot-*

through the relatively tough stipes. Some such method must have been used in Vedic times and here we have an explanation of the term of art, *aṃśū*. There was an imperious need for a word to serve that function. Do we not have it in *aṃśū*? Renou translates *aṃśū* felicitously by *tige*, stem or stipe.

1. Journal of the Warburg and Courtauld Institutes v.5:159-197, London. My quotation is from p 163. As a source Wittkower's paper is essential reading.

togastor), a *hapax*. The divine being, Soma, has only his torso to live in (apart from his Single-Leg), no head, and his eyes and nose and mouth must be in his torso.

Carl Ruck has identified the Greek mythological archetype of all the 'Tongues-in-belly': it is Iambe-Baubo, who enters into the *Homeric Hymn to Demeter* (ll. 200-210), in the famous scene where Metaneira offers her grieving guest wine to drink, but the Goddess says that to drink red wine would be a sacrilege. This was just after Iambe-Baubo had brought her a stool and had thrown over it a lamb's fleece for her to sit on:

> *Thus she remained until the scheming Iambe amused the holy lady with jokes and made her smile, then laugh, softening her heart – Iambe who in later times pleased her at her rites of Mystery.*

Iambe-Baubo is a strange character: she has no head and her face is in her torso. We here present three examples of this figure. 'Iambic' is the poetic meter used in ancient Greece for erotic verse and Baubo is doing what is expected of her in this scene with Demeter. We also learn that she played a role in the rites of the Mystery of Eleusis. Some scholars have held the view that Baubo is an androgyne: the legs are joined throughout their length, the arms are only suggested, and as head and neck are absent, the whole figure suggests an erect penis.

This common fund of evasive euphemisms is used for the mighty entheogen, whether in the Indus Valley, in Siberia, in Greece, or indeed in some cases in the far off highlands of Mesoamerica. The evasive euphemisms were understood and used throughout vast stretches of the world. We are now bringing this vocabulary to scholarly attention. Aristophanes was an outstanding playwright, popular, and when he used *Sciapodes* and *Englottogastor* in *The Birds*, we can rest assured that Aristophanes knew he would be understood. These words drawn from the sacred vocabulary are rare in surviving documents but their rarity does not tell the story of their oral usage. *Sciapodes* and *Englottogastor* serve in the strophe and antistrophe of the Chorus in *The Birds*: Ruck thinks that in the case of *Englottogastor*, it may have been invented *ad hoc* by Aristophanes. Either way, invention by playwright or not, it had multiple progeny many centuries later. Just as in Mexico today, the sacred vocabulary seldom erupts in large and mixed gatherings but recurs in private conversations among people well known to each other. To the end in ancient Athens plays were tinctured with religion, and Aristophanes used in his comedies a freedom of expression that would not have been proper in the Agora.

Fig. 10. Iambe-Baubo Figures. *Terra cotta*, Priene, Asia Minor, 5th century BC.

10. *Soma among the Mediaeval 'Monsters'*

It is surprising enough that these evasive euphemisms for the plant Soma occur in classical Greece; but, doubly surprising, throughout the Middle Ages the scriptoria of Western Europe were busy with the 'monsters' that dwelt beyond the limits of the known world. Occasionally they hit on genuine peoples such as the pygmies of Africa, but mostly the scribes and artists contented themselves with perpetuating the same fanciful 'monsters' down through the ages. They derive their inspiration largely from classical sources, notably from the *Historia Naturalis* of Pliny the Elder, who drew on the Greek sources that we are now familiar with. These illuminated manuscripts seem to have been immensely popular among the literate and many people at first may have half believed in the imaginary creatures that they read about and saw pictured. But there was never an edition that tried to explain our three 'monsters'.

Those three do of course appear separately but what impresses me is that they often appear together. In an especially fine manuscript in the Bibliothèque Nationale designated Fr. 2810, one of the early versions of Marco Polo's account of his travels to the Orient that was commissioned as a gift from John the Fearless to the Duke of Berry, there comes the point where Marco Polo tells about his visit to Siberia. Of course he does not mention any 'monsters' but nonetheless the Boucicaut Master in charge of the manuscript (volunteering irrelevant illustrations as was often done) offers us a miniature of a Cyclops, a Sciapous, and a Tongue-in-Belly in Siberia. They are placed in a mountain scene where Soma might be growing in Siberia. One inevitably asks oneself when confronted with a manuscript such as this whether some even in the late Middle Ages had information withheld from our other sources, in short whether there were individuals who knew what our three 'monsters' meant.

Shortly after the middle of the 14th century a book destined for great fame was dictated to an amanuensis in French in Liège purporting to be the story of the travels of a fictitious Englishman, Sir John Mandeville, Kt., as related by himself. This was the supreme travel yarn telling with mock solemnity of the monsters, just as Cervantes with Don Quixote, two and a half centuries later, made fun of the chivalry and knighthood that had lingered on into his day. *Sir John Mandeville, Kt.* was translated into almost all the languages of Europe including of course English and, with the invention of printing, was published in innumerable editions. In the 19th and 20th centuries a few such editions continued to appear but only as picturesque period pieces. Here was a book that expressed the increased scepticism of the Renaissance.

The question will surely be asked why people devised words such as Tongue-in-Belly, Cyclops, and Shade-foot when speaking of Soma. But the answer seems to me obvious: wherever religious feeling is deep and sincere as it was among the Brahmans in Vedic times and others who worshipped Soma, everything associated with the holy and especially the name of the mighty plant is subject to a religious tabu. The sacred words must not be spoken openly and commonly. Originally the three names of our 'monsters' could be pronounced freely in the presence of strangers, of *śūdras,* without danger that the Most Holy would be befouled by those unworthy clods, as the Brahmans considered all the lower orders to be. In the Middle Ages the pictures and the names had lost contact with their own origins and they were mere oddities. They were perhaps the 'science fiction' of their day.

Fig. 11. 'Monsters' repeatedly appearing in manuscripts of the late Middle Ages, reputedly from creatures living beyond the known world. As we have shown in the text, these stem from *A. muscaria*, difficult as this is to imagine, going back through classical Greece.

The three pictures on this page are all taken from *The Travels of Sir John Mandeville, Kt.*, Strassburg, 1501, p 71. Courtesy of The Pierpont Morgan Library, New York.

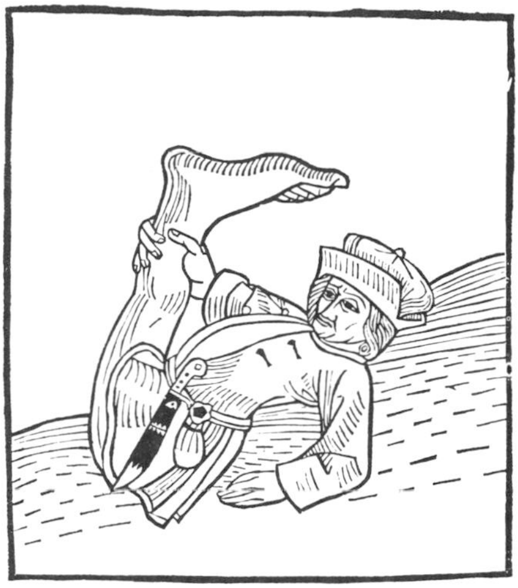

a. Single-footed man

b. Cyclopes

c. 'Tongue-in-Belly'

d. Drawing of group with other 'Monsters'
Taken from *Cosmographia*, by Sebastian Munster, Basel, 1544, p 628.
Courtesy of The New York Public Library, Rare Book Division.

e. Scene from mediaeval manuscript of Marco Polo's travels, ms. FR 2810,
Bibliothèque Nationale, Paris.

f. Nineteenth century reproduction of the 'Folk with but One Foot' from *The Travels of Sir John Mandeville, Kt.*, edited and illustrated by Arthur Layard, published by Archibald Constable, Westminster, in 1895.

11. *The Chukotka*

A Russian archaeologist, N. N. Dikov, who lives in Magadan, a city on the Pacific Coast of Siberia (as is only too well known to all Russians), in 1967-1968 discovered mushroom petroglyphs on the eastern bank of the Pegtymel' River. In many instances the mushrooms were associated with human figures, all apparently female, a mushroom crowning the head. The petroglyphs were small, some centimeters in height, and the mushrooms were larger in scale than normal. Did the mushrooms signify mushroom possession? Their size would suggest this. Collateral evidence permitted Dikov to speculate that the petroglyphs might date from the end of the stone age or the beginning of the bronze age, *ie* around BC 1000. The figures with mushrooms were far from isolated: reindeer, dogs (or wolves), foxes, a kayak, fish, and seals were also portrayed. The mushrooms were doubtless *A. muscaria*, and the women wearing them on their heads may have been engaging in a ritual dance, but I prefer a different explanation. In *SOMA* I quoted, pp 288 *et seq*, various tales in which the Kamchadali and the Koryaki introduce us to the 'little folk' of their entheogenic world as little girls, small, only a few centimeters high. (We are reminded of the 'little people' of the Oaxaca world, playing-card in size: see *The Wondrous Mushroom*, pp 136 *et seq*) I think the petroglyphs of the Pegtymel' River represent the 'fly-agaric girls', and the mushrooms serve to identify the pictographs. For me a striking feature of these petroglyphs was their location: the Pegtymel' River flows north into the Arctic Ocean in the eastern reaches of the Chukotka, the huge peninsula jutting out towards Alaska. The petroglyphs are only sixty kilometers from the river's mouth, in a ravine where the eastern bank of the river is a rocky formation rising high above the flowing water. Today this is Chukchi country and it may well have been so three millennia ago.

I thank Mr. Dikov for having sent me his writings about the petroglyphs and the pictures. The map was made by my cartographer, Jean Tremblay.

12. *The Fool's Mushroom*

In Magyar there is a phrase that circulates (in translation) in Southern Europe to this day, a conversational cliché, *bolond gomba*, 'fool's mushroom', as when one asks of a person behaving foolishly, 'Have you eaten of the fool's

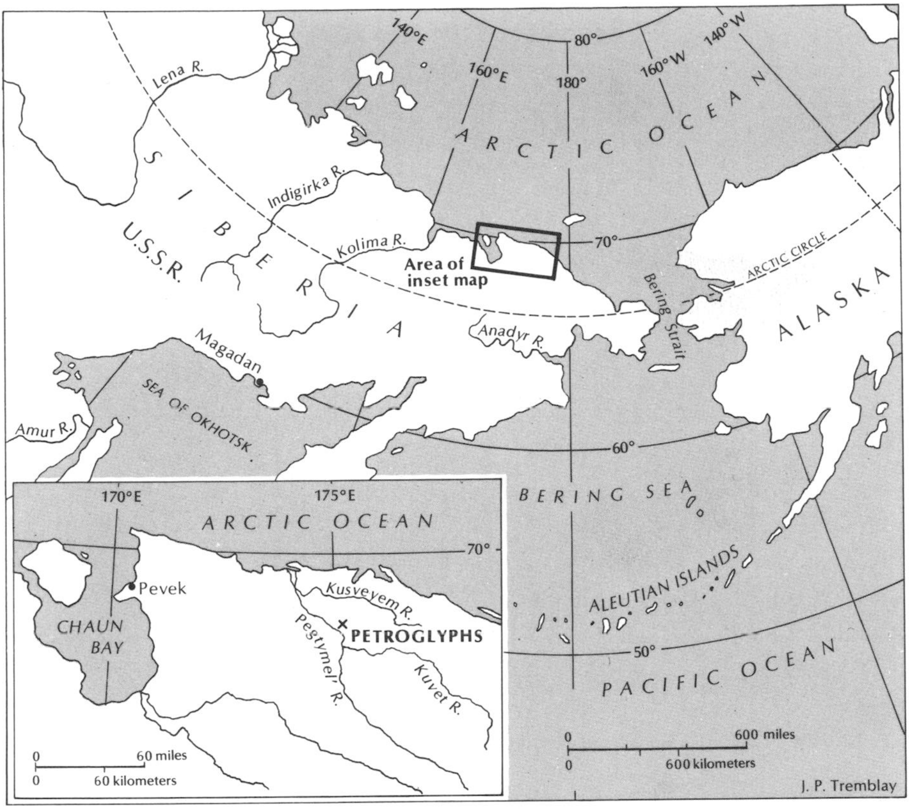

Fig. 12. Map of the Chukotka region and chart of mushroom shapes.

Fig. 13. N. N. Dikov, copying petroglyphs and view of mushroom carvings.

mushroom?', or when one rejects a proposition by saying, 'Do you think I have eaten of the fool's mushroom, that I should do such a thing?', or again, 'He is laughing as though he had eaten the fool's mushroom.' In Hungary the 'wise-woman', *javas asszony*, is said to use this same mushroom in love philtres, and the angry lover sends the philtre to the object of his passion. At our request considerable effort has been expended in Hungary to find out whether the peasants in any region of that country identify the *bolond gomba* with a particular species, with no success. But did the inquirers reach out to include the 'wise women'? They would be the last to lose this knowledge, though they would perhaps be reluctant witnesses.

Our sacred mushroom's peculiar virtue was widely known though its identity was perhaps intentionally lost. In Yugoslavia one still says, *Najeo se ljutih gljiva*, 'He has eaten enough of the fool's mushroom'. In Vienna one may hear, *Er hat verrückte Schwammerl gegessen*, 'He has eaten the mad mushroom', though having no particular mushroom in mind . . . How faint are these dying echoes of the Soma of the Aryans and of the *kakuljá hurakan* of the *Popol Vuh* in the Quiche Maya country!

In the spring and again in the summer of 1967 I visited Dr. János Gulya in Budapest, to consult with him in the field where he is the master, the Finno-Ugrian languages, and especially the Ugrian cluster – Magyar, Khanty, and Mansi. Out of his knowledge of these, to us, remote languages he drew to my attention a usage in Khanty (spoken in the valley of the Ob̦) that is relevant to our inquiry. The word *tulpanx*[1] occurs in two Heroic Songs in the Khanty tongue, formerly called Ostyak, in one as part of the hero's name, and in the second, repeatedly in the course of the narrative. Professor Gulya explained that '*tul-*' means 'fool' or 'foolish', *panx* meaning of course the entheogenic mushroom, Soma. This serves to nail down the source of expressions that have circulated in past centuries in many parts of Europe, but whose specific sense has long been up in the air. What we strongly suspected is now confirmed.

John Parkinson in his *Theatricum Botanicum* (1640) speaks of the 'foolish mushroom', but he is leaning on his Continental sources. The 17th century Polish poet Waclaw Potochki warns his readers in the *Unweeded Garden* against a kind

1. The citations are in *Osztják Hösénekek* [Ostyak Heroic Songs]. Reguly A. és Pápay J. hagyatéka [*The Legacy of Anton Reguly and J. Pápay*]. 1. kötet. (Vol. 1] Reguly Könyvtár I. [Reguly Library 1.] Edited by Miklós Zsirai, Budapest, 1944. The first citation is from the first heroic song, pp 2-165, on pp 2-3. The second citation is from the second song, pp 392, 398, 400. The first song was from Obdorsk, now Salehard. The second was from the northern Sosva river basin.

of mushroom called *szmer*, lest it render the eater foolish (*szaleć*) 'as from opium'. He was passing on hearsay as no mushroom could be confused with opium. A Slovak informant from the Tatra Mountains tells us that rejected mushrooms are variously called by his people *žabaci huby*, 'toad mushrooms' (inedible but harmless fungi?), *hadaci huby* and *hadunke huby*, 'viper mushrooms' (deadly mushrooms?), and *šalené huby*, 'mad mushrooms'. To the east of Slovakia, in the Ukraine, the natives call any wild mushroom that they reject *zhabjachyj hyrb* – 'toad-like mushroom'.

Names of Soma that reflect widespread knowledge of its psychic effects are numerous: in France in the Aude the *mijoulo folho*, around Toulouse the *mujolo folo*, in the Aveyron the *coucourlo fouolo*, in distant Trento *ovolo matto*, 'mad mushroom', and across the border in Cataluña, *oriol foll*, 'mad oriol', *oriol* being the name of *A. caesarea*, a delectable species, and *oriol foll* its evil counterpart. They both belong to the same genus *Amanita* and some people confuse them! In Crete, in modern Greek, we have come across a text that speaks of the 'mad mushroom', *trellomanitaria*, inebriating mushroom, probably Soma.

Almost ten years after my *SOMA* appeared I received a letter from a Catalan, a stranger to me, living in Barcelona, by name Josep Barba Formosa. He informed me that in Catalan the phrase is common, *Está tocat del bolet*, 'He is touched by the mushroom', meaning Soma and used precisely as the phrase is used in Austria, Yugoslavia, and Hungary. He attributes it to the refugees who crossed from France *ca* AD 1300, fleeing from persecution in western and southern France ('Occitania') in the course of the bitter religious war against those we generally call the Cathars or Albigensian heretics.

13. *'Happiness Mushroom'*

There is one instance of children's verses in Germany that I am at a loss to explain. Everyone born to German learns these verses and they stay with him throughout life:

Ein Männlein steht in Walde	A manikin stands in the wood
Ganz still und stumm.	Stock-still and mute.
Er hat von lauter Purpur	He has of purple pure
Ein Mäntlein um.	A mantle around him.
Sag' wer mag das Männlein sein	Say, who may the manikin be
Das da steht auf einem Bein?	Who stands there on one leg?

Alternative ending:

Sag' wer mag das Männlein sein	Say, who may the manikin be
Das da steht im Wald allein	Who stands there in the wood alone
Mit dem purpur roten Mäntlein?	With the purple red mantle?

Children:

Glückspilz! Fliegenpilz!	Happiness mushroom! Fly-agaric!

By a happy though perhaps a fortuitous chance, the answer posed by this riddle:

Say, who may the manikin be
Who stands there on *one leg*?

is our Soma who stands there *auf einem bein, ekapād, hurakan.* History is punctuated by ironies, and how ironical it is that a century and more ago, Max Müller, at a loss about the identity of Soma, and all later Vedists, plunged in problems of remote Sanskrit exegesis and Aryan Indian mythology, could have found the answer to Soma by listening to the children playing around their feet in the German world! As for the children's two answers, the first is clear, but the second, – *Fliegenpilz*, 'Fly-fungus' – its meaning is two-fold, – for most listeners it means simply the 'fly-killer', but originally, when Albertus Magnus first named and described it, with a pejorative twist, in the 13th century, the 'fly' may well have meant a psychic force. We have written on this at length in Chap. 13 'The Flies in the Amanita', of *Mushrooms Russia & History.*

Could children have originated these verses? I think not. Only adults would devise them. But what adults, and when, and why? Are the verses old, in what recensions? Are there dialectal variants? How far back do the verses go? The tone of the verses runs counter to European prejudices that date back centuries. Who can elucidate these verses? Am I wrong and did some German folk ingest Soma for its psychic powers, but who and when?

14. *The British and the 'Nameless Mushroom'*

The toad and Soma seem to be associated together from earliest times. In China Soma is called the *hama jun*, 'toad-mushroom'. In France there is a dialectal name, *crapaudin*, based on the name of the toad, but which also is Soma. The English 'toadstool' I think originally designated Soma, but the mushroom labored under such fearsome ignominy that the name came to be withdrawn from specific use and to be applied to the whole world of wild mushrooms, and since the English are mycophobes, this satisfied and reenforced their prejudice. Perhaps the most common mushroom and certainly handsomest is without a name – a shameful situation – that makes discussion of the plant difficult for those who do not know its Linnean name. I think I am the first to call attention to this tabu that leaves Soma without a name in English, and certainly the first to suggest that we call it 'Soma' out of respect for what it has represented for the human race, in the Old World and the New.

15. *The Vikings and Soma*

Samuel Ödman in 1784 first propounded the notion that the Berserkers' ragings were initiated by Soma. He had not the slightest evidence to substantiate this and none has been produced since then. According to his notion, Soma inebriation was simply a mightier alcohol, and since the north Europeans regardless of class were and are addicted to alcohol and obsessed with it, this explanation of the Berserk raging needed no study: it won the day almost without a fight. In my *SOMA* I demolished this yarn and I now reiterate my position. There is not a shred of historical evidence that the 'rages' were provoked by Soma. Nowhere in the Soma world, neither in the New nor the Old World, is there support for the notion that it made warriors better fighters. On the contrary, the evidence shows that it is a pacifying agent. Soma may have been consumed, and I think it was, by those who lived in Scandinavia, but this was two or three thousand years earlier: *vide* Reid W. Kaplan, 'The Sacred Mushroom in Scandinavia', *Man* (N.S.) 10.72-79. We know not who they were nor what language they spoke. Ödman must have been a mycophobe – all his compatriots were – and he knew nothing about mushrooms.

16. *The Tree of the Knowledge of Good and Evil*

I once said that there was no mushroom in the Bible. I was wrong. It plays a hidden role (that is, hidden from us until now) and a major one, in what is the best known episode in the Old Testament, the Garden of Eden story and what happened to Adam and Eve.

I suppose that few at first, or perhaps none, will agree with me. To propose a novel reading of this celebrated story is a daring thing: it is exhilarating and intimidating. I am confident, ready for the storm.

I hold that the fruit of the Tree of the Knowledge of Good and Evil was Soma, was the *kakuljá*, was *Amanita muscaria*, was the Nameless Mushroom of the English-speaking people. The Tree was probably a conifer, in Mesopotamia. The serpent, being underground, was the faithful attendant on the fruit. (See my *SOMA*, p 214) Please read the Biblical story in the light of all I have written on the awe and reverence that *A. muscaria* evokes, and how the knowing ones speak of it only when alone together, preferably by night. Gradually it will dawn on you that the 'fruit' can be no other than Soma. Everyone mentions the tree but its fruit is nameless. There were two trees in the Bible story, the Tree of the Knowledge of Good and Evil, whose fruit Adam and Eve were forbidden to eat, and the Tree of Life. Adam and Eve ate of the fruit of the Tree of the Knowledge of Good and Evil, but they were expelled from the Garden to prevent them from eating of the Tree of Life, which would have conferred immortality on them.

Now please read the following text, from the American revision made from the 1611 version, revised by the American Revision Committee in 1881-1885 and again in 1901. I give only the passages that are pertinent for our purpose. I quote from *Genesis*, Chapters 2 and 3.

> Chap. 2.9.: And out of the ground made Jehovah God to grow every tree that is pleasant to the sight, and good for food; the tree of life also in the midst of the garden, and the tree of the knowledge of good and evil. . . . 16. And Jehovah God commanded the man, saying, of every tree in the garden thou mayest freely eat; 17. but of the tree of knowledge of good and evil, thou shalt not eat of it, for in the day that thou eatest thereof thou shalt surely die. . . . 25. And they were both naked, the man and wife, and were not ashamed.

> Chap. 3.1-13: Now the serpent was more subtle than any beast of the field which Jehovah God had made. And he said unto the woman, Yea, hath God said, Ye shall not eat of any tree of the garden. And the woman said unto the serpent, Of the fruit of the trees of the garden we may eat: but of the fruit of the tree which is in the midst of the garden, God hath said, Ye shall not eat of it, neither shall ye touch it, lest ye die. And the serpent said unto the woman, Ye shall not surely die: for God doth know that in the day ye eat thereof, then your eyes shall be opened, and ye shall be as God, knowing good and evil. And when the woman saw that the tree was good for food, and that it was a delight to the eyes, and that the tree was to be desired to make one wise, she took of the fruit thereof, and did eat: and she gave also unto her husband with her, and he did eat. And the eyes of them both were opened, and they knew that they were naked; and they sewed fig-leaves together, and made themselves aprons. And they heard the voice of Jehovah God walking in the garden in the cool of the day:

> and the man and his wife hid themselves from the presence of Jehovah God amongst the trees of the garden.
>
> And Jehovah God called unto the man, and said unto him, Where art thou? And he said, I heard thy voice in the garden, and I was afraid, because I was naked; and I hid myself. And he said, Who told thee that thou wast naked? Hast thou eaten of the tree, whereof I commanded thee that thou shouldest not eat? And the man said, The woman whom thou gavest to be with me, she gave me of the tree, and I did eat. And Jehovah God said unto the woman, What is this thou hast done? And the woman said, The serpent beguiled me, and I did eat.

Therefore Jehovah God inflicted the penalties for their disobedience: on the serpent, he was to go for evermore on his belly; on Eve, she would suffer the pangs of childbirth; on Adam, he would undergo a lifetime of drudgery. We continue quoting from the text.

> Chap. 3.22-24: And Jehovah God said, Behold, the man is become as one of us, to know good and evil; and now, lest he put forth his hand, and take also of the tree of life, and eat, and live for ever – therefore Jehovah God sent him forth from the garden of Eden, to till the ground from whence he was taken. So he drove out the man; and he placed at the east of the garden of Eden the Cherubim, and the flame of a sword which turned every way, to keep the way of the tree of life.

Adam and Eve became self-conscious from eating the 'fruit' and wove fig leaves into aprons to cover themselves from each other and from Jehovah God. The story carries the mystical resonance of the early days, in Mesopotamia, where grew cedars and other conifers.

Some months ago I read the Garden of Eden tale once more, after not having thought of it since childhood. I read it as one who now knew the entheogens. Right away it came over me that the Tree of Knowledge was the tree that has been revered by many tribes of Early Man in Eurasia precisely because there grows under it the mushroom, splendid to look upon, that supplies the entheogenic food to which Early Man attributed miraculous powers. He who composed the tale for us in *Genesis* was clearly steeped in the lore of this entheogen: he refrained from identifying the 'fruit': he was writing for the initiates who would recognize what he was speaking about. I was an initiate. Strangers and also the unworthy would remain in the dark. Adam and Eve had eaten the 'fruit', being led to do so by the serpent, the faithful attendant on the 'fruit', what the mycologists call *Amanita muscaria*, what the initiates call by a variety of euphemisms, which change from time to time, and we have seen to what strange lengths the uninitiated go when these euphemisms are detached from the 'fruit' that they represent. The priestly redactor who set down the *Genesis* tale, an initiate and a believer, attributed to the 'fruit' the gift of self-consciousness, a remarkable observation because self-consciousness is one of the major traits that distinguish humankind from all other creatures. Is it not surprising that the composer of the story gave credit for this particular gift to our mushroom? It is unlikely that he was alone in doing so.

★

In various places of Eurasia where Early Man has been discovered revering a 'Tree of Life', he is fixing his attention on trees that harbor a mycorrhizal relationship with *Amanita muscaria*, the entheogenic mushroom. The Genesis story introduces an elaboration on this theme. The 'Tree of Life' in it confers on those who eat of it immortality, and Jehovah God, lest Adam and Eve eating of it become his equal, expels them from the Garden. Not surprisingly, no one has ever seen this 'Tree of Life'. But a 'Tree of the Knowledge of Good and Evil' is also introduced and the serpent gave of its fruit to Eve. This was the tree that is usually called the 'Tree of Life'. That Adam and Eve had eaten of its 'fruit' became clear when Jehovah God perceived the change in their behavior: they had acquired self-consciousness, which distinguishes mankind from all other creatures. Being naked in each other's presence and in Jehovah God's, they were embarrassed. They gave themselves away and confessed. They may have become aware of their nakedness, but their self-consciousness was key to far more than that.

Valentina Pavlovna and I were the first to become familiar with the entheogens and their historical role in our society. My discovery of the meaning of the Adam and Eve story came as a stunning surprise. That meaning was obvious. The larch of the Nivkhi (pp 60-62) is the Tree of Knowledge, and there are many species of tree that serve as host to *A. muscaria*. The tree is revered but only because it harbors the entheogen that grows at its base, and the entheogen is far too sacred to mention commonly, and in mixed company.

When my wife and I discovered the magnitude of what was revealed to us, what were we to do? We were profoundly grateful to our Indian friends for having given us their confidence. But, with the swift and thorough expansion of European culture, the few remaining islands of traditional entheogenic use will vanish. Valentina Pavlovna and I resolved to do what we could to treat our subject worthily, devoting our lives to studying it and reporting on it.

EPILOGUE
The Age of the Entheogens

My prime candidate for the earliest religion in the world is the cult that became known to us, much much later, as the cult of Soma. In our woodlands, Soma is one of the commonest of mushrooms, growing wherever conifers and birches grow, as well as with certain other trees. Soma is found also in the Tropics, at an elevation in the forested mountains. In the tundra of the north, it has been reported as living with dwarf birches. Soma is breathtaking in its beauty, both at a distance and close up, and it is fortunately not to be confused with any other mushroom. Soma is the supreme mushroom, and while all mushrooms seem mysterious, Soma is the most mysterious of all. Before mankind existed, our bestial ancestors must have known it: gathering herbs for food, they would have tried it and found it good, and they must have seen other herbivorous fellow creatures do likewise.

At the point in his evolutionary progress where we first call him 'Man' beyond a doubt – *Homo sapiens sapiens* – and when he came to know, also beyond a doubt, what awe and reverence were, he clearly felt that Soma was conferring on him mysterious sensations and powers, which seemed to him more than normal: at that point Religion was born, Religion pure and simple, free of Theology, free of Dogmatics, expressing itself in awe and reverence and in lowered voices, mostly at night, when people would gather together to consume the Sacred Element. The first entheogenic experience could have been the first, and an authentic, perhaps the only authentic miracle. This was the beginning of the Age of the Entheogens, long, long ago.

A little later, someone, perhaps an inspired poet, made the suggestion that the miraculous plant, clothed in radiant raiment, was the fruit of the coitus of the lightning strike in the moist mother earth, and the suggestion was welcomed and adopted by the neighbors, by all the users of the plant, and thereafter spread by descent, by parents to children, a gladly accepted dogma, the first Dogma. From early times there was a subsidiary belief: just as the lightningbolt hit mother earth with a single shaft, it gave rise to offspring with a single leg, not a plant because it had no seed, but a unique creature with a single leg or 'stipe' and with its radiant raiment, a spark of its almighty father. These beliefs still exist, in their pristine shape in areas where mankind is still far behind the times, and moribund among peasants who are not caught up with their own leaders. These beliefs are very old, antedating the settlement of America from Asia by millennia. They survive out of habit, demonstrating to us how slowly cultures used to change in our previous incarnation.

In prehistory, running back to paleolithic times, many tombs have been found over most of the Eurasian continent, in which the skeletons are covered with red ochre. A plausible explanation is that the cadavers were given ochre burials to express the fervent hope that Soma, the divine mushrooms of immortality, would keep the departed one in their good care. In China, in documents that tell of very old events, there is occasional mention that cadavers are covered with 'leaves'. Western readers are not apt to remember that 'leaves' have in Chinese the additional meaning of *pilei* of mushrooms. Is not this the meaning in those old documents? Any contemporary Chinese would grasp the meaning. Were they the *pilei* of *A. muscaria*?

★

Some Vedic scholars have raised a ballyhoo because we have declared Soma to have been the white-spotted scarlet mushroom. The Aryans were only one of many peoples, scattered world-wide, to have revered Soma, and they enjoy the unique distinction of having developed a cult and a culture surpassing all others in that period for richness and subtlety, a truly memorable religion that we can only admire and study thousands of years later, the flowering of a people not yet possessing an alphabet, who left to posterity a collection of hymns in their tongue – Sanskrit – a tongue that we are proud to say is a collateral ancestor of our European dialects. What an incredible achievement!

When Valentina Pavlovna and I, in August of 1927, started out on our pilgrimage in the Catskills, little did we dream that it would transport us so far. All *Rig Veda* scholars knew much about the *Rig Veda*, but things irrelevant for our purpose, and so when it comes to *A. muscaria*, they must admit that their ignorance is total. They denounce our *SOMA* as 'outrageous' and of course cite Brough's review article in the *BSOAS*. They know the tenor of his argument and did not even need to read it, accepting it enthusiastically on Brough's great authority. I have yet to meet any Vedist who has read it carefully. To approach the subject, one had to know what we now call the entheogens, and I can testify personally that Brough's knowledge of them was nil.

Does 'toadstool' date from before Christianity came to us, and did not 'toad' carry an endearing flavor to our remote ancestors, as it does still in China, and also in the remote areas of Lithuania – the Lithuanians being the last people in Europe to convert to Christianity? The prejudice against *A. muscaria* is so powerful that it has led many writers of mushroom manuals, mostly by mycologists, to say it is toxic, and even sometimes to cast anathemas on it – the distant rumblings of ancient religious disputes. Anyone who undertakes to study soberly its properties is inviting disaster to his career – a strange aberration in the scientific realm, really derived in all likelihood from the religious world.

*

A prodigious expansion in Man's memory must have been the gift that differentiated mankind from his predecessors, and I surmise that this expansion in memory led to a simultaneous growth in the gift of language, these two powers generating in man that self-consciousness which is the third of the triune traits that alone make man unique. Those three gifts – memory, language, and self-consciousness – so interlock that they seem inseparable, the aspects of a quality that permitted us to achieve all the wonders we now know. With our computers we seem bent on dispensing with human memory as we have known it in prehistory, and even in the modest degree that our parents knew it. I am asking myself whether Soma could have possessed the power to spark what I have called these triune traits.

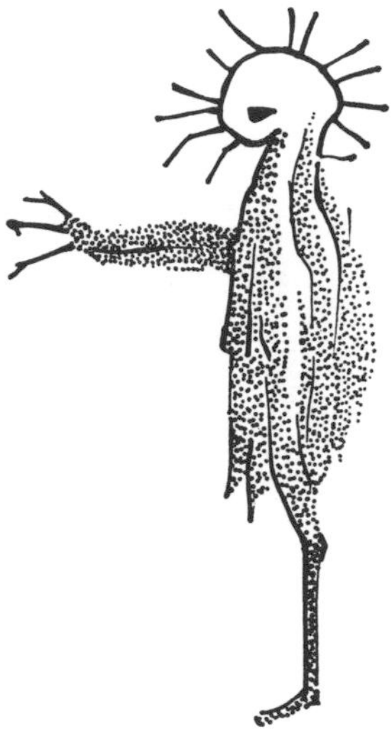

Fig. 14. One-sided man, or 'unilateral figure', or 'halfling': from monograph on the Chukchi by Vladimir Bogoraz, published by American Museum of Natural History in various editions at turn of the century. His 'one-sided man' was republished by Rodney Needham.

Rodney Needham of All Souls, Oxford, in 1980 has posed, in an elegant essay *Reconnaissances*, published elegantly by the University of Toronto Press, a problem that bears directly on our work. He draws attention to the wide dissemination of the 'Unilateral Figures' that are scattered around the world, from the Eskimos of the extreme North to the Yamaha of Tierra del Fuego, from the Nahua of Mexico to the folklore of Greece and Romania. He has dealt with a surprising number of instances, far more than I have cited. We reproduce his illustration of a 'Unilateral Figure' taken from Vladimir Bogoraz' opus on the Chukchi published at the turn of this century by the American Museum of Natural History. But Needham never mentions what we call the entheogens nor the supreme entheogen, Soma. If the cultures where Needham finds 'unilateral figures' there was knowledge of the entheogens, here then will be proof that this ancient religion has existed even more widely than I thought: I will be less surprised than overjoyed.

After their long and important history, Soma and the other entheogens have disappeared almost without a trace. How odd! The Divinity Schools seem not to know that they exist. Anthropologists have long had contact with them but have not specialized in their study.

UNFINISHED BUSINESS

One quasi-divinity or malign spirit in our world has been Satan. He also is a cripple, either a club- or a splay-foot is his deformity. In Old French Satan was often called simply *le bot*, now-a-days usually heard in the form *pied bot*, 'club foot'. *Le bot* served also for 'toad' and 'a mushroom'! Mark you, '*a* mushroom'. Not any mushroom. Was the French lexicographer unsure of the species, or did he possess no name for it, or was he inhibited by the same tabu that the English and most other West Europeans felt and feel, and so he refrained from saying it was what the French today call *le crapaudin*, or '*la fausse oronge*', as well as '*le tue-mouche*', and what we call Soma? How odd it would be if here we come, once more, upon One-Leg: *ekapād, hurakan, auf einem Bein*, in our familiar Satan! If so, when and how did he inherit (or usurp) this most ancient honor (or stigma)? Must we entertain the notion that by a prodigious feat of prestidigitation, acting true to character, he arrogated to himself the attributes of the Almighty Lightningbolt?

This may be only an aberrant idea of mine, but I think it is worth pursuing: why is Satan a Single-Foot?

CHAPTER TWO

LIGHTNINGBOLT AND MUSHROOM*

by R. Gordon Wasson

The inquirer who turns to Littré to learn about truffles, on reading the entry under *truffe*, comes upon a nugget of curious information that certainly fails to catch his attention. It seems in certain regions of France (presumably there where truffles abound) the country folk in thundery weather are wont to say, *Voilà un bon temps pour les truffes*, 'What fine weather it is for truffles!' Why in thundery weather? Not when it rains, mind you, but when it thunders. Nothing in Littré alerts the reader to the mystery that here lies hidden. The saying of these French rustics seems to be one of the surviving traces in Europe of a belief that reaches back in time deep into prehistory and in space wherever Eurasians or their descendants have lived. It is the end of Ariadne's thread that we propose to follow far and to a far-reaching end.

Pliny the Elder declared that truffles were disposed to grow in the time of autumnal rains, and above all (in the full-bodied Elizabethan translation of Philemon Holland) 'if the aire be troubled and disquieted with many thunders: during that season there will be good store of such Mushromes, &c, especially (I say) if it thunder much':

> *De tuberibus haec traduntur peculiariter: Cum fuerint imbres autumnales, ac tonitrua crebra, tunc nasci, & maxime e tonitribus.* [*Hist. Nat.*, Bk 19:37]

When Philemon Holland around 1600 rendered *tuberibus*, 'truffles', by 'mushromes', the word 'truffle' and the plant it represents were as yet unknown to the English-speaking world.

Juvenal wrote of the longed-for thunder in springtime [*sic*] that replenishes the table with truffles:

> *Post hunc tradentur tubera, si ver tunc erit et facient optata tonitrua cenas maiores.* [*Satire V:* 116-118]

* In 1956 I published 'Lightningbolt and Mushrooms: An Essay in Early Cultural Exploration' in a Festschrift: *For Roman Jakobson* (Mouton, The Hague) on his 60th birthday. It was my first paper on ethnomycology, a discipline that I founded. Here is that same paper, revised, reworked and shortened.

Strange: Juvenal speaks of tables laden with truffles in springtime, associated in men's minds as this season is with frequent thunderstorms. But in Italy truffles come in the fall and early winter until February. What was Juvenal thinking of? Was he conforming to a popular belief at the cost of doing violence to nature? Pliny had spoken of autumnal thunder-showers, adhering to the right season.

The *tuber* was an underground fungus, apparently embracing all species of both truffles and the genus *Terfezia*. The many species of *Terfezia* are often confused by travelers in the Mediterranean and Near East with truffles, but *Terfezia* and truffles, though both of course fungi, belong to different families, not merely distinct species. *Terfezia* flourish in the arid areas around the Mediterranean and eastward, and when classic writers refer to the Libyan truffles as especially good, they are speaking of *Terfezia*. In Greek the *tuber* was the *hydnon*, and Plutarch, in an essay now virtually forgotten, asked why people said thunder made the *hydnon* to grow. He asked why, not whether, the thunder made them grow, apparently accepting the fact, and he found no sure answer.[1] There was an underground fungus that the ancient Greeks called the 'lightningbolt' – *keraunion* – was it an alternative name for the *hydnon*? In Thrace *keraunion* was called the *oiton*: this word is a dialectal variant of *hydnon* and the mushroom presumably the same. Athenæus, writing in the third century after Christ, quotes Theophrastus five centuries earlier on these Thracian fungi:

> Concerning these a singular fact is related, *viz*, that they grow when autumn rains come with severe thunderstorms; the more thundering there is, the more they grow, the presumption being that this is the more important cause. [*Deipnosophists*, Loeb translation, Bk II:62]

(Theophrastus did not make Juvenal's mistake: he adhered to *autumnal* thunderstorms.) In ancient Greece and Rome we have to do with a notion that everyone accepted, a cliché, perhaps a tiresome conversational tag. 'It's not the rain, it's the thunder that makes them grow,' people would say, just as today in summer the New Yorker insists, 'It's not the heat, it's the humidity.' Did the Greeks and Romans arrive at this belief, which for them pertained to underground fungi only, by observing nature? The answer to this question had best be deferred until we have completed our pilgrimage throughout Eurasia and the lands to which in prehistory the Eurasian tribesmen emigrated, to wit, Polynesia and the New World.

This essay on its first appearance in 1956 prompted our friend Georges

1. Plutarch's *Moralia*, *Table-talk* IV, Question 2. Loeb Classical Translations, Vol VIII, p 316ff.

Becker, gifted *savant* and humanist of the countryside of eastern France, to recall an ancient belief surviving in and around his native village of Lougres: the people there hold that *Boletus satanas* and *Boletus luridus*, as well as those other species of mushrooms that turn blue on breaking, grow where lightning has struck, around isolated trees in meadows. Furthermore, he had a friend, an aged countryman, who often gave utterance, in the patois of Lougres, to an old saw:

> *Lou mâ temps, c'â lou bon temps des craipâs et pe des tchampégnôs.* (*L'orage, c'est le bon temps pour les crapauds et les champignons.*) (Thunderstorms are good weather for toads and mushrooms.)

The saying hides a pun: in the local dialect *mâ temps* means both 'bad weather' and 'thunderstorm' and therefore what is 'bad weather' for human beings is 'good weather' for toads and mushrooms.

The Piedmont in Italy is preeminent in that country for mycophilia, and immense quantities of fungi are marketed there and consumed. The towns of Alba and Cuneo are especially noted for their 'white truffles' (*tartufi bianchi*), *Tuber magnatum*. The reader will recall the classic tradition that links thunder with truffles. But in the Piedmont, strange to say, the 'thunder-mushroom', *trun*, (in Piemontese, 'thunder') is not the *tartufo bianco*. It is any market *Lactarius*, the common species being *L. sanguifluus* and *L. deliciosus*.

Among the English I have not yet found any trace of the ancient belief in a tie between mushrooms and thunder, but there is one quotation on the subject that should be carefully read. On 22 February 1774 Sir Alexander Dick, a retired physician, wrote to James Boswell a letter from which I will extract one sentence:[1]

> While I was at London, I alwise found plenty of Mushrooms at Covent Garden, good & reasonable during the Summer Season – this was the year 1760 and made Dr. Armstrong, quite of my opinion, who partook frequently of my Mushroom breakfasts – and *as Mushrooms often arise from Lightning, when they came well dressed to table we used to stile them Ambrosia ...*

I have italicized the ending. I feel fairly confident that this reference to mushrooms and lightning goes back to ancient Greece and Rome, rather than the Anglo-Saxons or ancient Britons. Dick was the educated 18th century Englishman, thoroughly grounded in the classics. Mushrooms in his mind were linked

1. By courtesy of the Editorial Committee of the Yale Editions of the Private Papers of James Boswell, New Haven, Conn.

to lightning and ambrosia was also; whence the playful association of mushrooms and ambrosia.

From our citations we see that the linking of thunder with mushrooms is not with *all* mushrooms but only with this kind or that, and the kind changes according to the region. In the temperate zone thunder is associated primarily with spring and early summer, but truffles are a product of the fall and early winter. Of course thunder *in spring* might produce truffles *in fall*, but no where in the classic sources is such a sophisticated idea hinted at. (Later we shall see that this very belief is actually entertained by the Bedouin of the Arabian desert.) While thunderstorms of course occur at all seasons, even in mid-winter, is it not odd that in classical times people sometimes linked springtime thunder and truffles? This bad fit in the popular belief must have been what led Juvenal and a few late writers to assert that the best truffles, contrary to fact, come in the spring. For example, Franciscus Marius Grapaldus in his *De Partibus Aedium*, *c* 1492:

> ... But truffles (= *tubera*) the pigs root out of the earth with their snouts. Truffles are surrounded on all sides by earth, without roots, neither thickly growing in [one] place nor cracking out among the dry and sandy thickets. [They] are to be called certainly nothing other than flesh of the earth. *Best at spring and more often during thunder, they are said to arouse dying love.* [Book II Chap. 3, italics mine.]

Grapaldus was forcing nature into the Procrustean bed of Juvenal's text and the popular belief.

The Germanic world yields us one pleasant citation associating mushrooms with thunderstorms. The Rev. Robert B. Reeves, Jr., Chaplain of the Presbyterian Hospital in New York, wrote me 9 March 1960 these words:

> In Harrisburg, Pa., where I lived from 1915 to 1923, my mother employed a Mrs. Tetzer, who was 'Pennsylvania Dutch', to bake Christmas cookies and help with the fall and spring housecleaning. She was full of country lore and would hold us children in fascination around the kitchen table or the stove, talking as she worked. One of the things she told us was that the time to gather mushrooms was after thunderstorms; that we should watch for the lightning, notice carefully where it struck, for wherever the lightning entered the ground mushrooms would spring up. These were the only kind that were fit to eat. The others, that grew without benefit of lightning, were toadstools and poisonous.

The Pennsylvania Dutch are descended largely from pioneers who hailed from the Palatinate. I have had no opportunity to take soundings there.

Many Polish and Czech friends of the recent emigration speak of a folk belief in their countries tying the growth of mushrooms to thunderstorms, but I have yet to find an informant who can pin down these beliefs in specific fashion. Similarly Ivan Sechanov, the Bulgarian mycologist specializing in the higher fungi, writes me that the Bulgarians link mushrooms with lightning, 'especially *Morchella* spp. and some others.' Probably field work in the west Slavic countries and in Bulgaria would yield more evidence than I present here.

The Great Russians, who know by cultural inheritance incomparably more about mushrooms than the classical writers did, call a particular kind of rain *gribnoj dozhd'*, 'mushroom rain'. Mushrooms, they say, come after a warm and steady and gentle rain, emphatically not the quick, violent, driving rain that we associate with thunderstorms. This 'mushroom rain' of the Russians leads to the growth of all kinds of mushrooms proper to the season, and mycologists agree with the Russians. For the Russians *gribnoj dozhd'* is a term used often to describe a particular kind of rain, even when mushrooms are not under discussion.

Roman Jakobson has drawn my attention to an obscure book by S. V. Maximov entitled *Lesnaya Glush'*, 'The Backwoods', published in St. Petersburg in 1909, in which the author dwells lovingly on the customs and beliefs that survived in the remote and impoverished village of Parfentief, some 300 miles northeast of Moscow. The villagers there were much given to mushroom-gathering and every year with the spring thaw an ancient of the village, Ivan Mikheich, would celebrate the event with a feast of morels. At that banquet without fail the host would explain, as a prelude, that the morel was good to eat only before the first thunder of spring. Thereafter, according to him, a snake would inject venom into the mushroom and cause it to rot and disappear. Only three times in his life had he heard thunder before trying out the fresh morels. . . . In the story of Ivan Mikheich the two essential elements are present, the thunder and a kind of mushroom. But here in the East Slavic world, far distant in time and space, our episode takes on a reverse twist. The morel is of course a springtime mushroom and thereby Ivan Mikheich avoided the uncomfortable discrepancy of Juvenal and Grapaldus. But with him the role of the thunder, while it is still vital, is unfavorable to the fungi. It casts an evil spell on them, and works hand in glove with the serpent, who now enters the scene for the first time.

The late Professor Georg Morgenstierne of Oslo has pointed out to me how widespread even now is the belief in our myth on the other side of our Indo-European world. He quotes an informant in Persepolis as saying that the *dum-*

balān are thought to grow in the desert after lightning;[1] *dumbalān*, literally 'sheep's fries', is apparently the name given to an underground species of *Terfezia*.

In Tadzhikistan, around Match and in the Yaghnob Valley southeast of Samarkand, Iranian dialects are spoken that come down from the ancient Sogdian language. In those two regions the belief persists that the thunder comes when the sky-borne divinity known as *Mama*, 'Grandmother', shakes out her bloomers, and then from her bloomers lice tumble down to earth, and from the lice springs up a crop of mushrooms.[2] (A similar belief about the genesis of mushrooms from the shaking of old furs is reported from the neighboring Turkic peoples.) At the thunderclap the children around Match cry out: *Puri, puri, xorč*, *puri* being the name of a plant, an annual, whose identity we do not know, and *xorč* being the word for the mushroom. There is reason to think *xorč* is the specific name of *Pleurotus fossulatus*; if so, *puri* must be a dead umbellifer, its saprophytic host. In the Yaghnob Valley the children's cry is different: *Katta xarčak man, pullja xarčak tau*, which is to say, 'The big mushroom is mine, the little one yours.' How enigmatic and tantalizing are these odd bits of our popular belief discovered in the heart of Asia! Perhaps they will fall into place as our pattern takes shape.

In the east of the Pashto-speaking area of Afghanistan the *zməkəy gošə*, 'earth meat,' grows 'with the first roar of thunder accompanied by rain.' This mushroom is certainly a morel, called by the Uzbeks in their Turkic language *qozaqarni*, 'baby lamb's belly,' and they too link its appearance with spring thunder and rain. In Farah, in the southwest, Pashto speakers associate thunder with a mushroom called *gobalakə*, whose identity I do not know but by the description given me think it is *Phellorina* sp. At Bargramatal, a town in the northeast of Afghanistan, in the Hindu Kush where they speak the ancient Katei language, an informant told us of a mushroom, *gokluk*, that he said was produced in spring by thunder. He drew it and his drawing strongly suggested *Coprinus comatus*.[3]

1. *BSOAS*, 1957, xx, p. 453. I take this opportunity to express my gratitude to Professor Morgenstierne for his help and counsel throughout my inquiries. His specific help mentioned in divers places in this paper does not begin to repay my indebtedness to this great scholar.

2. The Tadzhik and Yaghnob references appear in M. S. Andreev's 'Po Etnografii Tadzhikov,' a contribution in *Tadzhikistan, sbornik statej*, a volume edited by N. L. Korzhenevskij and published in Tashkent (1925), pp 172-3, which we consulted. Heinrich F. J. Junker uses the material in *Arische Forschungen: Yaghnobi-Studien*, I, p. 106 (= *Abhandlungen d. philol.-hist. Klasse d. sächsischen Akademie d. Wissenschaften*, Band xli, No. 2, Leipzig, 1930.)

3. For the Afghan fungal vocabulary I am indebted to M. Ch. M. Kieffer, the Alsatian specialist in the Afghan languages, for an invaluable 26 page memorandum prepared on my instigation in March 1965.

In Kashmir certain edible gilled mushrooms known in Kashmiri as *hĕḍur* and *hĕnḍa* are supposed to emerge after thunder, but this belief attaches above all to the morel, called locally *kana-gᵘ̈ch*, 'ear-mushroom'. The Kashmiri do not go out looking for morels until there has been thunder. They are clear about this, and also that the morels are powerful aphrodisiacs, to be eaten at weddings, if you can afford them. I gathered this information from Kashmiri informants when I was in Śrinagar in April 1965. Even more interesting are the verses in the Sanskrit lyric *Meghadūta*, 'The Cloud-Messenger', composed *c* AD 400 by *Kālidāsa*. In verse 11 the exiled *yaksha* or demigod addresses the raincloud drifting northward over India: 'When they eagerly hear thy sweet-sounding, fertilizing thunder, which can cover the earth with mushrooms . . . !' The *thunder* covers the earth with *mushrooms*! In the heart of this mycophobic Hindu people we find an outstanding poet giving voice to the same notion that we find elsewhere. But he does not suggest that the *mushrooms* replenish the tables: for upper caste Hindus, mushrooms are tabu. Here 'mushroom' is *śilīndhra*, a puzzling word of odd aspect that Professor Morgenstierne thinks was probably borrowed from some pre-Sanskrit language of India. From a variant of the poem it is clear that a mushroom with pileus was meant, and one lexicographer says that this mushroom was linked with cow-dung: these hints may point toward *Stropharia cubensis*. The ending *-dhra* could mean 'carrying' and *śilī-*, a rare and doubtful word, might mean a worm or a female toad. Such clues, having little weight by themselves, may become clothed with meaning in the context of other evidence. We recall that in India Hindus of the three upper castes are forbidden by their religion to eat mushrooms of any kind.

Now let us look beyond the confines of the Indo-European world.

In a personal letter to me dated 27 May 1950, Colonel H. R. P. Dickson, author of *The Arab of the Desert* and an outstanding authority on the life of the Bedouin, confirmed that the Bedouin are great lovers of *Terfezia*. He said that in the season of the *wasm* (October to early November) they look for heavy rains accompanied by *thunder and lightning*, and if the weather is propitious then, they know that some months later, in February and March, *Terfezia* will abound, and when the days are fulfilled, then the black-tent folk strike their tents and make their way across the desert to the places where grows the rug-rug bush, known to botanists as *Helianthemum Lippi*, for the *Terfezia* thrive close by this plant. Then at dawn and dusk, by the horizontal rays of the sun, the women and children and shepherds detect the shadows cast by the slight monticules caused by the swelling underground fungi, and gather them, and everyone feasts on them. . . . There is a metaphorical expression for a fungus found in a dictionary of classical Arabic,

بَنَاتُ الرَّعْدِ

BANĀT^{u}'R-RA'D', 'the Daughters of Thunder', but we are left in the dark as to the species so designated. It might be a name for the *Terfezia* that Dickson speaks of.

In India around Mysore, in Dravidian country, the thunder is said to be linked to the appearance of species of the genus *Phallus*. In the Northeast of India the Santal, an aboriginal tribe living on the western fringes of West Bengal, in eastern Bihar and in northern Orissa, call certain mushrooms *putka*, and the mushrooms so named grow always after thunder: so the Santal tell us. The mushrooms called *putka* are a *Scleroderma*, and also a false *putka* that is a puffball.

In Tibet by far the most popular mushroom is the *ser sha*, 'yellow flesh'; it is reputed to grow after thunderstorms. Despite our strenuous efforts we have failed to obtain a specimen of this mushroom and it remains unidentified. A painting of this mushroom in the Kew mycological collection was repudiated emphatically by my Tibetan friends in India.

Now let us turn to the Chinese. There came into my possession in 1951 a copy of a handwritten work in eight volumes on ethnomycology entitled in Japanese *The History of Mushrooms*, dated 1811 and composed by Karashi Masujima, who wrote under the pen names of Ranen, 'orchid garden', and Gushá, 'the fool.' (In choosing his field of research he preceded the Wassons by a century and a half!) He was a Japanese scholar teaching in Yedo at the school for samurai called Shoheiko. In this book are discussions of three kinds of Chinese mushrooms linked with thunder by the people of Suzhou and the Province of Juangzhou:

雷驚蕈	雷聲菌	雷菌
leijing xun	*leisheng jun*	*lei jun*
Thunder-aroused Mushroom	Thunderbolt Mushroom	Thunder Mushroom

The description of these mushrooms is insufficient for identification, but they all grow above ground. The three names may be variants for a single species. There is no reason to suppose that the thunder myth was confined to Suzhou and Juangzhou Province. When I was in Taiwan and Hong Kong in 1964-1966 the thunder association was commonly attributed to species of *Termitomyces*, a delectable table mushroom. The late Professor Roger Heim, the famous French mycologist and a gastronome, ranked them first among the edible mushrooms of the world. In the Philippines the mycologist José Miguel Mendoza reports in his *Philippine Mushrooms*[1] the common native belief throughout the islands that thunder and lightning cause the generation of mushrooms, and in the spring of the year, when people hear the thunder roll, they rush into the fields to gather the edible kinds. In the Pampango tongue, spoken in central Luzon, *Termitomyces albuminosus* (Berk.) Heim (formerly *Collybia albuminosa*) is called *payungpayungan kulog*, where the first element means 'parasol-like' and *kulog* is the word for thunder in both Tagalog and Pampango. This undoubtedly reflects the native belief to which Mendoza refers. I am told that the same association with thunder exists in Kyushu and the Ryu Kyu islands. The termites build their nests there and the farmers rate the termite-mushrooms highly. These offshore manifestations might easily mark the spread of a Chinese concept.

The thunder association of particular species of mushrooms runs all through the mycological writings of the Chinese. It seems to be more prevalent there than anywhere else. The sclerotia of *Omphalia lapidescens* Berk., which grow in Southern China as pellets of little balls on the roots of bamboo trees, are called 'thunder-balls' 雷丸, *lei wan* in Chinese or *raigan* in Japanese, and they were esteemed in Chinese medicine. The knowing-ones must have believed them to be aphrodisiacs. These balls were so highly regarded that the Japanese emperor Shōmu in the middle of the 8th century, when he and later his widow Kōmyō created the Shōsōin Temple in Nara, depositing in it all the treasures that he most prized, included in the collection some of these sclerotia.[2] At that time the Japanese Court was under strong Chinese influence and the 'thunder-balls' had probably been imported from Southern China. In China the famous *ling zhi* 靈芝, 'divine mushroom of immortality', has occasionally been called the *lei zhi* 雷芝, 'thunder zhi'.[3] In that idyllic text, *The Mushrooms of Wu*,

1. Published in *The Philippine Journal of Science*, LXV, Jan.-April 1938.

2. At the end of the second World War in the wake of the Japanese defeat these treasures were opened for inspection, and a few of the 'thunder-balls' were shown to a leading Japanese mycologist, Yoshio Kobayashi, on the staff of the Ueno National Science Museum. He confirmed their identity, twelve centuries after they had been deposited.

3. The Chinese *ling zhi* has been identified as *Ganoderma lucidum* by two Japanese mycologists, Iwao Hino in 1937 and Rokuya Imazeki in 1939. See *Transactions* of the Asiatic Soc. of

吳蕈譜 *Wuxun pu* written by Wu Lin 吳林 shortly after 1662 and published in 1703, in which the author dilates with love on the rich mushroom life of the countryside around his native village of Wu, the beneficial effect of thunder on certain mushrooms figures conspicuously. Let it be noted that in China, as well as elsewhere, the role of thunder always applies to particular species, never to the fungal world as a whole.

Now we shall shift the scene to Madagascar, where the indigenous cultures are dominantly Malayo-Indonesian, Professor Heim has reported an extraordinary practice of the Tanala people there.[1] They dry and convert to powder the giant sclerotium (known to mycologists as *Pachyma cocos*) of the mushroom *Lentinus tuber regium* Fries, on which the Tanala people bestow the name *olatafa*. Then when a thunderstorm of fearful violence breaks, the natives quickly put some of the powder moistened with water into their mouths, and as the lightningbolt streaks by, they spit forth the fungal paste into the teeth of the storm crying *Fotaka*! or else *Fotaka malemy*!, which is to say, 'Earth!' or 'Soft Earth!' The word *olatafa* appears to be related to *tafa*, meaning 'unbalanced' – a startling association of ideas, as we shall soon see. Professor Heim goes on to say that neighbors of the Tanala people in Madagascar – the Betsimisarakas, the Antimoros, and the Tsimihety – also make use of the *Lentinus tuber regium* to protect themselves against the fury of lightning, but they merely spread around them, on the ground, the dried powder of the sclerotium at the moment when the thunderstorm develops a frightening intensity. These three peoples like the Tanala speak languages of the Malayo-Indonesian family. Recent linguistic studies have indicated that they broke away from their kin in Southeast Asia before the Hindu influence made itself fully felt there, certainly before the 4th century AD,[2] perhaps much earlier.

The Maoris of New Zealand, pure Polynesians, possess the thunder link with mushrooms. In the Maori language *whatitiri* means 'thunder'. *Whatitiri* is a female ancestor of the Maori race. Her son (or grandson) Tawhiki was linked with lightning, which flashed from his armpits. In 1963, when I was in New Zealand, Kiri Maniapoto, a Maori woman of Rotorua, told me (and I paraphrase

Japan, 3rd series Vol. 11, 'Mushrooms and Japanese Culture', by R. G. Wasson, p 10; 'Japanese Mushroom Names', by Rokuya Imazeki, p. 40.

1. 'L'Olatafa', by Roger Heim, published in the *Archives du Muséum National d'Histoire Naturelle*, Volume du Tricentenaire, 6e Serie, Tome XII, 1935.

2. S. Thierry: 'A propos des emprunts sanskrits en malgache', *Journal Asiatique*, Paris, 1959, pp 311-348; Louis Molet: 'L'Origine des Malgaches', *Civilisation Malgache*, Tananarive, 1964, Série Sciences Humaines No. 1, Faculté des Lettres et Sciences Humaines, Université de Madagascar.

what she said) that when it thunders, the Spirits are defecating, and the turd falling to earth is the *tutae whatitiri*, the fungus ball that quickly expands into the strange, the astonishing, net- or basket-fungus common in New Zealand and called by mycologists the *Clathrus cibarius* (Tul.) Fischer. *Tutae* means 'faeces'.

*

In the course of my inquiries I have found only one chlorophyll-bearing plant linked to thunder or lightning: the mistletoe, – like the mushrooms, linked with religion.

My survey of the evidence is certainly not exhaustive. It comprises the documentation gathered intermittently by one man over a few decades. There must be many variants that I have missed. I have dealt only with the peoples of Eurasia and their offspring, the Polynesians. In black Africa I have taken soundings among the Baganda of Uganda, the Ibo and Hausa, and Fulani (= Peul) peoples. The results were wholly negative. If this prove true of all the peoples of black Africa, it would localize the origin of the myth in Eurasia. The Kumá people in the Wahgi Valley in the center of New Guinea know nothing of a fungus-thunder tie, though their empirical knowledge of the higher fungi is impressive.

An intelligent observer in Eurasia familiar only with the folk beliefs of his own area might naturally conclude that the local notion linking thunder with a particular species of mushroom derived from a subtle observation of nature on the part of his countrymen. But faced with the diversity of beliefs in various parts of the Eurasian world, he would have to pause and admit that the natural causes must be remote and involved. He would observe that except in two or three places such as Madagascar and the Maoris of New Zealand, the survivals are mere verbal fossils: nothing is left of them save a phrase repeated out of habit, thoughtlessly.

Our survey of the fossilized myth shows that in different regions it is linked with species of some fifteen genera:

Boletus	*Omphalia*	*Tuber*	(This includes the black truffle of Périgord and the truffle esteemed by the Romans, perhaps the *tartufo bianco* of contemporary Italy.)
Clathrus	*Phallus*		
Coprinus	*Phellorina*		
Lactarius	*Pleurotus*		
Lentinus	*Terfezia*	*Scleroderma*	thunder-engendered mushrooms called *putka* among the Santal of India
Morchella	*Termitomyces*	*Lycoperdon*	

and the genus represented by the unidentified Tibetan *ser sha*. The species include inedible (*eg*, *Phallus*, *Clathrus*) as well as edible kinds, and the myths show a wide variety in the details of the folk beliefs, the most elaborate of the myths being found among the Tadzhiks, the Tanala of Madagascar, and the Maori of New Zealand.

In every instance there is one common denominator: the link between a designated species of mushroom and the thunderbolt.

Of a belief associating mushrooms generally, regardless of species, to thunderstorms, we have found evidence in only two regions, both in Europe. In France, apart from the specific associations that I have already noted, belief in the favorable influence of thunder showers on the growth of mushrooms is widespread, as it seems also to be in Poland and Bohemia. Further inquiry on the ground would probably bring out added details corresponding to those we have found elsewhere. In the temperate zone thunder and lightning come mostly in spring and early summer though not exclusively, and mushrooms in late August and September, and the mythic belief makes no effort to reconcile this contradiction.

As for the mycologists, when confronted with the many faces of this belief, they offer no help in explaining them.

CHAPTER THREE

THE MAHĀVĪRA VESSEL AND THE PLANT PŪTIKA

*by Stella Kramrisch**

The Mahāvīra vessel is an anointed, empty earthen pot glowing red hot in the sacrificial fire. Its function, in the first and original part of the Pravargya rite of which it is the center, is symbolic. It is only in the second and subsequent parts of this rite that the vessel will be filled with milk, that it will be replete with perceptible contents.

Pravargya means that "which is to be put on the fire," *viz.* the Mahāvīra vessel. In the later Vedic age, in the White Yajurveda, the Pravargya sacrifice had been combined with the Ṛg Vedic Soma sacrifice, the Pravargya being performed just before or at the beginning of the Soma sacrifice. Myth and ritual of the two sacrifices were coordinated in one configuration. The head of this configuration is called the Head of Makha.

The Head of Makha of which the Mahāvīra vessel (*ukhā*) is the symbol, is the main and central sacred object of the Pravargya sacrifice. The vessel is made of clay to which four other ingredients are added. Pūtika plants are one of them and their significance is paramount in the myth and ritual of the Head of Makha. The Pravargya sacrifice requires a special initiation over and above that of the Soma sacrifice and it must not be performed by one who for the first time offers a Soma sacrifice (ŚB.14.2.2.44-46; Āp.ŚS.15.20-21).

THE SECRET OF THE CUT-OFF HEADS

The myth of the Mahāvīra vessel is told in several versions, that of the Śatapatha Brāhmaṇa being the most exhaustive:

> The Gods, Agni, Indra, Soma, Makha, Viṣṇu, and the Viśve Devāḥ perform a sacrificial session in Kurukṣetra in order to win glory. They agree that whoever amongst them through austerity, fervour, faith, sacrifice and oblations would first encompass the end of the sacrifice would be the most excellent among them and the glory should then be common to them all. Viṣṇu obtained it (ŚB.14.1.1-5).
>
> Viṣṇu is the sacrifice. But Viṣṇu was unable to contain the love of glory of his (ŚB.14.1.6).

* The Philadelphia Museum of Art and The Institute of Fine Arts, New York University.

Taking his bow with three arrows he stepped forth and rested his head on the bow. Then the termites of the Upadīka kind gnawed the bowstring, it was cut, the ends of the bow springing asunder cut off Viṣṇu's head (ŚB.14.1.1.7).

It fell and became the Sun. The rest of the body lay stretched out with the top towards east (ŚB.14.1.1.10).

The gods said: Our all-encompassing hero (*mahān-viraḥ*) has fallen. Therefrom the Mahāvīra vessel was named, and the vital sap (that flowed from him) they wiped with their hands (*sam-mṛj*). Whence the Mahāvīra is the Samrāj (the emperor) (ŚB.14.1.1.11).

The gods rushed forward to him, Indra applied himself to him, limb to limb, engulfed, encompassed him and became possessed of his glory [*ie* of that of the headless Viṣṇu] (ŚB.14.1.1.12).

The gods went on worshipping with that headless sacrifice (ŚB.14.1.1.17).

Dadhyañc Atharvaṇa knew this pure essence (the Madhu, the sweet [and secret] knowledge of the Pravargya), how the head of the sacrifice is put on again; how the sacrifice becomes complete again (ŚB.14.1.1.18 [*cf* 4.1.5.18]).

Indra threatens to cut off the head of Dadhyañc if he divulges the secret to anyone else [for Indra had obtained only the glory of the headless body.] (ŚB.14.1.1.19).

The Aśvins hear this and offer themselves as disciples to Dadhyañc (ŚB.14.1.1.20).

Dadhyañc refuses them, fearing Indra would cut off his head (ŚB.14.1.1.21).

However the Aśvins promise to protect Dadhyañc by the following scheme: when Dadhyañc would receive them as pupils they would cut off his head and replace it by a horse's head. Dadhyañc will teach them through a horse's head – which head Indra will cut off. Then they will replace Dadhyañc's own head (ŚB.14.1.1.22-24).

Dadhyañc Ātharvaṇa with a horse's head taught them the sweet [secret] (ŚB.14.1.1.25).

The god who does not honour an agreement and arrogantly keeps to himself the glory he undertook to share with the other gods is beheaded by his own bow. The decapitated god is Viṣṇu, in the Śatapatha Brāhmaṇa. His name is Makha in the Tāṇḍya Brāhmaṇa while in the Taittirīya Āraṇyaka he is called Makha Vaiṣṇava.[1] He is also called Makha Saumya (in ŚB.14.1.2.17). Viṣṇu and Makha are equated, they are one person for Viṣṇu is the sacrifice (ŚB.14.1.1.6) and Makha is the same as Viṣṇu (ŚB.14.1.1.13). Viṣṇu is particularly the Soma sacrifice.

Except in the above story, Makha does not figure amongst the gods. Makha's

1. Tāṇḍya B.7.5.6; Taitt. Ār.1.1-7; Śatapatha B.14.1.1-5; 14.1.2.17, a different version in Ait. B. 1.19; *cf* ṚV, 10.171.2 'Indra severed Makha's head from the skin' (body; and Taitt.S.1.1.8.)

head however is invoked in Taitt.S.1.1.8. and it is the very center of the Pravargya sacrifice. Makha's head means the Sun (ŚB.14.1.1.10) and has for its symbol the Mahāvīra vessel. Mahāvīra is here being translated as 'all encompassing hero,' with reference to the sun,[1] but also with regard to Makha whose cutoff head is restored by the Pravargya ritual to the sacrifice.[2] Makha, in the ŚB. is the deific name of the sacrifice.[3] The Sacrifice had its head cut off. Its headless body lies prostrate. This fallen hero is reconstituted by having his head sacrificially joined by the Pravargya ritual to the body, that is to the basic Soma sacrifice.

Who but Viṣṇu or Makha among the gods could encompass to its end the sacrifice? For Makha himself is the sacrifice and Viṣṇu is the sacrifice; subject and object are one. In its deific shape, as Makha or Viṣṇu, the sacrifice is the main figure in the myth. The myth is acted out in the form of the ritual. The meaning of the sacrificial myth, the staging and action of the sacrificial ritual, aim at the atonement of an initial wrong and at reintegration. In the present myth an arrogantly broken pledge is the initial wrong, the departure from integrity, a broken promise out of self-seeking niggardly pride. This initial disintegration that causes Viṣṇu-Makha, the sacrifice, to lose its head, wants to be undone by a reintegration, which is the purpose of the rites of the sacrifice.

The Pravargya sacrifice is added on to the beginning, or precedes the Soma sacrifice. The Pravargya is not known to the Ṛg Veda. It appears to have been a sacrifice originally independent of the Soma sacrifice. The two conjoint sacrifices have their mythical figure in Makha, the Pravargya being Makha's head. Its symbol is the Mahāvīra pot.

The Soma sacrifice has Viṣṇu for its mythical figure. When the Pravargya sacrifice is added to the Soma sacrifice, they form as it were one sacrifice of which the Pravargya is the head, Makha's head. Forming one albeit extended sacrifice, Viṣṇu becomes equated with Makha. The Pravargya preceding the Soma sacrifice, being in front of the sacrifice, it is the 'Head of Makha'; nowhere is it spoken of as Viṣṇu's head.

In the ŚB. version it was Viṣṇu who encompassed the entire sacrifice: this was his glory which identified him with the sacrifice. But in the elation of his triumph he literally lost his head. His bow cut it off. The head fell and became

1. J. A. B. van Buitenen, *The Pravargya*, Poona 1968, 35, translates Mahāvīra as 'Large Man.' The largeness being that of the sun, does not refer to its size, but to its all-encompassing power.

2. Pravargya is 'that which is to be put on the fire,' L. Renou, *Vocabulaire du Ritual Védique*, Paris, 1954, 111; *ie* the Mahāvira pot.

3. Makha has been variously translated; M. Mayrhofer, *A Concise Etymological Sanskrit Dictionary*, Heidelberg 1963, *s.v.* 'Sacrifice' and 'Hero,' both fit Makha in the present context.

the sun. The rest of the body lay stretched out towards the east. In this calamitous situation, Indra encompassed the prostrate body, lay down on it; limb to limb he embraced it and its glory was absorbed by him. It was a truncated glory of a headless body. The gods went on worshipping with that headless sacrifice and gained nothing by it.

Truly, the gods were cheated by Viṣṇu of the glory of the sacrifice. Moreover the identities in the ŚB. story do not work out squarely. Viṣṇu is the sacrifice and he who is the sacrifice is the Sun (ŚB.14.1.1.6,32). In itself however, and not by synecdoche, the cut off head becomes the sun. It is Makha's head which is represented by the Mahāvīra pot in the Pravargya sacrifice (Vāj.S.37.8; ŚB.14.1.2.1). One who teaches and partakes of the Pravargya sacrifice enters the light of the Sun (ŚB.14.1.1.26-32). By offering the Pravargya, the head of the sacrifice is replaced. (Tāṇḍya, 7.5.6, end)

Two equations hold good: Viṣṇu is the sacrifice; Makha is the Sun. The two conceptions are combined. They are linked in the ŚB. by the role of Indra. It is as problematic as it is imitative. It is moreover futile, for the gods sacrificing with the headless sacrifice do not obtain blessings. (Taitt.Ār.I.6) Dadhyañc, the Ātharvaṇa, the firepriest, comes to their rescue by telling the Healers among the gods, the Aśvins, the 'madhu-vidya,' the 'sweet' or secret magic knowledge how to replace the head of the sacrifice. The Aśvins, in possession of the secret knowledge, ask the gods for a boon and receive it in the shape of a libation of hot milk (*gharma*) out of the Mahāvīra pot (Taitt.Ār.I.7). They promptly replace the head of the sacrifice. Henceforward, Gharma, Mahāvīra, Pravargya and 'Makha's head' refer to the same complex reality. The Aśvins learned the Madhu Vidyā, the 'sweet' secret knowledge straight from the 'horse's mouth,' for it was with a horse's head that Dadhyañc spoke to them (ṚV.1.119.9).

Now Indra had entered also this part of the story. He had cut off the head of Dadhyañc, that is the horse's head (ṚV.1.84.14). Indra had to cut off the head which had divulged the secret to the Aśvins. In fact, Indra previously had threatened Dadhyañc that he would cut off his head should Dadhyañc ever betray the secret known only to Indra and Dadhyañc. By a ruse the Aśvins made Dadhyañc part with the secret and keep his head. That is, they themselves cut off Dadhyañc's original head and put on Dadhyañc a horse's head which told the secret. When Indra fulfilled his threat, he did cut off Dadhyañc's head but that was the head of the horse which had told the secret. Finally the Aśvins know how to restore the original head of Dadhyañc. This miraculous restoration these divine healers accomplished. Now, their knowledge further increased by the secret they had learned from the horse's head, they also knew how to restore the head of Makha. But did the 'sweet,' the Madhu, that only Indra and Dadhyañc[1] knew and that Dadhyañc announced to the Aśvins through the horse's head remain unchanged from the Ṛg Veda to the Brāhmaṇas?

The Ṛg Veda speaks of the 'sweet' (*madhu*) of Tvaṣṭṛ, it also speaks of the fly that gave away the Madhu, the 'sweet' (ṚV.1.119.9). Tvaṣṭṛ's sweet is Soma. Indra once stole the Soma from Tvaṣṭṛ (ṚV.3.48.4), whereas the fly betrayed the secret to the Aśvins. In the ancient story of the Ṛg Veda, the secret of Soma is betrayed to the Aśvins, by Dadhyañc, or else it is betrayed to them by a fly.[2]

Was the 'sweet' that Dadhyañc knew the knowledge of Soma and where the Soma could be found? The horse's head of Dadhyañc was submerged in Śaryaṇāvat.[3] Śaryaṇāvat is a lake or river in the mountains of Kurukṣetra. It is rich in Soma.[4] With the bone of that cutoff horse's head Indra slew nine times ninety arch enemies (Vṛtras).[5] That bone served as Indra's Vajra, his unfailing weapon. It was the thunderbolt.[6] The Madhu in the Ṛg Veda has the secret of Soma for its content. This secret, the repository of Indra's strength, is revealed by Dadhyañc to the Aśvins.

A later text[7] also tells us that Indra himself had imparted to Dadhyañc the magic secret (*brahma*) and had forbidden him to reveal it to anyone. This secret knowledge in post-Ṛg Vedic texts appears not to be the same pure essence, *viz* Soma, the innermost mystery and life elixir of the sacrifice, but another carrier of sacrificial transport, *viz* the secret of the Pravargya. This mystery is revealed to the Aśvins by the horse's head which was cut off by Indra. Another cutoff head, that of Makha and the life elixir which flowed away from the decapitated head of the sacrifice itself, have their own initiatory power. Soma, the drink of immortality, sweetness itself (*madhu*), is the original mystery.

The mystery now however is centered in the restoration of the head of Makha. The horse's head told the Aśvins the secret of how to restore the head of the sacrifice. The secret, however, shared originally by Indra and Dadhyañc is Soma. Secretly, by the horse's head, the sanctity of Soma was assigned to Makha's head in a duplicity of meaning, implying a transfer of significance from the Soma sacrifice to the Pravargya sacrifice. The Soma mystery is the primary secret. It is the 'sweet' of Tvaṣṭṛ, the maker of all form, the mystery of creativity itself, of which the Ṛg Veda sings.

1. ṚV.1.116.12; 1.117.22; 1.119.9; 9.68.5.
2. ṚV.1.119.9; R. Gordon Wasson, *SOMA: Divine Mushroom of Immortality*, The Hague, 1968, 61; K. F. Geldner, *Der Rig Veda*, I, p. 162, n. on ṚV.1.119.9.
3. ṚV.1.84.14.
4. ṚV.9.65.22,23; Sāy. on 1.84.14; *cf* 10.35.2.
5. ṚV.1.84.13-14.
6. *Cf* A. A. Macdonell, *Vedic Mythology*, Strassburg 1897, 142. Wasson, 40.
7. Bṛhad Devatā, 3.18-24.

The secret given away by Dadhyañc Ātharvaṇa, according to the Śatapatha Brāhmaṇa, is the knowledge of the restoration of the head of the sacrifice (ŚB. 14.1.1.18; 4.1.5.18). It is the secret of the restitution of wholeness which had become fragmented. The cause of the fragmentation, the cause of the lost head, was the overweening pride of the god himself who thus 'lost his head.' While Soma is creativity itself – in a state untainted by egoity – the secret of regaining the lost head belongs to a state in the godhead fallen from primal innocence, when guilt had come to be. This latter mystery – enacted in the Pravargya ritual – slides into the place of the divine Soma transport. The horse's head divulged secrets of the gods. They were not the same, one supplanted the other.

Makha's head was cut off by a divine act of retribution – the termites hence were divinized. His sacrificial death is an immolation. Makha is the sacrifice by expiation. The slaying of Soma however fulfills his inner destiny. In order to be consumed Soma must be killed. The Soma sacrifice is a passion whereas Makha was felled by his overweening selfishness. The demon in Makha was liberated, the dark face of the cosmic giant was severed from the trunk, the cutoff head was purified in the Pravargya sacrifice. In its flames the head of Makha was made to glow with the radiance of the sun.

The secret knowledge by which the Aśvins, the celestial Healers, restored the sacrifice is contained in the Mantras of the Hymn to the Light (ṚV.10.170.1-3). It is these incantations which are meant by the Divākīrtyas of which the Śatapatha Brāhmaṇa speaks (ŚB.4.1.5.15; SV.2.803-805; Ūhyagāna.2.2.9). By the power of these words addressed by the Aśvins to the Light radiating from the Sun the head of Makha is restored to the body of the sacrifice.

Significantly, the hymn ṚV.10.171.2 immediately following this laud of the celestial Light, the Sun's radiance, praises Indra who severed the head of raging Makha from his body.[1] The beheading of Makha underlies the rite of the Pravargya. It is also one of Indra's heroic deeds. The slaying of demoniac darkness and thereby turning into Light is celebrated in more than one version. Makha, in the Ṛg Veda is raging darkness from whose body Indra severs the head so that it may arise as sun.[2] No doubt the 'demon' Makha is cognate, *ab intra* with

1. See note 1; ṚV.10.171.2. Makha as raging darkness thus figures as the primeval sacrificial 'animal.' The transformation of the demon into the sacrificial victim leads one step further. As sacrificial victim Makha supplants King Soma.

At a time when the Soma sacrifice was waning and Soma not readily obtainable, the Pravargya was added on to, supplemented, expanded, and reoriented the ancient rites.

When Indra had severed the raging head of Makha 'he came to the house of one who had prepared Soma' (somin; ṚV.10.171.2).

2. Indra liberating the Sun is the subject not only of the Vala myth, but figures also in other

Makha, the sacrifice. The horse's head of Dadhyañc the fire priest, which the Aśvins – whose name derives from *aśva*, 'horse,' – had put on his shoulders, reveals the secret. The horse's head is the sun, itself. It is at the same time the head of the sun-horse. Through the mouth of Dadhyañc, the sun-horse's secret knowledge, the Madhu Vidyā is revealed, or, it is said, the sun-horse 'sings together with the Soma-inspired singers in heaven.'[1]

In the Pravargya ritual, the head of Makha, the severed head, the Sun, represented as the 'all encompassing hero,' the Mahāvīra pot, is hallowed by the horse even before the pot is made. A stallion leads those who go to collect the clay from a hole, significantly situated towards the sunrise, to the east of the Āhavanīya altar where the gods are invoked, the priest addressing the clay, 'Thou art the head of Makha,'[2] and the stallion is made to sniff at the clay.[3] When the Mahāvīra vessel has been shaped, it is fumigated with horse-dung burnt on the Gārhapatya altar.[4] And the Mahāvīra vessel glowing on the crackling fire is lauded: 'Loudly the tawny stallion neighed.'[5] Dadhyañc, through a horse's head that the Aśvins – having beheaded him in order to save his human head – had given him, reveals to these horse-involved saviours, the cutoff head, the Mahāvīra, the 'all encompassing hero,' the Sun. And thus its symbol is the earthen Mahāvīra pot.

images like that of raging Makha (ṚV.10.171.2), or also that of Indra striking down the chariot of Uṣas, the Dawn (ṚV.10.73.6) in her darkness-aspect *cf* A. K. Coomaraswamy, 'The Darker Side of Dawn,' *Smithsonian Miscellaneous Collections*, 64.1. Washington, 1935,6. *cf* RV.9.73.5, the dark skin which Indra hates and which is magically blown away from heaven and earth.

Taitt.S.1.1.8 invokes the head of Makha as the wide extended vessel which contains all life. This vessel however is made of potsherds (*kapāta*). The skin which is to be grasped by a god (not named), the victory over the demon appear in the same context, and Savitṛ, the Impeller or solar power is invoked to make ready (the vessel) in the highest firmament. The Pravargya ritual is adumbrated in the Yajur Veda.

1. RV.I.6.8, *cf* A Bergaigne, *La Religion Vedique*, II.380, fn. 2, or, the Sun is the hidden horse, ṚV.1.117.4-5, in its journey through the night.

2. Āpastamba Śrauta Sūtra 15.1.7; Taittirīya Saṃhitā 1.1.8.

3. Āp.ŚS.15.2.2.

4. Āp.ŚS.15.3.17; Vājasaneya Saṃhitā 37.9, *cf* K. Rönnov, 'Zur Erklärung des Pravargya,' *Le Monde Orientale*, Uppsala, 1929, XXIII, 125.

5. Vāj.S.38.22, The platters for the Rauhiṇa cakes which are baked at the Pravargya are 'horse-shaped.' They were made of the same clay-mixture as the Mahāvīra. This makes van Buitenen, p. 15, notes 49 and 50, think, with some reserve, of the little baked clay horses attendant on icons.

THE ELIXIR OF LIFE: SOMA AND PŪTIKA

When Viṣṇu or Makha or the sacrifice – they are synonyms – had his head cut off, sap flowed away and entered the sky and the earth. 'Clay is this earth and water is the sky. Hence it is of clay and water that the Mahāvīra vessel is made.'[1] The elements earth and water carry the sap of Makha's head into the substance of the Mahāvīra pot. It will dry in the sun and be baked in fire. Earth or clay as it is dug from a pit east of the sacrificial hut is the major but not the only solid substance that goes into the making of the Mahāvīra pot. Four other ingredients are added to the clay. Their importance is primarily symbolical, the relevant ingredient is a certain plant. ŚB.14.1.2.12 speaks of this plant:[2] 'Ādāra plants are Indra's might[3] for when Indra encompassed (Viṣṇu) with might, the vital sap of Viṣṇu flowed away. And he lay there stinking as it were after bursting open (*ā-dar*). The vital sap sang praises. The Ādāra plants originated and because he lay there stinking (*pūy*) therefore [they are also called], *pūtika*. When laid on the fire as an offering they are fragrant for they originated from the vital sap of the sacrifice.' The vital sap that flowed from the head penetrated heaven and earth and mid-air, all that lies under the sun. The vital sap that flowed from the beheaded body was pressed out from it by Indra's might. Indra's might is sustained by Soma. In the transport caused by that drink of immortality the inspired poets sing about Indra's deeds. Does the Ādāra plant here stand for Soma inasmuch as it is here called Indra's might? The Ādāra plant is not otherwise identified except that it originated then and there and that it is also called Pūtika. If the etymology of *ādāra* is hermeneutic, that of *pūtika* is correct, not only philologically[4] but also factually as will be shown.

In Indra's close embrace of Viṣṇu's body – limb by limb, he covered him – was Indra's power carried by osmosis into the fallen body of Viṣṇu-Makha? Was it too much for that beheaded and disintegrating body and did it burst open and plants spring forth?[5] These plants called either 'Ādāra' or 'Pūtika' are the most significant amongst the five ingredients that make up the clay of the

1. ŚB.14.1.2.9; 14.2.2.53.

2. *Cf* Taitt.Ār.5.1.3.5; Āp.ŚS.15.2.1; Mānava ŚS.4.1.11, ed. J. M. van Gelder, New Delhi, 1961.

3. Vāj.S.37.6; inspired and invigorated having drunk Soma, Indra performs his deeds.

4. Mayrhofer, *s.v.*

5. ŚB.4.5.10.4 speaks about the provenance of Ādāra or Pūtika. This passage does not treat of the Pravargya myth, but of substitutes for Soma. The Ādāra plant in this context is one of the Soma substitutes, when Soma cannot be had. It is said to have sprung from the sap which spurted from the head of the sacrifice when the head was cut off. The implications of the myth are lost or overlooked when a part of it only is taken out of context. ŚB.14.2.1.19 narrates somewhat vaguely 'when the sacrifice had its head cut off, its vital sap flowed away and therefrom those plants grew up'.

Mahāvīra pot. They represent the might (*ojas*) of Indra communicated to the body of Makha and transmuted into plants which will be ground and mixed with the clay out of which Makha's head, the Mahāvīra pot, will be formed.[1]

The other ingredients of the Mahāvīra pot are: earth from a termite hill[2] for these termites had been divinized and made 'first born of the world' in return for the part they played in the severance of Viṣṇu's head; earth turned up by a boar, for it was the boar Emuṣa-Prajāpati that raised the earth herself – she was quite small then – into existence.[3] These two additional kinds of earth establish mythically the consistency and existence of the substance of the Mahāvīra vessel from the beginning of things. The Pūtika plants are the third additional ingredient.[4] The sources do not reveal their identity. But the secrecy that surrounds them is not the only thing they share with Soma. The wrong identifications of the Pūtika plant are proportionate to those of the Soma plant, which is fair as the former is only a substitute for Soma.[5] Yet its relevance is

1. According to Mānava Śrauta Sūtra, 4.1.9-10, the Pūtika plants were ground. Another version of the origin of the Pūtika plant, though lacking the coherence of the Brāhmaṇa of a Hundred Paths tells that the Pūtika plant grew from a feather or leaf (*parṇa*) when Soma was carried through the air by the falcon (Tāṇḍ.B.9.5.1). This plant which properly is called Śyenābhṛta, 'carried hither by the falcon,' is Soma (ṚV.1.80. 2; 8.95.3; 9.87.6). ŚB.4.5.10.2-6 however, enumerating the substitutes for Soma speaks of Śyenābhṛta and Ādāra as two different substitutes of Soma. Taitt.Ār.5.1.3.5 presents yet another name and story: 'Makha leaning on his bow smiled overbearingly and his warmth of life (*tejas*) left him. The gods wiped it on the plants. The plant Śyāmaka originated therefrom. Also his manly power (*vīrya*) flowed out.' Makha here is not decapitated, Indra is absent from the story. The Śyāmaka plant which may be a kind of grain or corn, does not otherwise figure in the story of Makha nor amongst the substitutes for Soma. Makha pays with his life for his hubris, his vitality goes to the plants.

2. ŚB.14.1.2.10; Vāj.S.37.4; Taitt.Ār.4.2.3; Āp. ŚS.15.2.1.

3. *Cf* 25. These two earth admixtures are not always enumerated in the same sequence. Their proportionate amount is not indicated and seems to have not been relevant to the texture of the clay of which the pot was made. Like the ground Pūtika plants these ingredients had more ritual-symbolical than technical importance similar to the presence of gold and silver in the metal alloy called aṣṭadhātu (eight substances) of later day Indian bronze images.

4. Vāj.S.37.6; ŚB.14.1.2.12; Āp.ŚS.15.2.2; van Buitenen, p. 57 quotes from Baudhāyana ŚS., a variant of Pūtika, namely Bādāra [*Ādāra*?] stalks. For references here given to Āp.ŚS. *cf* van Buitenen, *passim*.

5. Sāyana on Tāṇḍ.B.9.5.1 considers the Pūtika plant to be a creeper; Pūtika is explained as the flowers of the Rohiṣa plant by the commentary on Kātyāyana ŚS. An impressive array of wrong identifications of the Soma plant is given by W. Doniger O'Flaherty in Wasson, 93-130. According to ŚB.4.5.10.2, one of the Soma substitutes, the Phālguna plants, deserve mention. Of their two varieties, one with bright red flowers, the other with reddish brown flowers only the second was considered eligible. In this connection the observation in the Atharvaprayaścittāni, J. von Negelein, *JAOS* 34, 254-256, is of interest. Red Soma is said to grow in the Himalayas and brown Soma on Mūjavant. If the fly-agaric, the mushroom identified by Wasson, has a red as well as a brown variety it would appear that in post-Vedic time the latter was in demand. Pūtika is cited among the substitutes by W. Doniger O'Flaherty.

such that it confirms the drink of immortality to have been pressed from a mushroom. This mushroom has been identified as the fly-agaric, *ie Amanita muscaria*.[1]

The fourth ingredient added to the clay, making altogether five components of the Mahāvīra pot, is goat's milk (ŚB.14.1.2.13) or hairs from a she goat or black antelope (Āp.ŚS.15.2.1), for the goat and antelope are sacrificial animals, 'born of fire,' symbols of heat.

King Soma was killed in that he in the shape of the Soma plant was pressed.[2] 'In the slaying of Soma the sacrifice is slain, with the sacrifice the sacrificer.'[3] In the Soma sacrifice the sacrificial significance of Soma was enhanced by his royal status. In the course of the Pravargya sacrifice, King Soma having been enthroned, that is a bundle of Soma plants having been placed on the seat of a high four-legged stool, the *rājāsandī*, which reaches to the navel of the sacrificer, a similar throne that may be higher, even shoulderhigh, is placed near King Soma's throne. This is the Emperor's throne (*samrāḍāsandī*) on which the Emperor, the 'All-encompassing Hero,' the Mahāvīra vessel will rest.[4]

The Emperor, the All-encompassing Hero, Mahāvīra, the Sun, is the Great God of the Pravargya. His throne faces east, for nothing must come between Mahāvīra and the sun.[5] Symbolically they are one, Makha's head is the Sun.[6] This is the meaning of the Mahāvīra vessel. It has no other 'content.' Its fiery glowing shape encompasses its cavity, its vastness. Only after the pot has achieved its greatest heat and splendour is hot milk poured into it, the offering to the Aśvins.[7] The All-encompassing Hero, the Sun, of the Pravargya, being joined to the Soma sacrifice, is the head of the sacrifice. 'The head of the sacrifice has become joined in the same manner in which the Aśvins restored it.' (ŚB.14.2.2.43) Just as the Aśvins knew how to put the horse's head on the shoulders of

1. Wasson, *passim*.

2. Taitt.S.6.4.4.4; 6.6.7.1.

3. Taitt.S.6.6.9.2.

4. ŚB.14.1.3.10; 3.3.4.21; *cf* van Buitenen, p. 15; the three Mahāvīra pots, two of them in reserve, – should the empty, red hot glowing pot crack during the sacrifice, – are placed on the Samrāḍāsandī, the emperor's throne.

5. The emperor's throne is placed south of the Āhavanīya fire where the gods are invoked and receive their offering and north of King Soma's throne, ŚB.14.11.3.8,12. Notwithstanding these rites, raising Mahāvīra above Soma, the Śatapatha Brāhmaṇa, ritually, though not logically, sums up its entire section on the Pravargya with the words 'The Pravargya indeed is Soma' (ŚB. 14.3.2.30). In this identification the Pūtika plant plays the main role.

6. Vāj.S.38.24; ŚB.14.1.3.3-6.

7. Āp.ŚS.5.9.10-12; 15.10.1-5. In the course of the sacrifice curds are offered to Indra and other gods. The curds offered to Soma should be curdled with Pūtika plants (TS.2.5.3.5) in the first place, or with bark while other curdling agents such as rennet, curds, rice, or buckthorn should be used for the offering of the curds to other gods. – In more than one ritual context is Pūtika linked with Soma.

Dadhyañc whose human head they had to cut off and then restored to Dadhyañc his human head, so they restored the head of the sacrifice. It was the horse's head that taught them this secret.

This is how the Śatapatha Brāhmaṇa presents the Madhu Vidyā, the sweet, secret knowledge that Dadhyañc's horse's head betrayed to them. In the Ṛg Veda however, it was another secret that Dadhyañc betrayed to the Aśvins. This secret was 'Madhu,' the innermost 'sweetness,' Soma. (ṚV.1.116.12; 1.117.22)

More than half a millennium lies between the two meanings of the Madhu Vidyā in the Ṛg Veda and the Brāhmaṇas. The Sun cult of Mahāvīra, the All-encompassing Hero, was combined with the Soma sacrifice. The meaning of this combined sacrifice revalued the ancient secret of the horse's head, of Dadhyañc and of the Sun.

The substitution of contents and the continuation of the original Soma sacrifices has a ritual analogy in the relation of the Soma plant, identified by Wasson as the fly-agaric, *Amanita muscaria*, and its substitute, Pūtika. King Soma has not been dethroned, but his throne is further from the sun than that of Emperor Mahāvīra. Into the making of Mahāvīra went the Pūtika plant. This symbolically essential ingredient of the Mahāvīra pot has an unsavory connotation accounted for by the myth, told in the Brāhmaṇa of a Hundred Paths. However, its offensiveness is turned into fragrance when the plant is laid on the fire. This transfiguration in and by the ritual is similar to that of the juice of the Soma plant itself, which is made palatable ritually by an admixture of milk.

Mythically, however, the purification of Soma is effected by Vāyu, the Wind. He blew with the gale of the spirit when Indra freed the cosmos from the Asura, the non-god, the Titan, Vṛtra the Serpent. Soma was in Vṛtra (ṚV.10.124.4) and Indra slew Vṛtra, the ophidian Asura. Slain Vṛtra stank to heaven, sour and putrid. Vāyu blew away that foul smell – 'the smell of King Soma.' He was neither fit for offering, nor was he fit for drinking (ŚB.4.1.3.5-8).

Agni, Soma and Varuṇa were in Vṛtra, the Asura. They were ensconced in the ambience of this ancient cosmic power. Indra slew this dragon, his antagonist. Agni, Soma and Varuṇa were liberated. They went over to the young conquerer god. The rule of the world had changed. But inasmuch as Soma was in Vṛtra he was slain with him who had contained him. However, he came out of the decomposing carcass. Its odor clung to him. Vāyu blew on him and made him palatable (ŚB.4.1.2.10).

The preoccupation of this account with the stench of the decomposition of the flesh of the World Serpent and of King Soma smells of guilt, the guilt of murder. The odor associated with the putrid smell of dead bodies was not unfamiliar it seems to the priests after animal sacrifices. The gods themselves dispelled some of the smell of King Soma and laid it into [dead] cattle. (ŚB.4.1.3.8) In fact, the priests had chosen the plant Pūtika and endowed it with a myth of its own (ŚB.14.1.2.12) in the context of the sacrifice. In this myth stench as a symbol of evil is implicated in and purified by the sacrifice. The plant Pūtika, however, when laid on the fire as an offering is said to become fragrant, it acquires the odour of sanctity.

PUTKA AND THE SANTAL OF EASTERN BIHAR

In Eastern Bihar there live aboriginal people, the Santal, occupying a stretch of country called the Santal Parganas, and we find scattered villages of Santal also in the adjacent regions of Orissa and the western marches of West Bengal. The Santal number some millions. Until recently they were a hunting and food-foraging folk. Their language is not derived from Sanskrit nor is it Dravidian: it leads the third, smaller group, the Munda family. A trait of these languages is that their nouns are not classified into genders – masculine, feminine, neuter – but are either animate or inanimate, either possessing a soul or not possessing a soul. The whole vegetable kingdom is inanimate, soulless, except for one word that designates a certain mushroom. That noun is *putka*: it is animate, a soul possesses it.

P. O. Bodding in the preface to his *Santal Dictionary* (Oslo, 1929-1936, 1, xiv) draws atttention to a noteworthy fact: 'Strangely enough, the Santals use some pure Sanskrit words, which, so far as I know, are not heard in present day Hindi.' He might have added that, at least in the instance we are considering, the word has disappeared from all Sanskrit vernaculars. We may owe this survival to the mycophilia of the Santal, whose knowledge of the fungal world is reflected in a substantial fungal vocabulary. By contrast the Hindus are mycophobes: the twiceborn castes are expressly forbidden to eat mushrooms, whether growing on trees or from the earth (Manu 5.5.19; 6.11.156; Āp.ŚS.1.5.14.28).

Among the Santal the *putka* is a mushroom and, alone in the whole vegetable kingdom, possesses a soul.[1] Did not *putka* inherit this sacred character

1. Roger Heim and R. Gordon Wasson: 'Les Putka des Santals, champignons doués d'une âme.' *Cahiers du Pacifique* 14, 1970, pp. 59-85. *Putka* appears to be a Santalized version of Sanskrit *Pūtika*, the name in Sanskrit having a long or short 'i'. In the light of this discovery in Santal, one would like to inquire whether the same word with the same attributes is current in the sister language Ho, and in other languages of the northern group of Munda languages and, if so, whether it is present in the southern group.

from long ago when it was an ingredient of the Mahāvīra pot, which was ritually 'animated,' endowed with sense organs, with a soul? Is not *putka* the Sanskrit *Pūtika*?

The second peculiarity of *putka* is its revolting smell when gathered and left for a day or two exposed to the air.[1] In Dumka (Santal Parganas) a Santal woman in answer to questions put to her by Wasson said that she thought she might know why *putka* was animate; the Santal consume *putka* in their curry, but at the end of a day or two should any *putka* have been left over, the remains of the leftover *putka* stink with the stench of a cadaver.[2] She did not know the meaning of the word *putka* nor the myth of Pūtika in the Brāhmaṇas. Wasson himself did not link *putka* with Pūtika though he supplied the evidence for the identity of this mushroom.

The third peculiarity of *putka* in Santal culture is the Santal belief that the *putka* are generated, not from seed, as are the generality of the vegetable world, but by the thunderbolt; in short, generated by divine intervention. Soma itself is generated by Parjanya (ṚV.9.82.3) apparently when his thunderbolt strikes the earth (*cf* ṚV.5.83.1,2,7).

Pūtika, the foremost, and possibly the only direct surrogate for Soma, is a mushroom. When the fly-agaric no longer was available, another mushroom became its substitute. It had acquired a myth of its own. Nothing is known about any psychotropic virtue Pūtika may have. However, no drink was made from it. Instead it was crushed, mixed with the clay of the pot. Its transubstantiation

1. Heim and Wasson, p. 65. The only other reason supplied by many Santal to justify the unique status of *putka* was that it was commonly found in the sacred village grove of *sarjom* trees (*ie* *śāl* in Hindi; *Shorea robusta*). But the *sarjom* itself is not animate; why therefore the *putka* around it, especially as the *putka* is not confined to *Shorea robusta*?

2. *Ibid* p. 85. The Santal distinguish three kinds of *putka*. (1) *hor putka* in which *hor* means 'man' or 'human being' or any Santal; (2) *seta putka*, *seta* meaning 'dog'; and (3) *rote putka*, *rote* being a 'toad' or 'frog.' It emerges from the Heim-Wasson paper that these authors consider the first as variations in usage and the terms are applied interchangeably, the usage varying in different villages and possibly with different stages of growth. The third is a puffball that appears suddenly after thunder storms. Many Santal have never heard of the *rote putka* and of those who had, few were able to identify it. The puffball does come in response to thunder, but the belief in thunder as the generative agent applies equally to the *hor putka* and *seta putka*. The *hor* and *seta putka* is an hypogean species, harvested when it finally breaks the surface of the ground. It has often been called a truffle, or 'truffle-like', which it is not. The Frog or *rote putka* calls to mind the Hymn to the Frogs (ṚV. 7.10.3.8). There reference is made to the Gharma, the offering of hot milk and to the officiating priests, the Adhvaryus. In the ŚB. the Aśvins who had not been invited to the sacrifice became the Adhvaryu priests of the sacrifice after they had restored the head of the Sacrifice by the mantras of the Hymn to the Sun (ṚV. 10.170.1-3).

In the paper by Heim and Wasson, Professor Heim describes the *putka* mycologically and gives them their scientific names.

into the 'All-encompassing Hero' came about through fire, for it is said that the plants themselves strewn on fire become fragrant 'because they originated from the sap of the offering';[1] moreover, integrated into the substance of the fire-baked vessel, anointed with butter, they glow in glory in the fire of the Pravargya.

None of the other alleged substitutes for Soma has a myth of its own. Pūtika sprung from the slain body of the sacrifice is a resurrection, as it were, of Soma. The other plants have no myth of their own except the Śyenābhṛta plant which, as the name tells, is Soma itself. The name Śyenābhṛta meaning 'carried by the falcon' conveys the myth of Soma having been brought from heaven by a falcon (ṚV.8.82.9; 10.144.5) when a feather or leaf, fell to earth[2] and the plant sprang from it. Regarding the other substitutes of Soma nothing but a similarity of colours connects certain flowers; or the fact that they were used in the sacrifice, certain varieties of grass, *viz* Kuśa and Dūrvā grass.[3] A mushroom is foremost among the substitutes of Soma. Moreover, a mushroom is a significant ingredient in the sun-cult of Makha's head, added to the Soma sacrifice. Pūtika though secondary in its role, being a surrogate for Soma, occupied a position of eminence in its own capacity as an essential ingredient of the substance of the Mahāvīra pot. Pūtika was raised into the region of the sacred as a surrogate for Soma, the most exalted plant in Vedic rites which indeed had Soma for their center. Pūtika, however, did not succeed Soma, did not become hallowed by the same rites but was integrated into the substance of the Mahāvīra vessel. Soma was meant to be drunk. The Mahāvīra vessel was meant primarily to be made and seen. Its communion with the sacrifice was by a craft and ultimately by sight only.

The identification of Pūtika, the Soma surrogate, supplies strong evidence that Soma indeed was a mushrom. Pūtika integrated into the Mahāvīra pot played its part in the mystery of the Pravargya sacrifice. That Putka-mushrooms should be known, to this day, as 'endowed with a soul' witnesses amongst the Santal of Eastern India a memory of the numinous emanating from the indigenous Indian Soma substitute.

Mixed with the clay and the other ingredients Pūtika is part of the substance of which the Mahāvīra vessel is made; it is dried in the heat of the sun, baked in the fire, placed on a silver dish and anointed with butter. The vessel is heated

1. ŚB.14.1.2.12.

2. Tāṇḍya B.9.5.1 assigns to Pūtika the myth of Śyenābhṛta, saying that Pūtika is the plant which grew from a feather (or leaf, *parṇa*) that fell to earth when Soma was carried through the air in contrast to the far more telling myth of ŚB.14.1.2.12 about the origin of Pūtika.

3. ŚB.4.5.10; 14.1.2.12.

at the peak of the Pravargya to a red-hot glow, when the golden plate that had covered the mouth of the Mahāvīra pot is removed. The 'All-encompassing Hero,' the 'Head of Makha,' the vessel that contains all life,[1] that is flame, glow, and heat, is the Sun.[2] Mahāvīra, is 'Lord of all the worlds, Lord of all mind, Lord of all speech, Lord of all tapas [the fiery strength of asceticism], Lord of all brahman [the power of the sacred word], Lord of creatures, Spirit of poets.'[3]

THE MAHĀVĪRA VESSEL

The Mahāvīra vessel is prepared at the sacrifice itself. The making of the earthen vessel is itself part of the ritual.[4] The pot is shaped by hand; it is not thrown on a potter's wheel. Its height will be a span[5] and it is Makha's Head. Its shape however does not resemble any head or face, though part of it is called its mouth, but is also spoken of as opening[6] or outlet or as an outlet for pouring into.[7] The shape of the vessel resembles the Vāyavya, the wooden vessel which held the libation for Vāyu, the Wind.[8] The mouth or opening or top of the pot is also metaphorically called a nose for the Mahāvīra pot. It is contracted in the middle and projects outward, widening toward the top.[9] These metaphors do not aim at conjuring up a physiognomy. They refer to a human face as much or as little as does the measure of a span.

The wooden Vāyavya vessel is named after Vāyu, the Wind. The gods rewarded Vāyu with the first libation of Soma from this vessel because he was the first to tell them that Vṛtra had been slain (ŚB.4.1.3.4). Subsequently when Vāyu had made Vṛtra-Soma fit for offering and fit for drinking the libation vessels belonging to other gods were also called Vāyavya or Vāyu's vessels (ŚB. 4.1.3.10). Vāyu, the Wind, had made Soma sweet. 'Therefore what becomes putrid they hang out in a windy place' (TS.6.4.7.1).

The Mahāvīra vessel conforms with the libation vessels called Vāyavya. While these are carved out of wood the Mahāvīra pot is built up of clay.

The lump of clay for the pot is divided into three parts, one part to be the

1. *Cf* TS.1.1.8.
2. ŚB.14.1.3.17,26.
3. Āp.ŚS.15.8.15-16; tr. van Buitenen, 92; matter in brackets added.
4. ŚB.14.1.2.2.
5. ŚB.14.1.2.17.
6. Aśv.Gr.S.4.3; *bila* commented as *garta*, 'a hollow.'
7. Kāty.ŚS.26.1.16; *āsecana*.
8. Āp.ŚS.12.1.4; a libation vessel for an offering to Vāyu; Renou, s.v. the same as Ūrdhvapatra, a high vessel in the shape of a mortar. *Cf* Kāty.8.7.5.
9. ŚB.14.1.2.17. The references to facial features do not conjure up the image of a face. They enliven single features of the pot.

bottom. The clay, pressed down with the thumbs and flattened, is addressed with the words 'you are the two feet of the sacrifice.'[1] Obviously no similarity to any feet is intended here. The lowest part of the pot supports the vessel as the two feet support the human figure.

The second part of the clay is used for building the walls of the vessel up to the height of its collar (*parigrīvā*). The clay is laid on in three, five or an indefinite number of *uddhis* (elevations), that is, in coils or rings.[2] They seem to decrease in diameter towards the middle of the height of the vessel and increase towards its top. The contracted middle is referred to as *lagnam*. This is not to be understood to be a joint but denotes an intersection of planes.[3]

The third portion of the original lump of clay goes into the making of the top portion of the vessel which flares out to a height of two or four thumb widths above the collar (*parigrīvā*) or girdle (*mekhalā*)[4] laid on in high relief around the pot.[5] At the conclusion of the rites of Makha's Head, milk will be poured into the pot.[6]

Once the vessel is completed it must not be touched by hand.[7] It is held, raised, and transferred by tongs. The high relief of the collar or girdle would have prevented a slipping of the tongs.

The shape of the Mahāvīra pot is not anthropomorphic: it has neither the shape of a head, face, or figure of man. It is not an icon but a symbol in the shape of a vessel. To the officiating priest and to the sacrificer it means the Head of Makha, the Sun, and its mystery is experienced by them in the ritual. While they enact it, this mystery pervades their entire being, Mahāvīra comes to life in them and they live in him. 'Like the two eyes, like the two ears, like the two nostrils thus he [the priest] places the senses in him.'[8] The Pravargya is a mystery rite, it requires a special initiation over and above the one for the Soma sacrifice.

The Pravargya is a complex ritual. Its first part, the Pravargya proper, is a sun ritual. Its main symbol is the red hot, glowing Mahāvīra, 'the All-encom-

1. Āp.ŚS.15.2.14; Taitt.Ār.4.2.6. *cf* R. Garbe. 'Die Pravargya Ceremonie nach dem Āp.ŚS.' *ZDMG* 34, 1880, 319.

2. Āp.ŚS.12.1.4.

3. Baudhāyana (van Buitenen, 10) gives a clear description, *cf* also Āpastamba (*ibid* p. 9). The number of *uddhis* or 'rings,' *ie* superimposed parts varies from three to four or more.

4. Taitt.Ār.5.3.5 *parigrīvā*, also *rasnā* or 'girdle' (Āp.ŚS.15.2.17) are here synonymous.

5. Garbe, p. 329.

6. Van Buitenen, 10f; based on Baudh.ŚS. [see also drawing on p. 11]. Van Buitenen understands the three portions of the lump of clay to have been shaped as two small balls one on top of the other, and supported on a broad calotte shaped base, suggesting the shape of a man seated cross legged. This reconstruction is not according to the texts nor would it serve the purpose of the Mahāvīra pot.

7. Van Buitenen, 15; Āp.ŚS.15.4.6-8.

8. Ait.B.4.1.21.

passing Hero,' who encompasses as sun the horizons of heaven,[1] unbounded space, all the world.

The second main part of the sacrifice begins when the vessel, having been made to blaze and having been hymned, is filled with milk. This part of the sacrifice belongs to the Aśvins: it is the offering of hot milk due to them, the Gharma proper.[2] In this capacity, the Aitareya Brāhmaṇa lauds the Gharma as divine intercourse. The vessel is the member, milk is the semen, ejaculated – while boiling – into the fire as the divine womb, the birthplace of the gods, as generation.[3] Extending beyond the sacrifice, into the cosmos, Mahāvīra, creator, procreator, by begetting extends from the bottom to the top, penetrates and supports heaven and earth.[4]

The coincidence within the same visual symbol, the Mahāvīra vessel, of tropes taken from the shape of man is not to be seen as an overlapping of physical features. Each evocation conjured up an inner experience, valid in itself and not an image. The function of the lowest part of the pot is being felt as akin to that of feet; the top of the vessel, its opening, functions as mouth for liquid to be poured in and out. Or the entire pot is felt to function as the cosmic, procreative member, aggrandized as cosmic pillar. In another context, however, the Mukhalinga symbol of Śiva is a visually materialized form of such coinciding tropes. In this visualized symbol, the liṅga however had no procreative meaning. On the contrary, the concept of the ascending, not ejaculated but transubstantiated, semen as the substance of illumination is the motivating belief or experience that conjoins the shapes of phallus and head. The Mahāvīra vessel is not anthropomorphic. It releases in the ritual the experience of the creative power of the Sun by the conception of 'Makha's Head' and again by an upsurge of procreative empathy of which the vessel becomes the liṅga-like symbol.

The allusion to the figure of man however is implied throughout the sacrifice. In the Pravargya, at the conclusion of the entire sacrifice the implements of the sacrifice are assembled around the Mahāvīra pot either in the shape of man[5] or in that of the sun. This alternative implies the transfiguration of man, the sacrificer, which is the purpose of the sacrifice. The sacrificer has reached the

1. Āp.ŚS.15.6.2; 15.8.15-16.

2. In the Ṛg Veda, the Gharma was offered to the Aśvins in a metal cauldron (ṚV.5.30.15) which has no original connection with the Mahāvīra clay pot. The Pravargya includes finally also an offering to Indra, of hot curds, the Dadhigharma. The Ṛg Vedic offering of hot milk to the Aśvins became combined with the ritual of the red hot Mahāvīra pot.

3. Ait.B.4.1.22.

4. Śāṅkh.ŚS.5.9.4; Aśv.G.S.4.6.1, *cf* AV.4.1; 2.4; *cf* van Buitenen, p. 67. This recitation accompanied the first part of the Pravargya.

5. ŚB.14.3.2.2; 14.2.2.16-22 and Baudhāyana; *cf* van Buitenen, p. 130, note 6.

sun, 'the radiant face of the gods, the eye of Mitra, Varuṇa and Agni.'[1] 'With the sun's eye I gaze upon thee,'[2] the priest had addressed the Mahāvīra vessel when it had been baked in the fire and he had lifted the pot on the gravel kept ready for it. 'Were not the eye sun-like, never could it perceive the sun,' thus Goethe worded a knowledge expressed by the priest in the ritual sun-gaze of recognition of the completed Mahāvīra vessel. This cosmic realization comprises all beings. Mahāvīra, the sun, the All-encompassing Hero is addressed: 'Mahāvīra, may all things regard me with the eye of a friend. May I regard all beings with the eye of a friend. With the eye of a friend do we regard one another.'[3] 'Long may I live to look on thee.'[4] 'Through a hundred autumns may we see that bright eye, god appointed, rise.'[5]

THE LATER AND SEPARATE LIVES OF MAHĀVĪRA AND PŪTIKA

Mahāvīra, the All-encompassing Hero, is also the name of the last Jina or Conqueror of the twenty-four Jinas or Saviours (*tīrthaṅkara*) in the heterodox Jaina religion. His mythical life story is the exemplar for that of the other Tīrthaṅkaras. Before his birth his mother had fourteen prognostic dreams. In one of them she beheld a vessel, a 'brimming vase.' This vessel of abundance is a symbol of ultimate knowledge.[6] In another frame of reference this vessel is also the Sun as vessel containing all time.[7] The brimming vase is common to the art of Buddhism and Hinduism. It is shown brimming with lotuses. They are particularly associated with the Lotus Goddess, Lakṣmī, Goddess of Plenty. The Mahāvīra vessel, however, held no tangible contents. This sacred vessel as the All-encompassing Hero, the Sun, rules over space and time. In its Jain context it also holds that one supreme knowledge which has overcome the separateness of space and time, the manifoldness of the world.

The iconology of the prognostic dream vessel seen by the mother-to-be of the Saviour and which prefigures his life on earth, however, differs from all the other sacred vessels represented in Indian art. It is known to us in the Western Indian school of painting after the fourteenth century. There it is shown flanked, at the height of its neck, by wide open, far-seeing eyes. They are painted

1. Āp.ŚS.15.16; ṚV.1.115.1.
2. Āp.ŚS.15.4.6-8; Mānava ŚS.4.1.26.
3. Vāj.S.36.18.
4. Vāj.S.36.19.
5. Vāj.S.36.24; ṚV.7.66.18.
6. *Kevala-ñāṇa daṃsana*; A.K. Coomaraswamy, 'The Conqueror's Life in Jaina Painting,' *Journal of the Indian Society of Oriental Art* 3, 1935, p. 136f; Pls.35,2;36.
7. AV.19.53.3; *cf* note 69.

next to the vessel, whatever be its shape, not on it. Together with it, they form an inseparable configuration showing with utmost clarity the vessel with the eyes that belong to it. Visually, this configuration combines, as a truly creative symbol, the presence of the sacred vessel and that of the all-seeing eyes which are its own. Floating on a monochrome coloured ground, they gaze, charged with the mystery of the sacred vessel, with the power of Mahāvīra.[1]

The Mahāvīra vessel and the Pūtika mushroom are significant elements in the fabric of Indian tradition. Pūtika starts with being a substitute for Soma, the drink of immortality, the elixir of life. Pūtika qualifies for this part because Pūtika is a mushroom reddish brown in colour. This mushroom amongst other reasons was chosen when the Soma plant, the fly-agaric, gradually became unavailable, in preference to other indigenous mushrooms for its being conspicuous or noticeable by the bad smell the cut mushroom develops. Hence also its name Pūtika. Once chosen in lieu of Soma, Pūtika usurped as its own the name 'Śyenābhṛta' and the myth of Soma's origin from on high. The substitute became authenticated as the original.

A gap of more than two and a half millennia, a transfer from Aryan priestly symbolism to tribal belief, the tribe adopting a Sanskrit name with but little change into its own language, the survival of this name in a Munda language, in a region at a considerable distance to the east from the ancient center of Brahmanical sacrifices, all this did not impair the ongoing myth of Pūtika. This species is known to the Santal as 'endowed with a soul.' It is distinct from other mushrooms, from all the vegetable kingdom as being numinous. The odor of sanctity clings to this mushroom, however pejorative its telling name.

The sanctity of the Mahāvīra vessel as artifact and symbol, judging by the pristine technique of shaping the earthen pot, would belong to an age far beyond the age of the Brāhmaṇas. Deified, the Mahāvīra pot is the center of a ritual, entirely its own. The very making of it is part of the ritual. In this respect this pottery ritual may be grouped with the 'brick piling' ritual of the Vedic altar,[2] but also with the function of the potterpriest in South India today.[3]

1. In some of the paintings the vase and the flanking eyes are combined into a phantasmagoric 'face' (Coomaraswamy, Pl. 35,2.) comprising further subservient devices. On the other hand, the conception of the Suneye, as eye '*per se*' more or less independent of the face of the figure is one of the main factors in the style of the Western Indian school of painting, *cf* S. Kramrisch, 'Western Indian Painting,' under publication by Bhagawān Mahāvīr 2500th Nirvāṇ Mahotsava Samiti, Bombay, 1974.

2. The square *ukhā* made of clay which held the heads of the five sacrificial victims was part of the sacrificial pile. It was neither the central cult object nor even a cult object in its own right.

3. S. Kramrisch, *Unknown India*, Philadelphia Museum of Art, 1968, 57.

The Mahāvīra pot is not in any way like a head urn, nor does it resemble a human figure: it refers to the sun, – not by virtue of its shape but by the process of making it. The vessel is dried by the heat of the sun and baked in a fiery pit. In the culminating ritual its validity is established in glowing glory wreathed in flames as symbol of the Sun or the Head of Makha, the cosmic giant.[1]

The worship and disposal – the whole ritual – of Mahāvīra, though part only of the total Pravargya sacrifice are organised with the finality of perfection. The incongruity of an empty earthen vessel as symbol for Makha's head, the Sun, seems inexplicable. Yet a symbol is what one makes it to mean. The mouth or nose of the pot are as suggestive as are the implements in the final laying out of all the paraphernalia of the Pravargya, where they are understood to reconstruct the shape of man. Three pots (the original and the two reserve pots should the original crack) form the 'head,' the unclipped broom that had been used in the ritual is placed above the head, so as to form a hair tuft, the tongs are the shoulders, and so on, the straws of the other broom are scattered over the configuration that embodies the essence of man, so as to form its muscles.[2] Whatever took part in the sacrifice, becomes part of the transfiguration of sacrificial man. The configuration of the paraphernalia of the sacrifice is vested with their composite magic. If the implements are arranged in a way so as to conjure up an image of the sun, the same purpose is fulfilled.

The head of sacrificial, transfigured man is represented by the three Mahāvīra pots, each of them is the head of the sacrifice – even though only one played its role. Though there are three they mean one and the same only. In the sacrifice Makha's Head is the sun, the pot is Makha's head, the pot is the sun. The pot is the head though it is unlike a head. The pot is made by the priest, the Adhvaryu, or he delegates this task to a potter (*kartṛ*, 'the maker'). The pot is the sun, is Makha's head, the head of the sacrifice not by a likeness of its shape but by that of another quality which has its maximum effect at the culmination of the sacrificial heating of the vessel. It is then that Mahāvīra, anointed with butter and, heated to the highest degree, attains the fieriness of the sun. It had been covered with a golden dish so that it should protect heaven from its heat.[3] The 'All-encompassing Hero, glowing gold-colored, encompasses as sun, the horizons of heaven.'[4]

In South India of the present day, the cult of Aiyanar requires clay images

1. *Cf* Ṛ̣V.10.171.2; and, above, p. 225.
2. Āp.ŚS.15.15.1.
3. Āp.ŚS.15.8.5a; Kāty.ŚS.1.6.24; Śāṅkhāyana ŚS.5.9.13; van Buitenen, 77.
4. *Cf* Āp.ŚS.15.6.2.

of Aiyanar and his retinue. They are made by the village potter who is at the same time the officiating priest. He is a Kusavan by caste, son of a Brāhman father and a Śudra woman. Did clay, being baked in the fire and turning from earth to glowing splendor, effect in a potter-priest an initiation through the potter's craft, familar only with his sundried output? Did he behold the fiery sun glowing in his own work? Did the sun cult of the Mahāvīra pot arise amongst potters and make them priests of their calling? Was it a cult indigenously Indian where the heat of the sun is as powerful as its splendor so that transposed into a rite the glow of the earthen pot and the vehemence of the flames are intensified by the anointing of the vessel? It was made by hand, the clay pressed into shape by the thumbs without a potter's wheel. This pristine technique was hallowed. It had arisen from direct contact, preserved the shape and the manner in which the vessel had been fashioned when the sediments of more than one myth were integrated in its substance and when the Sun vessel once-finished was not to be touched by human hands. It was not to be touched by human hands for its heat would have burnt them. The vessel was not to be touched because it was sacred. It was not to be touched so that the only contact with the sacred object was by sight, sight intensified to the exclusion of all other sensory perceptions, a rite of 'seeing' a communion by vision.

An indigenous sun cult celebrated by the ritual of its craft became the 'Head of the sacrifice' and Makha's head was joined to its body. Symbols live their own lives, draw to themselves their affinities, coalesce with them and emerge showing in various facets an identity of ambience of meaning. Mahāvīra, in the Aitareya Brāhmaṇa, encompasses all creation, in the intensity of the climactic moment of procreation. The vessel now stands for the Liṅga. Head and procreative organ are coterminous yet do not overlap in the vision of the Brāhmaṇas.

Through long stretches of Indian thought and imagery, the symbolism of Liṅga and head combined in the creation of a visual whole. The Mukhaliṅga of Śiva, the phallus with a head or heads, is a concretely realised sculptural form perduring for two thousand years of Indian art, though with a total reversal of the implied meaning which here extols antithetically the power of creative heat as fervor of ascetic sublimation not as a spending into the fiery lap of all gods-to-be but as a self-contained rarification and ascent of this power.

On another facet of its meaning, Makha's head, the Sun, the All-encompassing, All-seeing eye of the world, fastens its steady gaze on all and everyone. The brimming vase sends forth this glance in eyes that are painted outside its shape, bestowing the power of sight and insight. Two vessels overlap in this Jain rendering of ancient themes. The one is the Mahāvīra pot, which the 'Unbounded,' Aditi, is invoked to encompass.[1] It contains ultimate knowledge and all time. These are intangible contents. The other vessel is the 'full pot' (*pūrṇa ghaṭa*), the brimming vase of plenty, Lakṣmī herself.

The symbolism of the Mahāvīra vessel is deeply ensconced and has manifold connections in Indian thought and art. Pūtika, on the other hand, only contributes to the substance of the vessel. The mantle of King Soma had fallen on this notable mushroom, which inherits the glory of Soma for whom it is a surrogate. Its heyday is in the Pravargya ritual. Then the mushroom is lost to us in a millennial darkness from which, miraculously, it emerges 'endowed with a soul' amongst the aboriginal Santal of Eastern India in our own day.

1. Taitt.Ār.4.2.6; Aditi, 'the Boundless,' is invoked to comprise its cavity, ŚB.14.2.7; Mānava ŚS.4.3.1 invokes the cow as Iḍā, Aditi and Sarasvatī. While on one level the cow whose milk will fill the pot is Aditi, on the highest level Aditi remains Boundlessness itself.

CHAPTER FOUR

THE LAST MEAL OF THE BUDDHA

by R. Gordon Wasson

WHAT WAS *SŪKARA-MADDAVA*?

Upwards of a dozen scholars[1] in the past century have commented on what the Buddha ate at his Last Meal, *ca* BC 483, and the puzzling mystifications in the evidence. The meal was served to him and his suite of monks by his host the metal-worker Cunda at Pāvā, a village that lay near Kusinārā where the Mahāparinirvāṇa – the 'Great Decease' as the Rhys Davidses translated it – was scheduled to take place some hours later. The canonical Pāli Text says that Cunda served his august guest *sūkara-maddava*, a hapax in Pāli. Walpola Rāhula, the Buddhist monk and scholar residing in the West, has assembled in a memorandum for us the relevant Pāli texts with his translations and notes, and this document is appended to our paper.

The first part of that compound word, *sūkara-*, is simple: 'pertaining to swine,' *sūk-* being cognate with Latin *sus*. The second element is generally

1. 1896 and earlier. Karl Eugen Neumann: *Die Reden Gotamo Buddho's aus des Mittleren Sammlung Majjhimanikāyo des Pāli-Kanons*, Leipsig, 1896, pp xix-xxii. Neumann cites earlier writers: Friedrich Zimmermann, who in turn refers to an article in the *Journal of the Maha-Bodhi Society*, Vol. 1, No. viii, pp 2-3, Calcutta, 1892, wherein the editor of this *Journal* reproduces statements by 'Rhys Davids, Bigandet, Rockhill, and Colonel Olcott,' laying stress on the proper meaning of *sūkara-maddava*. We have seen none of these earlier discussions.
1910. T. W. and C. A. F. Rhys Davids, and later editions. *Dialogues of the Buddha: Part II*. Translated from the Pāli of the *Dīgha Nikāya* by T. W. and C. A. F. Rhys Davids. One of the series of the Sacred Books of the Buddhists. Published for the Pāli Text Society by Luzac, London. (All of our quotations from the *Dīgha Nikāya* are from the 1959 edition.)
1916. Coomaraswamy, Ananda K.: *Buddha and the Gospel of Buddhism*, p 79, George G. Harrap, London.
1931-2. Arthur Waley. 'Did Buddha die of eating pork?' *Mélanges chinois et bouddhiques*, Vol. I, pp 343-354. Brussels.
1942. Fa Chow. 'Sūkara-maddava and the Buddha's Death.' *Annals of the Bhandarkar Oriental Research Institute*. Edited by R. N. Dandekar, pp 127-133.
1948. E. Waldschmidt. *Beiträge zur Textgeschichte des Mahāparinirvāṇasūtra*, pp 63-85: 'Die Letzte Mahlzeit des Buddha.'
1948. E. J. Thomas. *Indian Culture*, XV, pp 1-3: 'Buddha's Last Meal.'
1949. A Foucher. *La Vie du Bouddha*. Paris, Payot. pp 304-308: 'Le Dernier repas à Pāvā.'
1968. André Bareau. 'La Nourriture offerte au Buddha lors de son dernier repas,' *Mélanges d'Indianisme*, Paris, Editions E. de Boccard. pp 61-71.
1970. André Bareau. *Recherches sur la biographie du Buddha*. Tome I. Notably Chapter VII 8 & 9, pp 251-281. Paris. Ecole Française d'Extrême-Orient, Vol. LXXVII.
1970. P. Demiéville. Review of R. Gordon Wasson: *SOMA: Divine Mushroom of Immortality*. *T'oung Pao*, LVI: Livr. 4-5, pp 298-302. E. J. Brill, Leiden.
This list does not pretend to be exhaustive.

thought to mean tidbits, dainties, but whether as a specially delicate part of the pig's meat or as a food of which swine were specially fond, whether a subjective or objective genitive, no one can say. Rhys Davids, noticing that in Bihar there was a common edible underground fungus, translated *sūkara-maddava* by 'truffles.'[1] This was a successful pitch, considering that by 'truffles' he meant an underground fungus common thereabouts, although no truffle (= *Tuber*) has been discovered so far in Bihar. His underground fungus was a *Scleroderma*, a little snow-white ball that is gathered just as soon as it appears on the surface. There are a number of genera of underground fungi of which truffles are one, and each genus has many species.

The two canonical Pāli Commentaries discuss but do not agree on the meaning to give to *sūkara-maddava*. One of them is the canonical Pāli Commentary on the *Dīgha Nikāya, Sumaṅgalavilāsini*, and the other, the *Paramatthajotikā*, the canonical Commentary on the *Udāna*. These Commentaries took their present form in Pāli under the guidance of the celebrated monk Buddhaghoṣa early in the fifth century of our era, mostly from Sinhala sources available to him. Each of these commentaries suggests various dishes as possibilities. Both include pork and an 'elixir' (a chemical preparation) in the list of choices. The canonical Pāli Commentary on the *Dīgha Nikāya* adds soft rice with the broth of the five products of the cow. The canonical Pāli Commentary on the *Udāna*, deriving its authority from the Great Commentary (now lost) that dates from the third century BC, offers two further choices: bamboo shoots (sprouts) trodden by pigs, and *mushrooms grown on a spot trodden by pigs*.

That the Buddha was eating his last meal was known to everyone thereabouts: nothing that happened there could have escaped those within eye-reach nor have been forgotten by them, not least because of the awesome event to take place a few hours later, the Buddha's translation to Nirvana that he had been predicting for that night since he was in Vaiśali three months before.

Dr. Stella Kramrisch, building on the work of the late Professor Roger Heim and me in eastern India, has identified with finality the *sūkara-maddava* as the *Pūtika*,[2] a plant that figures conspicuously in the Brāhmaṇas and other early post-Vedic sacred Sanskrit texts. In this paper I will examine the Last Meal at Pāvā and the death of Gautama the Buddha at Kusinārā in what is today northern Bihar. I will focus attention on what he ate at his Last Meal – a matter of little theological importance to the Theravadin branch of Buddhism and none at all

1. See note 1, entry under 1910, p 137 ftnt.

2. Stella Kramrisch: 'The Mahāvīra Vessel and the Plant Pūtika,' *supra* p 95.

to the Buddhists of the Greater Vehicle, but pertinent to our mushroomic inquiries and notably, as I shall show, to the identity of Soma.

Of all the scholars who have dealt with the Last Meal of the Buddha, I believe only one, André Bareau, has addressed himself to the surprising anomaly offered by the possibility of either pork or mushrooms being served to the Buddha at this meal. Here is what Bareau has to say:

> En effet, la viande de porc et plus encore les champignons sont des choses pour lesquelles les Indiens imprégnés de culture brahmanique, comme l'étaient le Buddha et une grande partie de ses disciples, éprouvent un profond, un insurmontable dégout et que ne consomment guère que certains tribus sauvages ou des gens de basse caste, rejetés par la bonne société et pressés par la faim. L'idée d'offrir au Bienheureux, pour l'honorer et le régaler, comme un mets de choix, . . . de la viande de porc ou des champignons est aussi insolite que si, dans une légende occidentale, on offrait à quelque éminent personnage un festin dont le plat principal serait une cuisse de chien ou une purée de goémon, des sauterelles frites ou des chenilles grillées; cela paraîtrait à juste titre une plaisanterie ou ferait croire à une erreur de copie. [*Recherches sur la biographie du Buddha.* Tome I, p 267. Paris. 1970. Publications de l'Ecole Française d'Extrême Orient, Vol LXXVII]

Confirming what Bareau says, Chap V-5 of the laws of Manu, believed to have been committed to writing around the beginning of the Christian era, declares that:

> garlic, leeks and onions, mushrooms and (all plants) springing from impure (substances), are unfit to be eaten by twice-born men.

and this proscription is repeated in V-19:

> A twice-born man who knowingly eats mushrooms, a village-pig, garlic, a village-cock, onions, or leeks, will become an outcast.

Here the prohibition carries a dire penalty. Mushrooms are forbidden in two further clauses, VI-14 and XI-156. The repeated prohibition applies expressly to twice-born men, which embraced the three upper castes.

The ban on mushrooms was no dead letter. Sir William Jones quotes from a commentator on the laws of Manu named Yama:

> . . . the ancient Hindus held the fungus in such detestation that Yama . . . declares 'those who eat mushrooms, whether springing from the ground or growing on a tree, fully equal in guilt to the slayers of Bráhmens, and the most despicable of all deadly sinners.' [*The Works of Sir William Jones*, Vol V, pp 160-161, London, 1807.]

This is the most extravagant outburst of mycophobia that we have found anywhere, surely the most extravagant to be found in the Indo-European world, which is saying a good deal. The learned Brahman tells us that the simple mushroom-eater is as bad as the murderers of Brahmans! Why such passionate, such exaggerated censure? Bareau, in comparing the Hindu eater of mushrooms to one among us who eats dog's flesh, was engaging in understatement.

Three months before the Last Meal at Pāvā and before his Mahāparinirvāṇa, the Buddha had been sojourning at Vaiśali and thereabouts. While in the vicinity of Vaiśali he had suffered a grave illness, attributed from ancient times to a chronic gastric upset, probably dysentery; had felt the weight of his years, had called himself an 'octogenarian,' and had announced his intention to go to Kusinārā and there three months later to experience the Mahāparinirvāṇa, the Final Extinction. He was predicting the time and place of his own end. He made his way to Kusinārā with his followers on foot, teaching the doctrine as was his wont, and it took him three months to cover the 140 kilometers. To his disciples and the villagers he made freely known his purpose: he never wavered in his resolution, nor did he hide it from anyone.

The day before the Buddha reached Kusinārā he arrived at the nearby village of Pāvā and passed the night in the mango grove belonging to one Cunda, a metal-worker or blacksmith, and therefore a śūdra, the lowest of the four castes in Hindu society. Cunda, appearing almost immediately, inquired what the Buddha desired. According to one of the Chinese recensions of the Buddha's life, the Buddha explained that he was to undergo the Mahāparinirvāṇa in Kusinārā: lamentations followed. Cunda invited the Buddha and his many followers to take their single meal the next day with him, and by his silence the Buddha accepted. Cunda withdrew to assemble the food and prepare it. In the morning Cunda came to summon the Buddha and his followers to the meal that he had prepared.

Cunda, as we said before, was a śūdra, a man of the lowest caste. On the other hand, as the metal-worker of the region he was a technician, comfortably off, extending hospitality on a moment's notice to the Buddha and his numerous followers, one accustomed to meeting and mixing with travelers including individuals of what are today called the 'scheduled castes,' – aboriginal tribesmen who were not Hindus and therefore not a part of the dominant Hindu society. His forge may well have been the *raison d'être* for Pāvā. When the Buddha arrived at Cunda's dwelling-place and was seated in the place prepared for him, he (according to the *Dīgha Nikāya*) addressed Cunda saying,

> As to the *sūkara-maddava* you have made ready, serve me with them, Cunda, and as to the other food, sweet rice and cakes, serve the monks with them. [Chap IV, ¶18, p 138]

The Buddha then said to Cunda,

> Whatever *sūkara-maddava* are left over to thee, those bury in a hole. [¶19]

In a hole, not just throw away, and we are told that the surplus *sūkara-maddava* Cunda buried in a hole. Apparently Cunda had brought *sūkara-maddava* for the whole company, as he had thought all would share in them, so there must have been an ample surplus.

Then the Buddha added these remarkable words,

> I see no one, Cunda, on earth nor in Mara's heaven, nor in Brahma's heaven, no one among the Samaṇas and Brāhmaṇas, among gods, and men, by whom, when he has eaten it, that food can be properly assimilated, save by a *Tathāgata*. [¶19]

Obviously the Buddha had recognized at once what he was being offered, the *sūkara-maddava*, and he knew the mushrooms were of a species that would shortly smell bad ('stink') if they were not eaten or buried in a hole. (To this day the custom among some Santal seems to survive to bury any surplus *sūkara-maddava* in a hole.) Perhaps it was the first time in his life that the Buddha, of kṣatriya origin, was being offered mushrooms to eat. But these particular mushrooms were familiar to him because of their unique role in the Hindu religion in which he had been brought up.

André Bareau appreciates to the full the solemnity of this dish of *sūkara-maddava*, though he did not know what it was. He says:

> . . . cette nourriture, la dernière que consomme le Bienheureux avant son Parinirvāṇa, est une nourriture en quelque sorte sacrée, dont les riches qualités, la puissance essentielle, vont lui permettre d'accomplir cet exploit surhumain, la suprême Extinction. Cette richesse, cette puissance sont trop grandes pour être supportées par les autres êtres, hommes ou dieux, qui n'auront jamais, et de loin, à exécuter une action comparable. [*Recherches sur la biographie du Buddha.* Tome I, p 271. Paris, 1970. Publications de l'Ecole Française d'Extrême-Orient, Vol LXXVII]

Here was the Buddha, at one of the two supreme moments of his life, unexpectedly offered at his last meal a dish that Hindus of the upper castes were forbidden to eat, an edible mushroom, a dish that was the surrogate for Soma when formally sacrificed in an utterly different manner and setting. Buddhaghoṣa quotes the Great Commentary (*Mahā-aṭṭhakathā*) as saying of Cunda's motives in offering this dish to the Buddha and his monks:

> They say that Cunda, the smith, having heard that the Exalted One would attain *parinibbāna* that day, thought it would be good if he could live longer after eating this dish, and offered it wishing for the Master's longevity. [p 138 *infra*]

Walpola Rāhula's comment on the Great Commentary from which we have extracted this quotation is as follows:

> The *Mahā-aṭṭhakathā* (Great Commentary) is the most important of the ancient original Sinhala commentaries dating back at least to the 3rd century BC, on which are based the present available Pāli commentaries of the 5th century AC, including the Commentaries on the *Dīgha Nikāya* and the *Udāna* from which these two commentarial passages are taken.

The Great Commentary cites hearsay ('They say . . .') as the reason that Cunda served those particular mushrooms on that day. The hearsay may be right, but if indeed Cunda felt the dish of *Pūtika* would extend the life of the Buddha, he must have confused the properties of *Soma* and of the *Pūtika*. The *Pūtika* enjoyed a unique status as the exalted surrogate for *Soma*, but, whereas *Soma* was consumed, the *Pūtika*, as Kramrisch quotes the sources, were mixed with the clay and then fired ritually in the making of the Mahāvīra pot and there is no reason to think that the Hindus of the three upper castes or even the Brahman hierarchs ate these fungi. Does not the text of the Great Commentary permit another interpretation? Cunda, a śūdra accustomed to eating the *Pūtika*, served them because it was the season of the rains (which had started when the Buddha and his suite were in Vaiśali) and the mushrooms, which he had known all his life, were fresh from picking. If so, it was the Buddha who at once recognized them because of their role in the Hindu religion and stopped Cunda from serving them to the others. The Buddha was certainly not accustomed to eating mushrooms of any kind, and here he was being invited to eat those slimy mucoid excrescences, as the twice-born Hindus with loathing would view them. May not this, combined with the emotional tension of his imminent extinction, have provoked a recrudescence of his intermittent attacks of dysentery?

I now interrupt our account of the Buddha's progress on his last day to set forth certain discoveries bearing on *sūkara-maddava*.

THE SANTAL AND THE *PUTKA*

By an accident of fortune the Santal people living now in eastern Bihar and Orissa have preserved for us, as though in a time capsule, the identity of the Sanskrit *Pūtika*, a plant until recently unidentified, an ingredient in the clay of the Mahāvīra vessel that was fired in the course of the Pravargya sacrifice. The *Pūtika* is known as having been the surrogate for Soma,[1] though probably today by no Santal, and it figures conspicuously in the Brahmāṇas and other early sacred Sanskrit texts. As I said before, it was identified by Kramrisch on the strength of evidence produced by Heim and me.[2] (Roger Heim, outstanding French mycologist, had served as President of the Académie des Sciences and was Director of the Muséum National d'Histoire Naturelle: he accompanied me on many of my field trips.)

The late Georg Morgenstierne, the Norwegian linguist, specialist in the Kafir and Dardic languages, also a Sanskrit and Persian scholar, first called my attention to an oddity of the Santal language of special interest to me, as it affected their mushroom vocabulary. Santali was not a specialty of his but he was a vast reservoir of general linguistic knowledge.

The Santal, who number some millions, live in villages scattered in the area of eastern Bihar known as the Santal Parganas, in the western north-and-south strip of West Bengal, and in Orissa as far south as the Simlipal Hills. The Santal are slight in build, neat in dress, with sleek, black hair and dark almost black regular features, their houses of red earth ornamented with curious painted geometric patterns and neatly disposed within and without, in these respects contrasting with the Hindus. By tradition they are food gatherers, hunters, fishermen, but are now taking to agriculture.

From the Indo-European point of view, the Munda languages, of which Santali is the biggest member, are peculiar: in Santali there are no genders, – no masculine, feminine, neuter. Their nouns are either animate or inanimate – endowed with a soul or without a soul. The entire animal kingdom is animate, has a soul. The whole of the mineral kingdom is inanimate, without a soul. There are oddities: *eg* the sun, moon, stars are animate. Strangely, the vege-

1. See Manfred Mayrhofer: *A Concise Sanskrit Etymological Dictionary*, entry under *pūtikaḥ*, also Vol 3, p 761.

2. *Cahiers du Pacifique* #14, September, 1970: 'Les putka des Santals, champignons doués d'une âme,' p 77. For those interested, the mushroom was *Scleroderma hydrometrica* (Pers.) H. var. *maculata* (Pat.) H. In Europe it breaks out into an *Astraeus*, but in India remains closed, a *Scleroderma*.

table kingdom – herbs, shrubs, trees, the fungal world – is inanimate, but *with a single exception*, one species of mushroom, the *putka*. The Santal do not know why the *putka* is animate, or so they say. The *putka* is an underground fungus that is gathered for eating just as it appears, a snow-white little ball, in mycology identified by Heim as a *Scleroderma*, well known in Europe. In season it is commonly highly prized as food by the Santal, and much sought for by women and children.

For the last century the Norwegian Lutherans have made a vigorous play to be helpful in India by missionary activity among the Santal. The Rev. P. O. Bodding, a resident of the Santal Parganas from 1890 to 1934, mastered their language and compiled an admirable Santal-English dictionary in five large volumes, pointing out among other things the oddity of *putka*, which enjoyed in the vegetable kingdom the unique attribute of a soul. He could not explain this anomaly, nor did he venture an etymology for *putka*. But in the preface to his dictionary Mr. Bodding observed a noteworthy fact:

> Strangely enough, the Santals use some pure Sanskrit words, which, so far as I know, are not heard in the present day Hindi.

I visited Dumka in the Santal Parganas for the first time in January 1965. The Rev. A. E. Strønstad, Mr. Bodding's successor, and Mrs. Strønstad put me up and Mrs. Strønstad graciously served as my interpreter. We asked elderly and knowledgeable Santal in Dumka and the surrounding villages why *putka* was animate. No one could tell us. Our best informant turned out to be Ludgi Marndi, the widow of a native Lutheran pastor. She told us that there was one entheogenic mushroom.[1] Was it the *putka*? No, not at all. It was merely *ot'*, 'mushroom' of the soulless class. No one was able to find an example of this inebriating mushroom, but the description (big, growing only in dung mostly of cattle, and white reaching an intense cream color in the umbolate center) tallied with *Stropharia cubensis*. Neither were there any *putka* at the time of my visit: they would come after the monsoon broke. Ludgi Marndi and some other informants suggested that the *putka* was animate because it was found regularly in the sacred grove of *sarjom* trees near every village. (Santali *sarjom* =

1. 'Entheogen' is a word devised by some of us for those plant substances that inspired Early Man with awe and reverence for their effect on him. By 'Early Man' we mean mankind in prehistory or proto-history, before he could read and write, whether long long ago or since then or even living today in remote regions of the earth. 'Entheogen' (or its adjective 'entheogenic') has the advantage that it does not carry the odor of 'hallucinogen,' 'psychedelic,' 'drug,' *etc*, of the youth of the 1960s. See *Journal of Psychedelic Drugs*, Vol 11 (1-2), Jan-June 1979, pp 145-6.

Hindi *sāl* = *Shorea robusta.*) But the sacred *sarjom* trees were not animate so why should a mushroom growing from their roots be? Furthermore, the *putka* grew also in mycorrhizal relationship with other species of trees. Ludgi Marndi seemed an especially good informant and just before we were leaving for New Delhi, defeated as we thought, I asked if I might talk with her again. We went over the same ground. Suddenly she leaned forward across the table to Mrs. Strønstad and in a whisper (as translated to me) said that she would tell her why she thought the *putka* were animate: 'You must eat them within hours of gathering *for they will soon stink like a cadaver.*' She spoke under considerable emotion. We knew not what this meant but at once I jotted down her translated words in my notebook and her remark appeared later, somewhat toned down, in the paper[1] that Heim and I published.

My 1965 visit was followed by another with Heim in July-August 1967, he flying from Paris to Calcutta and I from New York. We started our quest in the Simlipal Hills and the village of Bisoï in Orissa, where the Santal and their close linguistic kin the Ho intermix, as well as several other peoples. Again we questioned the natives about why the *putka* were animate. In Nawana in the Simlipal Hills I spent the evening with Ganesh Ram Ho, the chief of the village, and he, as Ludgi Marndi had done, volunteered the information that there was an entheogenic mushroom, and his description tallied with Ludgi's; his testimony confirmed that it was probably *Stropharia cubensis* or a close cousin. (That these two excellent informants volunteered to speak of an inebriating mushroom, doubtless *Stropharia cubensis*, is a lead not to be neglected: it may have played a part in the cultural past of the Santal and of Soma.) But, just as before, it was '*ud*' and soulless. '*Ud*' is 'mushroom' in Ho.

We published the account of our trips to the Santal country in *Les Cahiers du Pacifique*, #14, September 1970. Kramrisch in time saw our paper and she grasped immediately that the *putka* of the Santal was the *Pūtika* of the Brāhmaṇas, of the Pravargya sacrifice and the Mahāvīra pot. The *Pūtika* had been the surrogate for Soma and naturally it would possess a soul! Kramrisch deserves a rich accolade for discovering that Santali *putka* was a loanword from the Sanskrit *Pūtika*. When Soma was being abandoned, probably over a long period that ended shortly after B.C. 1000, the *Pūtika* took its place, not as an entheogenic drink like Soma in the earlier sacrifice but as a component with the clay in the ceremonial firing of the Mahāvīra vessel. Its stench (of which Ludgi Marndi had spoken) was turned into fragrance when the pot, held by tongs, was fired in

1. See p 123, fn 2, p 65.

the course of the rite. No one had ever known what plant it was. We now know that, like Soma, it was a mushroom, but a common mushroom, and it possessed divine qualities though less than Soma's.

In Santal culture not only is the *putka* animate, endowed with a soul: it possesses another of Soma's attributes. The belief is apparently universal among the Santal that the *putka* is generated by (mythological) thunderbolts.[1] Long after the Brahmans have lost any use for or knowledge of this mushroom, and have lost all special contact with the Santal, these humble, hardworking people, untouchables, still believe that the *putka* is procreated by the lightningbolt, as the Vedic Brahmans believed that Soma was procreated by the Vajra of Indra, or Parjanya, the god of lightning. Here is another manifestation, another proof, of the breathtaking cultural intensity millennia ago of the religion of the hierarchs of the Aryans. The lightningbolt was thought of as the sperm, the spunk, fecundating the soft mother earth with the entheogenic mushrooms.

The Santal believe there are two kinds of *putka*, the *hor putka* and the *seta putka*, one smooth and the other rough. Heim said the two kinds were merely different stages in the life cycle of the one species. The *hor putka* is the 'man *putka*,' not in the sense of male but of a human being, or of the 'Santal' whom they naturally regard as *par excellence* the human being. The *seta putka*, which is rough, is the 'dog *putka*,' the dog not being despised as it is in Hindu culture. A few of the Santal spoke to us of a third *putka*, the *rote putka* or 'toad *putka*.' Most Santal did not recognize this term and of those who did, most could not say what kind of mushroom it meant. But when we were in Kathikund, a village in the Santal Parganas, we witnessed from our veranda a violent midday thunderstorm and within hours and then throughout the night a host of puffballs appeared on the plain before our bungalow. One of our Santal companions told us with assurance that these were indeed *rote putka*. In this instance the puffball was *Lycoperdon pusillum* but probably any other puffball coming in response to a thunder shower would be a *rote putka*. In short, the *rote putka*, which is not eaten by the Santal, is a false *putka* . . . The entheogenic mushrooms of which Ludgi Marndi and Ganesh Ram Ho had told us, probably *Stropharia cubensis*, are not *putka*: they are merely *ot'*, or *ud* in the Ho language, enjoy no grammatical distinction in the languages, and so far as I learned no distinction in folklore. But it is imperative that this be explored much further. Does its entheogenic virtue account for the colored geometrical designs, endlessly varied, that decorate the exteriors of many Santal houses?

1. See p 123, fn 2; *SOMA: Divine Mushroom of Immortality*, pp 39-40.

Throughout our visits to the Santal country the people we spoke with said that pigs dug for the *putka*, thus confirming what the canonical Pāli Commentary on the *Udāna* says of *sūkara-maddava*. But I was seeking a quotation and after returning to New York the Rev. Johannes Gausdal, a retired missionary living in Oslo, put me in touch with Mr. Gora Tudu, principal of Kaerabani High School, and we asked Mr. Tudu through Mr. Gausdal whether swine sought out the *putka* in the forest. Here is what he replied:

> Whether the pigs eat *putka* or not? In this case also I got some *putka* from the forests. I tried them on a few pigs—the old *putka* were not liked, but the new ones seemed to be delicacies of the pigs. They ate them with relish. Also in the forest I found at several bushes where *putka* usually come up several marks of upturned earth, indicating that the pigs had been digging for the *putka*. [Letter in my *Munda* file]

I was careful not to divulge the reason this question was being asked. There are a number of genera of underground fungi divided among scores of species, and I should be surprised if they all drew pigs but perhaps they do.

Mr. Gausdal asked also about the smell of aging *putka*. Mr. Tudu replied, with unconscious humor:

> I collected some *putka*, both *hor putka* and *seta putka*, and put them in dishes in dry condition as well as wet, just to see what the smell would be like after decomposition. In both the smell emitted was that of decomposing wood material, not at all bad in the sense of any blooded being. The smell was never too strong or filthy. The worst I could compare, the smell was that of rotting jute in muddy water.

Kramrisch tells me that rotting jute in muddy water creates a fearful stench. Mr. Tudu possesses the endearing quality of dirt farmers everywhere: their fondness for the smell of dung heaps, for example, is powerfully colored by what dung means for the crops. The earthy smells of farm yards also possess a likeable integrity.

The Gausdal-Gora Tudu correspondence was conducted in Santali, but my questions and his answers to them were in English.

We know that the Santal have not always lived where they do now. Six hundred years ago they lived to the west of Benares on the Chotā Nāgpur plateau, and tradition has it that long before then the Santal had lived much further to the West, just where no one knows, but possibly near the ancient center of Brahmanical sacrifices, where they could have had close relations with the Aryans, perhaps serving them before and through the shift from Soma to the *Pūtika*. This would also explain the other Sanskrit words in Santali that Mr. Bodding notes. Indeed he remarks in his preface to his Santal Dictionary that 'the description of the Dasyus in the Vedas and the Mahābhārata seems to be adaptable to many a Santal.'

THE DEATH OF THE BUDDHA

Having completed the Santal interpolation, we will now revert to the text of the *Dīgha Nikāya* as translated by the Rhys Davidses.

After the discussion of the *sūkara-maddava*, the Rhys Davids translation continues with an astonishing development:

> ¶20. Now when the Exalted One had eaten the rice prepared by Cunda, the worker in metals, there fell upon him a dire sickness, the disease of dysentery, and sharp pain came upon him, even unto death. But the Exalted One, mindful and self-possessed, bore it without complaint. [Chap IV]

This was a disconcerting turn of events, since the Omniscient One has but lately said that he sees no one, save a Tathāgata, who can properly assimilate the *sūkara-maddava*, which he has just eaten. If the circumstances were invented, as Bareau thinks, what a strange set of circumstances for utterly devoted followers of the Buddha to have invented! The mushrooms, now that we know precisely, were sound and there was never a risk: moreover, aged *Pūtika* would declare their age by their stench! And Cunda was a responsible man to buy and cook them. However, let us remember that in the upper Hindu castes where the Buddha had been brought up and lived out all his early life, even though he was now free from food tabus and caste distinctions, all mushrooms would be shunned as inedible; but here, at a critical moment of his life, he was being offered *Pūtika*. Did Cunda know the role of the *Pūtika* in the religion of the twice-born castes? Did he perhaps know it by rumor, inaccurately? Or did he not know it at all and was he serving these mushrooms solely for the excellent reason that they were fresh and in season? It is clear from the testimony of the *Dīgha Nikāya* that the attack suffered by the Buddha was sudden; it was violent; it alarmed the whole company; it was virtually over quickly, for not long afterward the Buddha instructed the faithful Ānanda that they should walk on to Kusinārā close by. But what could be more natural than a violent reaction in one brought up as a kṣatriya to consider mushrooms inedible? And with his large intestine being chronically inflamed with dysentery, his diarrhoea was a natural sequence. 'Dysentery' is a translation of the Pāli *lohita-pakkhandika*, which means 'bloody flux' in old-fashioned English.

The account in the *Dīgha Nikāya* is as though written to order for this explanation. Two quatrains, apparently independent of each other, are inserted in the text of the *Dīgha Nikāya* (¶ 20, p 139) at this point. Buddhaghoṣa adds a note: 'It should be understood that these are the verses by the Theras [Elders] who held the Council' – the Council that took place at Rājagṛha, at which some months later the initial plans were laid for mobilizing detailed recollections of the Buddha's teachings and for organizing the Buddhist religion. The first quatrain shows how those present murmured against Cunda, and, according to the second, there was also murmuring about the mushrooms. Here are the quatrains in the Rhys Davids translation:

> When he had eaten Cunda's food,
> The copper-smith's – thus have I heard –
> He bore with fortitude the pain,
> The sharp pain even unto death.
>
> When he had eaten, from the mushrooms [= *sūkara-maddava*] in the food
> There fell upon the Teacher sickness dire,
> Then after nature was relieved the Exalted One announced and said:
> I now am going on to Kusinārā.

After the episode the Exalted One went out of his way to exonerate Cunda of blame, thus making even more tenable my explanation of his illness. For if Cunda had been guilty of negligence in choosing the mushrooms, why should the Omniscient One have exonerated him?

> 42. And the Exalted One addressed the venerable Ānanda, and said: – 'Now it may happen, Ānanda, that some one should stir up remorse in Cunda the smith, by saying: – "This is evil to thee, Cunda, and loss to thee in that when the Tathāgata had eaten his last meal from thy provision, then he died." Any such remorse, Ānanda, in Cunda the smith should be checked by saying: – "This is good to thee, Cunda, and gain to thee, in that when the Tathāgata had eaten his last meal from thy provision, then he died." From the very mouth of the Exalted One, Cunda, have I heard, from his own mouth have I received this saying: – "These two offerings of food are of equal fruit, and of equal profit and of much greater fruit and much greater profit than any other – and which are the two? The offering of food which, when a Tathāgata has eaten, he attains to supreme and perfect insight; and the offering of food which, when a Tathāgata has eaten, he passes away by that utter passing away in which nothing whatever remains be-

hind – these two offerings of food are of equal fruit and of equal profit, and of much greater fruit and much greater profit than any others. There has been laid up by Cunda the smith a karma redounding to length of life, redounding to good birth, redounding to good fortune, redounding to good fame, redounding to the inheritance of heaven, and of sovereign power." In this way, Ānanda, should be checked any remorse in Cunda the smith.' (p 147-8)

Bareau concedes that Cunda and Pāvā may be original elements but, if so, thinks that they are the sole original elements in the narrative of the Buddha's stay in Pāvā:

> Deux siècles après le Parinirvāṇa, ces deux noms, ici Pāvā et Cunda, étaient les deux seuls éléments anciens, peut-être même historiques, de l'épisode du dernier repas du Buddha. Aucun souvenir n'avait donc été conservé ni des incidents qui avaient pu s'y produire ni de la nature précise des aliments qui avaient été servis alors au Bienheureux. [Tome I, p 258 in his *Recherches sur la biographie du Buddha*, Ecole Française d'Extrême Orient]

Perhaps in the light of our discoveries Bareau may grant more to the history of the Buddha's Last Meal in Pāvā as told in the *Dīgha Nikāya*. Too many had witnessed the episode with the mushrooms to permit the Theras to suppress it: his sudden illness had provoked too much talk.

Here is the account of the Buddha's death according to the *Dīgha Nikāya*, Chap V:

> 1. Now the Exalted One addressed the venerable Ānanda, and said: – 'Come, Ānanda, let us go on to the Sāla Grove of the Mallas, the Upavattana of Kusinārā, on the further side of the river Hiranyavatī.'
>
> 'Even so, lord!' said the venerable Ānanda, in assent, to the Exalted One.
>
> And the Exalted One proceeded with a great company of brethren to the Sāla Grove of the Mallas, the Upavattana of Kusinārā, on the further side of the river Hiranyavatī: and when he had come there he addressed the venerable Ānanda, and said:
>
> 'Spread over for me, I pray you, Ānanda, the couch with its head to the north, between the twin Sāla trees. I am weary, Ānanda, and would lie down.'
>
> 'Even so, lord!' said the venerable Ānanda, in assent, to the Exalted One. And he spread a covering over the couch with its head to the north, between the twin Sāla trees. And the Exalted One laid himself down on his right side, with one leg resting on the other; and he was mindful and self-possessed.

In a note on this passage the Sinhala commentator added an explanation:

> Tradition says that there was a row of Sāla trees at the head of that couch, and another at its foot, one young Sāla tree being close to its head, and another close

to its foot. The twin Sāla trees were so called because the two trees were equally grown in respect of the roots, trunks, branches, and leaves. There was a couch there in the park for the special use of the (periodically elected) chieftain of the Mallas, and it was this couch which the Exalted One asked Ānanda to make ready. (Ftnt p 149)

In the last watch of the night the Buddha died, precisely as he had been predicting for three months, since he was in Vaiśali.

There have been individuals in various parts of the world, and especially among the holy men of India, who have acquired by 'concentration' (*samādhi*) control over some of the muscles that ordinarily function in response to stimuli beyond the human will. A. L. Basham has remarked on this in *The Wonder That Was India*, p 327:

> The ancient mystical physiology of India needs further study, not only by professional Indologists, but by open-minded biologists and psychologists, who may reveal the true secret of the yogī. For whatever we may think about his spiritual claims there is no doubt that the advanced yogī can hold his breath for very long periods without suffering injury, can control the rhythm of his own heartbeats, can withstand extremes of heat and cold, can remain healthy on a starvation diet, and, despite his austere and frugal life and his remarkable physical contortions, which would ruin the system of any ordinary man, can often survive to a very advanced age with full use of his faculties.

Basham fails to mention that occasionally death is the goal of this 'concentration,' but there is no reason to question that death can be the purpose of such an act of will. In recent years, when death has been the end result of this manifestation of will power, *mahāsamādhi* has sometimes been the term used when speaking of it.

The Buddha predicted the day of his death three months before and thenceforward announced freely the time and place of his own extinction. After his Last Meal the narrative says that on his initiative he walked the short distance to Kuśinārā. Since the time of his death, no Hindu, no Buddhist, has ever suggested that he died of mushroom poisoning. His death has not provoked discussion among Buddhists. Knowing as we now do what the mushrooms were that Cunda served, they could have provoked a stomach upset in a Hindu mycophobe but they could not have caused his death. He died of his own will power, of his own *mahāsamādhi*. Or, rather than provoking his own death, did he not use yogic power, under trying circumstances, to postpone his translation to *nirvāna* until he had reached his place of choice?

The surrogate for Soma explains and justifies the extraordinary words used by the Buddha in limiting to himself alone this dish. By consigning to a hole the surplus *Pūtika*, he showed himself familiar with its everyday properties. Now that we know the precise properties of this mushroom, its etymology as cognate with 'putrid' is clarified, and its strong link with Soma is a good explanation for the Santal belief that it is generated by the divine lightningbolt.

Up to this point we have concentrated on only one source – the canonical Pāli Text of the *Dīgha Nikāya* – for our details about the life of Buddha. It is the Holy Scripture of the Theravadin branch of Buddhism with its headquarters in Śrī Laṅka. There are, in addition, five other master recensions of his life, four in Chinese and one in Sanskrit. All five mention the stop in Pāvā and name Cunda as the host there, but none of them mentions *sūkara-maddava*. An obvious explanation for this omission is that the Chinese are natural mycophiles: they eat with relish all kinds of edible mushrooms and they know their mushrooms. They would not understand why the Buddha honored the *Pūtika*, saying he alone could digest it. For the Chinese all this would have been incomprehensible.

The Buddha and his followers were mostly Hindus of the upper castes who had withdrawn from obedience to the Hindu religion. When the Theras assembled at Rājagṛha, they were inevitably, even if they were rebels, heirs to the infinite complexity of habits, practices, subtle ways of thinking and feeling of the Brahmanic religion. When Buddhism became a world religion, it liberated itself from the Brahmanic religion and this included the mighty tradition of Soma and the Vedic hymns, and of course from the less powerful hold of the *Pūtika*. In the early days of Christianity, before it became a world religion, the pull of Jewish ways such as circumcision and the ban on pig-meat exerted influence on Jewish converts to Christianity, and the early Church faced a parallel conflict.

THE BUDDHA'S LAST MEAL

The episode at Pāvā lends itself to various explanations; the written record contains a number of anomalies. If we were to offer the solution that we think is most likely, here it is.

There is only the Commentary on the *Udāna*, which Buddhaghoṣa presented as hearsay, to show that Cunda the śudra knew of the use made by the Brahmans of the *Pūtika*. Cunda certainly knew this mushroom as a universal favorite among mushroom eaters when it was in season and it was in season right then:

he was taken aback when the Buddha recognized the mushroom and asked him, in astonishing language unfamiliar to his ears, to serve them to the Buddha only. Cunda had done himself proud in assembling mushrooms for the whole company, and now he was forbidden to give them to the guests or even to himself.

Shortly after the Buddha had eaten his mushrooms with rice he fell violently ill. This must have caused Cunda consternation and chagrin. Alarm was felt, and there was murmuring against Cunda and the mushrooms in the assembly, for all or almost all were twice-born men and had been indoctrinated against mushrooms. We can imagine Cunda's embarrassment but we have no information: an opaque cloud of silence falls over him.

In the *Dīgha Nikāya* the Buddha exonerates Cunda, somewhat stiltedly under the circumstances. Perhaps everyone remembered that the Buddha had spoken up for Cunda and many had heard him but none could recall what precisely he had said. Someone seems to have drafted the paragraph much later. The fitting exoneration of Cunda demonstrated the thoughtfulness and the nobility of the Buddha under most trying circumstances.

Was not '*sūkara-maddava*' introduced in place of *Pūtika* at Rājagṛha to avoid confusing people as to the Buddha's attitude toward the Old Religion? He showed an attitude toward the *Pūtika*, and he reacted to them, in a way that we today, under the circumstances, can understand for the first time.

And as for the diverse explanations in the two canonical Commentaries for *sūkara-maddava*, they may have been introduced at Rājagṛha also, or perhaps more likely late in Aśoka's reign when the need for an explanation became increasingly felt by the Buddhist community. No theological importance was ever given, then or later, to the Pāvā episode because, after all, the Buddha was under acute stress at the time, what with his illness, his imminent extinction freely predicted since he was in Vaiśali three months before the episode at Pāvā, and the unexpected dish of *Pūtika* that suddenly confronted him. There had been far too much talk among those present to suppress the episode, but obviously the *Pūtika* was not to be identified plainly. The *sūkara-maddava* was a way to tell the truth but still to interpose obstacles to its understanding. The word may have been a neologism invented *ad hoc*.

Now we see for the first time in how dramatic a predicament the Brahman proscription on mushrooms for the twice-born castes accidentally involved the Buddhist religion at the very moment of its birth. We still do not know – we will probably never know – when that proscription came into force, perhaps over centuries while the Vedic hymns were being composed, or possibly when the hierarchs among the Brahmans learned of the entheogenic virtues of *Stropharia cubensis* as known to the lower orders living in India, or when Soma was finally abandoned and the *Pūtika* adopted as its surrogate. But we do know how effectively the Buddhist Theras fudged the facts in the *Dīgha Nikāya*, until an inquirer 2,500 years after the event appeared, assembled the evidence, and with the help of Georg Morgenstierne, Roger Heim, Stella Kramrisch, Wendy Doniger O'Flaherty, and above all of the Santal people, fitted together the jigsaw pieces.

THE INDUS VALLEY AND KASHMIR

When we published *SOMA: Divine Mushroom of Immortality* in 1968 I pointed out in it that in the 1028 hymns of the *Rig Veda* there was never a mention of the blossoms, fruit, seed, leaves, branches, bark, or roots of the plant – a telling clue where to look for the divine herb. But there was another botanical fact that deserved full recognition, but I had not yet focussed on it.

Botanists divide plants between phanerogams and cryptogams. The phanerogams include all flower- and seed-bearing plants, whether trees, shrubs, creepers or climbers, herbs and grasses, whether cultivated or uncultivated. The cryptogams are lower orders of vegetation, less developed along the evolutionary trail, and the mushrooms are the cryptogams that interest us. Only in recent centuries have three or four species out of thousands lent themselves to commercial exploitation, and a meager handful also to expensive cultivation in laboratories. In Aryan times, in the Indus Valley and Kashmir, there was the widest variety of climate, owing to the variety of accidented terrain therein – lofty mountains, low lying plains, valleys, wetlands, arid stretches – and any needed phanerogam could probably have been grown in some part of that large country. *But only those mushrooms grew there that the country produced spontaneously.* Since we know that the supply of Soma was limited at best to the mountains and must have been further reduced when the monsoon failed, conforming to what we know about Soma in Vedic times, this points to the entheogenic mushroom *Amanita muscaria* for their Soma. That the birch and also the conifers act as hosts to *A. muscaria* was not realized by anyone among the Aryans, and therefore no one thought of planting the host trees to see whether by this means man could thus increase the yield of the holy plant.

Other fungal entheogens grow at the lower levels. They come in cattle dung, are easily identified and gathered, and are effective. But they fail to conform to Brahman practices: they are known to tribals and śudras. Soma on the other hand exacts self-discipline of the priests, a long initiation and training: it is, for proper exploitation, an affair of a priestly *élite*. But the possible role of *Stropharia cubensis* growing in the dung of cattle in the lives of the lower orders remains to this day wholly unexplored. Is *S. cubensis* responsible for the elevation of the cow to a sacred status? And for the inclusion of the urine and dung of cows in the *pañcagavya*? And was that a contributing reason for abandoning Soma? Given the ecological conditions prevailing in the Indus Valley and Kashmir, only a few of the Aryans could know by personal experience the secrets of the Divine Herb. The cult of Soma must have been shaped by the peculiar circumstances prevailing in the area, but ultimately those circumstances must have doomed that cult. Today it lives on in India only as an intense and glowing memory of an ancient rite.

Under the British Raj the rich and diverse vegetation of India was admirably studied, and George Watt's encyclopaedic *Dictionary of the Economic Products of India*, 1889-1896, in eleven volumes, edited and partly written by him, is a major legacy of the British rule in India. However, the mycophobic British did little to advance knowledge of mycology, and the Hindus nothing. No one ever suggested a mushroom for Soma, let alone *A. muscaria*. Our *SOMA* came out in 1968 but no *A. muscaria* since then has yet been found in Pakistan or Kashmir: there have been numerous reports of finds but voucher specimens have not been deposited in herbaria. Dr. Roy Watling, mycologist of the Royal Botanic Garden of Edinburgh, spent three weeks in the field in 1978 on a general survey of the Kashmir area, in the vicinity of Srinagar. He collected in stands of birch in two areas but he arrived there late in the growing season and moreover the season was dry. In his printed report[1] he writes, 'The species *A. muscaria* is almost certainly native to the *Betula*-zone of northern India.' There he found *Betula utilis* from 9,000 feet up to the timber line at 10,500 feet but no *A. muscaria*. In the Northwestern Himalayas the birch grows intermixed with Rhododendron in scrub-vegetation up to 11,500 feet.

We may think we are feeling the frustrations of the Aryans but by comparison with them we are making only lackadaisical efforts to find a few voucher specimens, whereas the Brahmans must have developed urgent need for quantities of fruiting bodies to dry, and then to reflate, and bring to the pressing stones. Their needs must have been constantly increasing with the increasing population. Whatever may have been the case later, the relations at first with

1. Watling, Roy and Norma M. Gregory: 'Larger Fungi from Kashmir,' *Nova Hedwigia*, Band xxxii, Brunswick, 1980, J. Cramer.

the natives were surely hostile. The natives seem to have come to occupy the intermediate mountain heights, precisely where *A. muscaria* grows and where the *Rig Veda* time and again says Soma grows. As we know from the *Śatapatha Brāhmaṇa,* the Brahmans depended for their Soma supplies, in large part at least, on the natives living in the mountains. The supply depended on the weather and the state of the relations with the natives, whereas the needs were swelling with every generation. The Brahmans must have found it in their interest to cultivate the Dasyus and the Dasyus would have found it advantageous to discover every spot where *A. muscaria* grew, above all the stands of birch but also other host trees. (*A. muscaria* has been reported lately from Tamilnadu, especially from the Nilgiri Hills, in Southern India, but its presence there has been attributed by mycologists to plantings of exotic conifers in the past century.) Most of the Soma sacrifices must have used make-do phanerogamic substitutes and in the post-Vedic Brāhmaṇas and other writings we learn how the priests from early times faced this scarcity with such make-do plants.

The Brahmans probably continued to trade with the mountains of Afghanistan seeking Soma, and with the Hindu Kush, but there is no knowing whether these tribesmen were friendly, perhaps intermittently. The *Afghanistan Journal* 6.2, 1979, announced the finding of *A. muscaria* in Nuristan, in the Shetul Valley high in the Hindu Kush in the extreme northeast of the country. The authors, Gholam Mochtar and Hartmut Geerken of Kabul, talked with three old codgers, ostensibly *habitués* of the "ravens' bread," claimed to be *A. muscaria* from which an inebriating concoction is made. The episode is insufficiently documented to permit conclusions about its bearing on *Amanita muscaria* and the Soma question. Their report antedates the Russian invasion.

The use of substitutes by the Aryans must have been a reluctantly adopted practice from the start. They are mentioned for the first time in the last batch of hymns incorporated into the canon, Mandala X 85 through to the end, 191. In *SOMA* we failed to take into consideration these hymns of Mandala X, since they were admitted to the canon at a late stage, shortly before the Vedic age ended. But some years ago Professor Clifford Wright, in a lecture delivered at Cambridge University, took the position that many of those hymns, the last to be admitted to the canon, on strong stylistic ground were by no means the last to be composed. There is a verse in these hymns that speaks of the substitutes. That hymn may well have been composed centuries earlier:

Rig Veda X 85.3: One thinks one drinks Soma because a plant is crushed. The Soma that the Brahmans know – that no one drinks.

This conforms to our present thinking: the scarcity of Soma was not to be explained by the spread of the Aryans southward, then eastward down the Yamunā and beyond the confluence with the Ganges. The scarcity had always existed, and the make-do substitutes had been a chronic problem.

MEMORANDUM BY WALPOLA RĀHULA ON THE EARLY SOURCES FOR THE MEANING OF *SŪKARAMADDAVA*

The original Canonical Pāli passage from the *Mahāparinibbānasutta* of the *Dīgha-nikāya*, Pāli Text Society edition (London 1966), Vol. II, p 127:

Atha kho Cundo kammāraputto tassā rattiyā accayena sake nivesane paṇītaṃ khādaniyaṃ bhojaniyaṃ paṭiyādāpetvā pahūtañ ca sūkaramaddavaṃ Bhagavato kālaṃ ārocāpesi: 'Kālo bhante, niṭṭhitaṃ bhattan'ti.

Then at the end of that night, Cunda, the smith, having made ready in his house hard and soft delicious food, and also a big quantity of *sūkaramaddava*, announced the time to the Exalted One, saying: 'The time, Lord, has come, the meal is ready.'

In explaining *sūkaramaddava* in this passage the Pāli Commentary of the *Dīgha-nikāya*, *Sumaṅgalavilāsini*, Pāli Text Society ed. (London, 1971), Vol. II, p 568, gives three different opinions:

Sūkaramaddavan ti n'ātitaruṇassa n'ātijiṇṇassa ekajeṭṭhakasūkarassa pavattamaṃsaṃ. Taṃ kira muduñ c'eva siniddhañ ca hoti. Taṃ paṭiyādāpetvā sādhukaṃ pacāpetvā'ti attho. (Colombo ed. of the *Sumaṅgalavilāsinī*, Part 1, (1918) p. 395 adds within brackets): [*Eke bhaṇanti: sūkaramaddavaṃ pana muduodanassa pañcagorasa – yūsapācanavidhānassa nāmam etan'ti yathā gavapānaṃ nāma pākanāmaṃ. Keci bhaṇanti: sūka-*

Sūkaramaddava means meat available (in the market) of an excellent (first-rate) pig neither too young nor too old. This is soft and fatty. 'Having made it ready': having cooked it well is the sense. (Some say: *sūkaramaddava* is the name for a culinary preparation of soft rice made into a broth with the five products of the cow,[1] just as *gavapāna* is the name of a culinary preparation. Others say: *sūkaramaddava* is a chem-

1. Five products of the cow: 1) milk, 2) curd, 3) buttermilk, 4) fresh butter, 5) clarified butter (ghee). W.R. [Walpola Rāhula is a Buddhist monk of our day and he renders in English the Sanskrit word *pañcagavya* as befits our times. In the past, for millennia *pañcagavya* represented: 1) milk, 2) coagulated or sour milk, 3) butter, 4) urine, and 5) dung. R.G.W.]

ramaddavaṃ nāma rasāyanavidhi, taṃ pana rasāyanasatthe āgacchati, taṃ Cundena Bhagavato parinibbānaṃ na bhaveyyā'ti rasāyaṃ paṭiyattan'ti.]

ical preparation [elixir]. It is found in the science of chemistry. That chemical preparation [elixir] was made by Cunda thinking that the *parinibbāna* of the Exalted One might not take place.)

The story of Cunda offering *sūkaramaddava* to the Buddha occurs exactly in the same way in another canonical Pāli text, *Udāna*. The *Paramatthajotikā*, Commentary on the *Udāna* (Colombo, 1920), p 279, in explaining *sūkaramaddava* gives four different opinions:

Sūkaramaddavan'ti sūkarassa mudusiniddhaṃ pavattamaṃsan'ti Mahāaṭṭhakathāyaṃ vuttaṃ. Keci pana sūkaramaddavan'ti na sūkaramaṃsaṃ, sūkarehi madditavaṃsakalīro'ti vadanti. Aññe: sūkarehi madditappadese jātaṃ ahicchattan'ti. Apare pana sūkaramaddavaṃ nāma ekaṃ rasāyanan'ti bhaṇimsu. Tañ hi Cundo kammāraputto ajja Bhagavā parinibbāyissati'tī sutvā 'appeva nāma naṃ paribhuñjitvā cirataraṃ tiṭṭheyyā'ti Satthu cirajīvitukamyatāya adāsī'ti vadanti.

It is said in the Great Commentary (*Mahāaṭṭhakathā*)[1] that *sūkaramaddava* is soft and fatty pork (flesh of pig) available (in the market). But some say: *sūkaramaddava* does not mean pork (flesh of pig), but bamboo shoot (bamboo sprout) trodden by pigs; others say that it is mushroom grown on a spot trodden by pigs; still others have maintained that *sūkaramaddava* is a certain elixir. They say that Cunda, the smith, having heard that the Exalted One would attain *parinibbāna* that day (lit., today) thought that it would be good if He could live longer after eating this (preparation), and offered it wishing the Master's longevity.

EPILOGUE

When I began working with Gordon Wasson on *SOMA*, almost twenty years ago, we had, at first, no suspicion that Soma might have been a mushroom: we just wished to collect the texts relating to Soma and look at them with a botanical as well as an Indological eye. It was only when I casually mentioned

1. The *Mahāaṭṭhakathā* (Great Commentary) is the most important of the ancient original Sinhala commentaries dating back at least to the 3rd century BC, on which are based the present available Pāli commentaries of the 5th century AC, including the Commentaries on the *Dīghanikāya* and the *Udāna* from which these two commentarial passages are taken. W.R.

to RGW the urine-drinking, Soma-drinking episode in the *Mahābhārata* that he thought of *Amanita muscaria* as a possible identity for Soma, but from that moment on he became increasingly convinced that this was the case. I was certain that the evidence proved Soma was an entheogen (we called it an hallucinogen then), and that it was not a form of alcohol (as had been theretofore widely believed) but was a drug provoking an ecstasy of a very special kind. Here is a truth of great importance in the study of later Indian religion and this was the major contribution that RGW had made to Vedic studies.

I was, however, not yet convinced that Soma was a mushroom. I felt that the arguments rested primarily on the interpretation of adjectives, many of them words for colors, and mythological traits, many of which applied to other gods as well, permitting other interpretations as well as the interpretation that identified Soma with the fly-agaric. As an Indologist, rather than a botanist, I still feel that the broader hypothesis – that Soma was an entheogen – is more significant than the narrower one – that it was a mushroom. Over the years, however, the new evidence that RGW has brought to light, particularly the evidence linking the Buddha's last meal to Soma through the double links of the Vedic *Pūtika* and the Santal *putka*, does in fact make it seem likely that Soma was a mushroom, as RGW believed from the first moment, and, when we recall the religious role of urine mentioned above, specifically the fly-agaric. But each of the three levels of the hypothesis – that Soma was an entheogen, a mushroom, and the fly-agaric – adds a valuable dimension to our understanding of both Vedic and post-Vedic religion.

WENDY DONIGER O'FLAHERTY

Chicago
January 15, 1982

CHAPTER FIVE

CARVED 'DISEMBODIED EYES' OF TEOTIHUACAN

by Jonathan Ott[1]

Situated a few hours' drive northeast of Mexico City are the magnificent ruins of Teotihuacan, dating from the beginning of the first millennium AD. Best known for two large, stepped pyramids (Pyramids of the Sun and Moon) and the smaller, more ornate Pyramid of Quetzalcoatl, the ruins abound in numerous low, labyrinthine buildings which are decorated with beautiful and complex mural paintings. The comparatively well preserved Tepantitla murals are best known to scholars, a prominent segment having been restored and repainted in the Teotihuacan room of the Museo Nacional de Antropología in Mexico City by Augustín Villagra Caleti. Portions of many other murals survive at Teotihuacan, while some, such as the important Zacuala murals, which are unprotected from the elements, are scarcely visible today.

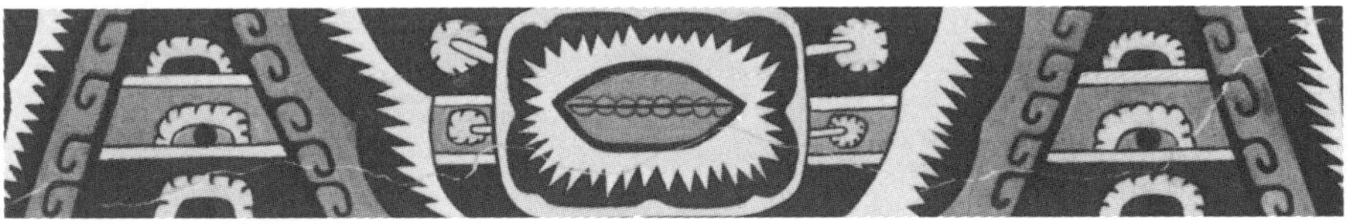

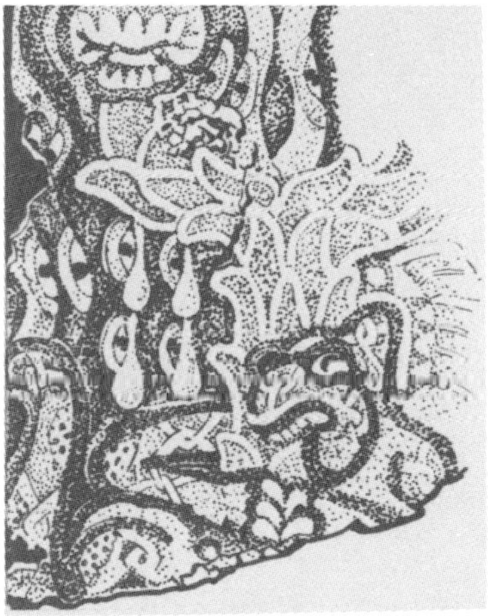

Fig. 1. 'Predella' from Zacuala, Teotihuacan, repainted by Abel Mendoza, who caught them before they disintegrated. Notice 'disembodied eyes' flanking central motif representing four mushrooms surrounding the radiant 'logos'.

Fig. 2. Drops of entheogenic potion with appended 'disembodied eyes' from Teotihuacan murals. Reproduction by Margaret Seeler.

1. President, Natural Products Co., P.O. Box 273, Vashon, Wa., 98070.

Fig. 3 & 4. Drops of entheogenic potion and appended 'disembodied eyes' issuing from entheogenic flowers. Reproduction of fragments of Tepantitla murals by Margaret Seeler.

Fig. 5. Gold ring of Isopata near Knossos, greatly enlarged. Scene depicts epiphany of goddess (presumably Artemis) on the right, and four worshippers, all represented as anthropomorphic bees. Note 'disembodied eye' in center, and plants (presumably entheogenic) surrounding goddess.

In his 1973 book *The Mural Painting of Teotihuacan*, Arthur G. Miller[a] drew attention to the prominence of the 'disembodied eyes' that occur repeatedly in the mural paintings of Teotihuacan. Figures 1-4 illustrate some typical examples of the recurrent 'disembodied eyes' motif. During a recent visit to Teotihuacan, I was struck by the ubiquity of these 'disembodied eyes', indeed, it was difficult to escape the sensation of being watched constantly.

I here comment on the existence of 'disembodied eyes' in relief carvings at Teotihuacan. The carvings are found on columns in a courtyard of a structure known as the Palace of Quetzalpapálotl,[1] located at the west corner of the square adjacent to the Pyramid of the Moon (Fig. 6 & 7). The face of each column in the courtyard is adorned with two rows of four 'disembodied eyes' arrayed above and beneath a carving of a bird (Fig. 8). The carved eyes are realistic

Fig. 6. Looking north at Teotihuacan, with Pyramid of the Moon at right and Palace of Quetzalpapálotl at left in foreground.

1. The Palace of Quetzalpapálotl was excavated in 1962 and summarily restored under the direction of Mexican archaeologist Jorge R. Acosta. The structure dates from the sixth century AD, belonging to the Teotihuacan III and IV eras. Details of the excavation and restoration can be found in Acosta's book *El Palacio del Quetzalpapálotl* (Instituto Nacional de Antropología e Historia, México, 1964).

Fig. 7. Entrance to Palace of Quetzalpapálotl at Teotihuacan.

Fig. 8. Column showing Quetzalpapálotl chimera and 'disembodied eyes'.

and are inlaid with obsidian 'pupils' (Fig. 9 & 10). The identification of the carvings as eyes is unequivocal – witness the corresponding inlay of obsidian to the eyes of the creature in the carvings, which represents a chimera called Quetzalpapálotl, 'quetzal bird/butterfly' (Fig. 8). It is perhaps significant that the eye of the bird is round, as in nature birds' eyes appear, whereas the 'disem-

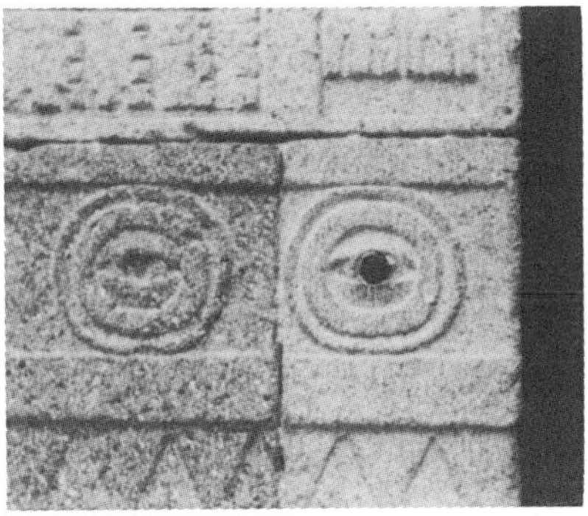

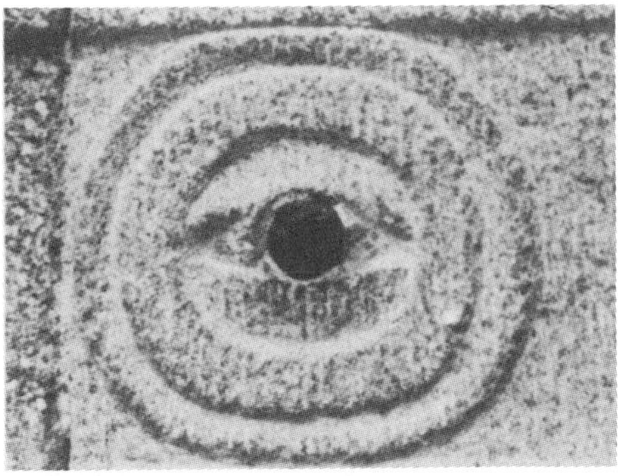

Fig. 9 & 10. Closeups of 'disembodied eye' from column. Note inlaid obsidian 'pupil' and anthropomorphic 'eyelids'.

Fig. 11. West column with frontal view of avian creature and 'disembodied eyes'.

bodied eyes' are distinctly anthropomorphic, with upper and lower 'eyelids' giving the 'eyeballs' an ovoid shape. On the north, south, and east sides of the courtyard, the columns identically depict the avian chimera in profile (Fig. 8), whereas the columns on the west side show a frontal view, possibly of the

Fig. 12. West side of courtyard, showing columns surmounted by painted lintel and carved stone 'combs'.

same creature (Fig. 11).[1] The columns are surmounted by a broad lintel painted with a repeated motif, which in turn is crowned by a series of carved stone 'combs' (Fig. 12).

In his book on the murals of Teotihuacan, Miller drew no conclusions as to the meaning of the 'disembodied eyes' or of the murals as a whole. R. Gordon Wasson has proposed that the 'disembodied eyes' represent the visionary sight

1. Scholars have differed on the question whether one or two birds are here depicted. In a recent paper (*Ethnos* 32: 5-17, 1967) Arthur G. Miller summarizes the evidence and concludes that the bird depicted frontally represents an owl, whereas the bird depicted in profile represents the quetzal. Acosta, in his comments regarding his reconstruction of the columns, identified the profile birds as quetzal bird/butterfly chimeras, hence the name Quetzalpapálotl.

of the shaman or participant in an agape involving ingestion of a potion compounded of entheogenic mushrooms, morning glory seeds, or other plants with allied effects. This interpretation is based on the occurrence of mushrooms, flowers, and seeds in juxtaposition with the 'disembodied eyes' (*vide* Figures 1-4), and the association of the eyes with green drops issuing from the flowers (green, the color of jade, signifies religious value), drops which are symbolic of the entheogenic potion. This theory is laid out in detail in *The Wondrous Mushroom: Mycolatry in Mesoamerica*,[b] which further suggests that the labyrinthine buildings of Teotihuacan, decorated with these entheogenic motifs, were groups of cenacula in which sacramental ingestion of entheogens took place. The carved 'disembodied eyes' of the Palace of Quetzalpapálotl are further evidence confirming this hypothesis.

The 'disembodied eye' motif is not restricted to Mesoamerican art. Figure 5 illustrates the design on a gold ring, *circa* 1500 BC, from Crete. The scene probably depicts an epiphany of the Great Mother goddess Artemis (the figure on the right) in the form of an anthropomorphic bee.[c] The hierophants who attended the Ephesian Artemis were called *Essenes* or 'King Bees' and the later Greek mother goddesses, such as Rhea and Demeter, were attended by priestesses called *Melissae*, 'Bees'.[d] It would seem that the four figures on the left of the ring represent the *Melissae*, bee-priestesses worshipping the goddess. A 'disembodied eye' is clearly represented near the center of the composition, between the goddess and her devotees. Here we have a representation of a visionary scene, from an Old World culture and antedating by two millennia the murals of Teotihuacan, yet accompanied also by a 'disembodied eye'. We now know that the Greek culture practiced religious rites based on ingestion of entheogenic potions,[efg] and it is not unreasonable to assume that earlier cultures, such as the Minoans and Mycenaeans, had similar rituals. Does not the Minoan ring from Crete depict an entheogenic vision of the goddess and her devotees in their mythological forms, as human/bee chimeras? It is significant that the goddess on the ring is surrounded by plants, presumably the source of the entheogenic potion.

The carvings of 'disembodied eyes' in the Palace of Quetzalpapálotl echo a motif common in murals found throughout the ruins of Teotihuacan. What can the 'disembodied eyes' represent, other than the visionary eye of the seer under the influence of one or other of the well-known pre-Columbian entheogens? Indeed, the image of the 'disembodied eye' suggested itself to Wasson as a natural metaphor for the state produced by ingestion of entheogenic mushrooms. Written more than 25 years ago, in 1957,[h] long before the appearance of Miller's book and without his having seen the 'disembodied eyes' of the murals or columns, R.G.W.'s words are apposite:

> *There I was, poised in space, a disembodied eye, invisible, incorporeal, seeing but not seen.*

REFERENCES

a. Miller, A. G. *The Mural Painting of Teotihuacan*. Dumbarton Oaks, Washington, D.C., 1973.

b. Wasson, R. G. *The Wondrous Mushroom: Mycolatry in Mesoamerica*. McGraw-Hill, New York, 1980.

c. Gimbutas, M. *The Gods and Goddesses of Old Europe*. University of California Press, Berkeley and Los Angeles, 1974.

d. Ransome, H. M. *The Sacred Bee*. Houghton Mifflin, Boston and New York, 1937.

e. Wasson, R. G., A. Hofmann and C. A. P. Ruck. *The Road to Eleusis: Unveiling the Secret of the Mysteries*. Harcourt Brace Jovanovich, New York, 1978.

f. Ruck, C. A. P. Mushrooms and Philosophers. *Journal of Ethnopharmacology* 4: 179-205, 1981. Reprinted here as Chap. 6.

g. Ruck, C. A. P. The Wild and the Cultivated: Wine in Euripides' *Bacchae*. *Journal of Ethnopharmacology* 5: 231-270, 1982. Reprinted here as Chap. 7.

h. Wasson, R. G. Seeking the Magic Mushroom. *Life*, 19 May 1957, p. 109.

PART TWO

Poets, Philosophers, Priests: Entheogens in the Formation of the Classical Tradition

by
Carl A. P. Ruck

CHAPTER SIX

MUSHROOMS AND PHILOSOPHERS

Toward the end of Aristophanes' comedy, the *Birds*, Prometheus, the mythical figure who stole fire from the gods, arrives on stage, shielding himself from the view of his arch-enemy Zeus, the god directly overhead in the heavens, by hiding himself beneath the shade of a parasol. This episode of the comedy is completed by a dance in which the chorus of birds describes the philosopher Socrates in a swamp, where he is summoning up spirits from the dead in the company of a strange race of people called the 'Shade-foots'.

> Amidst the Shade-foots, there is a certain swamp where Socrates, unwashed, summons up souls. Amongst his clients came Peisander, who begged to see a spirit that had foresaken him while he remained alive. He had a camel-lamb as victim for sacrifice, and, like Odysseus of old, he slit its throat, whereupon to him from the depths there came up toward the camel's trench a spirit, Chaerephon, the 'bat'. [lines 1553-1564]

Who were these Shade-foots amongst whom the famous Greek philosopher is supposed to be performing this rite of necromancy? They can be found still attending such rites in modern times and hence their identity may give us a key for understanding what Socrates was really doing.

SHADE-FOOTS

The Shade-foots were said to be a grotesque tribe of people who had only a single leg with a broad webbed foot like that of geese. They customarily lay on their backs, protecting themselves from the heat of the sun by resting in the shade cast by their single, up-raised, parasol-like feet. At other times, however, they displayed extraordinary vigor, leaping up and down with prodigious strength on their solitary legs. We first hear of them in the sixth century B.C. from a traveler named Scylax, who, according to Herodotus (4.44), wrote a description of a trip down the Indus and thence along the coast to Suez in the reign of the Persian king, Darius I. Nothing remains of Scylax's book, but a fragment of another work from the end of the next century is still extant, in which they and their bizarre characteristics are again mentioned. This is a book by Ctesias (60 Jacoby), a Greek physician from Cnidos who served at the Persian court and wrote an account of a similar voyage. Both of these early travelers claimed that India was the homeland of the Shade-foots.[1]

The tribe was called by other names as well. They appear to have been the same people that we hear of even earlier from the seventh-century poet Alcman, who knew them as 'Cover-foots' (148 Page). Another name, although Greek, is preserved only in Latin sources. The Shade-foots were also known as Monocoli or 'One-Legs' (Pliny, *Natural History* 7.2.23; Aulus Gellius 9.4.9).

This latter name is particularly interesting because when we find these people in modern times, they will be a particular plant involved in Asiatic shamanism. Monocoli in Greek was an epithet of plants (Theophrastus, *How Plants Grow* 2.25, *Enquiry into Plants* 9.18.8). In modern times, the prodigious strength of their single leg will also be remembered from ancient traditions.

THE SCENE OF NECROMANCY

Before tracking them down today, however, we should look at the other details of the scene described by Aristophanes. Two other historical figures are also said to be present, Peisander and Chaerephon. The choice of these two is the point of the joke.

Chaerephon was the frequent and usually over-enthusiastic companion of Socrates. It was his impetuous consultation of the Delphic oracle that had elicited the famous response that Socrates was wiser than other men, an enigmatic

1. The real identity of the Shade-foots had become a futile topic for grammarians by the Christian era. Even as early as the fifth century, some people thought of them as African or Libyan (Antiphon 80 B 45 Diels; Archippus 53 Edmonds), and it was there that the scholars of the Hellenistic age placed them, for their parasol-like feet could be rationalized as a peculiar adaptation to the African heat, a bias that even endowed these poor suffering creatures eventually with the normal complement of limbs, the better to crawl about from exhaustion on all fours in the desert (scholia to Aristophanes' *Birds* 1553).

The valley of the Indus, however, must have been their original homeland, for that was the testimony of the earliest travelers, and even the fifth-century orator Antiphon, who thought they were Libyan, had apparently read of them in our earliest source, the Indian travels of Scylax (Antiphon 80 B 47 Diels). The confusion between an Indian and African homeland for the Shade-foots is understandable in view of the map made by the sixth-century Hecataeus, who placed the Ethiopians in the East along the entire region bordering the sea that separates Africa from India. By the Hellenistic age, however, these 'African' Shade-foots were reinterpreted as living in what was then considered to be Africa, the torrid regions to the west of Alexandria.

In identifying the Shade-foots' homeland as the Indus valley, I follow Roscher, *Ausführliches Lexicon der Griechischen und Römischen Mythologie*, and differ from the judgement recorded in Pauly-Wissova, *Real-encyclopädie der classischen Altertumswissenschaft* (see articles on 'Sciapodes').

reply that led to Socrates' life-long quest for someone wiser than himself, only at last to conclude that the oracle must have meant that all men are stupid, but that he alone knew it and thus, by that little bit, was wiser. We know of Chaerephon not only from the Platonic dialogues, but also from parodies of him in other comedies. He was an excitable and frenzied person (Plato, *Apology* 21a, *Charmides* 153b), a pederast (Aristophanes 377 Hall and Geldart) who could be called a 'child of Night' (Aristophanes 573), both characteristics that would make appropriate his metamorphosis into a bat as he impersonates the spirit that Socrates summons in the necromantic rite. He was also a pale person of notoriously slight and weak build, as dry and fragile as a moth's crysalis (Aristophanes 377; Anonymous 26 Edmonds), someone whom Aristophanes had described already as 'half-dead' years ago in his parody of Socrates' teaching in the *Clouds* (504).

It is this physical frailty that Aristophanes refers to as the culmination of the scene in the swamp, for Peisander, who was satirized as a coward in another comedy produced at this same festival of drama (Phrynichus, *Monotropos* frg. 20 Edmonds; cf. hypothesis for Aristophanes' *Birds*), apparently because of some otherwise unknown action in battle (Eupolis, *Exempt from Service* or *The Women Men* frg. 31 Edmonds), has come to Socrates' rite of necromancy in order to attempt to regain his own spirit that had failed him through cowardice. Instead of a miraculous return to bravery, however, he succeeds only in getting the squeaking bat-like weakling, Chaerephon.

PEISANDER AND THE AFFAIR OF THE PROFANATIONS

More important than the joke for our purposes, however, is the veiled accusation that Aristophanes is making against Socrates by describing this imagined scene of necromancy. To understand this we must know something more about Peisander and about what was going on in Athens at this time. The *Birds* was produced at the City Dionysia in March of 414 B.C. Athens was engaged in fighting a great and lengthy war with Sparta and its allies, and just the previous year had sent its armada against the Sicilian city of Syracuse. Just prior to the sailing of the fleet on that expedition, an event had occurred that had thrown the city into confusion. It was discovered that some group of people had gone through the city, knocking off the phalluses on the stone representations of the god Hermes, the so-called herms, that were commonly placed before public and private buildings as magical guardian figures. This mutilation of the herms was not only an act of sacrilege, but it seemed to indicate that some political group had bound its members to secrecy through mutual complicity in the crime in order to prepare the way for an attempt to overthrow the democratic government. Peisander[1] was a leader in the official investigation into the whole affair, and it was he on the board of inquiry who had interpreted the crime of vandalism as just such an act of conspiracy (Andocides, *On the Mysteries* 36). The investigation, moreover, was broadened to include other instances of sacrilege, and it came to light that a number of prominent citizens had been illegally performing the initiation ceremony for the Eleusinian Mystery in their private homes with dinner guests. Amongst those implicated was Socrates' famous disciple, Alcibiades, who was accordingly recalled from his generalship on the Sicilian expedition, whereupon he fled into exile in Sparta, the city that headed the coalition of states opposed to Athens and its empire in the war. He was condemned *in absentia* and his property was confiscated and sold at public auction.

Prior to this scandal, Alcibiades had been one of the most promising younger leaders of the democracy, but his flight to Sparta revealed that his demagoguery had masked his underlying sympathies for his own aristocratic class. He supported the populace merely to advance his own career. Apparently Aristophanes thought the same was true of Peisander, for a few years later, he was to emerge as a leader of the oligarchic faction that attempted to arrange for the restoration of Alcibiades. Peisander was to be prominent amongst the so-called group of Four Hundred oligarchs who seized control of the city in an attempt to come to terms with Sparta, and he too was to flee to the enemy at the frontier fortress of Decelea when the regime fell in September of 411 (Thucydides 8.49, 98.1), whereupon his property was confiscated (Lysias 7.4) and he is not heard of again.

1. The Hellenistic scholars believed that there were two Peisanders, one who was slight and the other big (Eupolis, *Marikas* frg. 182 Edmonds; Plato Comicus, *Peisander* frg. 101 Edmonds). There can be no doubt that the one in the necromancy scene is the famous cowardly demagogue, but it is also probable that the other one was nothing but an invention of the scholarly tradition to explain the apparent distinction between a Peisander called the 'big one, the mule-driver' and another described as the 'twisted one'. The distinction is actually a misunderstood joke, comparing the penis of the offensive Peisander to that of someone of no account (see Aristophanes' *Thesmophoriazusae* 516); hence in Hermippus (*Artopolides* frg. 9 Edmonds), 'the big Peisander mounted in silence a pack-ass with olive-wood sinews, like the one for the wood at the Dionysia', with a pun on the sexual meaning of 'mount' and the action of mounting the speaker's platform. The 'bigness' of a politician, even though he be cowardly is an indication of the trouble he can cause the Demos (see *Birds* 1477, on the demagogue Cleonymus). See also Danny Staples, *Pea Pteroenta: Plot and Metaphor in Aristophanes* 78 (unpublished dissertation, Boston University, 1978).

During his few months as one of the Four Hundred, Peisander arrested a fellow aristocrat, the orator Andocides, who originally had secured immunity in the earlier investigation into the mutilation of the herms and the profanation of the Mysteries by turning state's evidence and naming many of his associates (Andocides, *On his Return* 14). Although this informer was himself secure from prosecution at the time, a decree aimed specifically at him had later been passed, prohibiting anyone who had confessed to impiety from taking part in religious or commercial activities in the city, and he had accordingly been forced to withdraw into exile. While away from Athens, the informer had amassed a fortune as a merchant and had attempted to buy the good favor of what he thought was the rising political faction by an act of largesse to the fleet at Samos, only to find himself on the wrong side when he returned to an Athens controlled by the new group of Four Hundred oligarchs. Andocides' arrest and maltreatment by Peisander testifies to the degree of enmity that these wealthy citizens three years after the affair of the mutilation of the herms continued to direct toward someone who had caused themselves and their families so much trouble by his revelations and betrayal. Certainly Peisander, the former chief prosecutor in the investigation of the mutilations, would seem to have been acting out of character in supporting the guilty Alcibiades' restoration and, at the same time, persecuting the former star witness, unless, as is probable, the investigation into the mutilations had gotten out of hand by being linked to sacrileges in general, a broadening that went beyond the immediate problem of the suspected conspiracy and netted many who simply were discovered, like Alcibiades, to have been treating the forbidden Mystery ceremony as a private social event for the entertainment of their dinner guests.

As far as the comedian Aristophanes was concerned, Peisander was a hypocrite, both in persecuting the profaners and again at this very time that he was involved in making preparations for the transfer of the city to the oligarchic faction in 411 in order to facilitate the return of Alcibiades. As Aristophanes says in his *Lysistrata*, which was produced at this time, Peisander's changeable policy indicated that his demagoguery was for sale (489), an accusation he had first made fifteen years earlier in one of his first comedies, the *Babylonians* (81 Hall and Geldart). Moreover, again it appears that the Mystery profanations and political conspiracy are linked, for Peisander and his oligarchic associates are accused of performing the forbidden ceremony. The Eleusinian Mystery involved the drinking of a special drink, the so-called *kykeon* or 'mixed potion', and that is precisely what the hypocritical former prosecutor is accused of doing with Alcibiades and his aristocratic cronies, for, as Aristophanes claims, the whole politics of the city has become a 'mix-up' because these plotters are again 'mixing up' some 'up-set' for the stomach, an accusation that puns by these words upon the Eleusinian 'mixed' potion (489-491).

THE SWAMP OF DIONYSUS

What Peisander was suspected of doing in 411 is merely a continuation of his earlier misdeeds in consulting the notorious Alcibiades' teacher Socrates at the necromantic seance in the swamp with the Shade-foots, for a number of considerations will lead us to conclude that the Shade-foot parody with which we began can only be a reference to the cowardly demagogue's suspected complicity in the very scandal that he found himself hypocritically investigating. The swamp, first of all, is a clear indication of what Socrates actually is said to have been doing. The place is not in some remote exotic land, for it is but one in a series of similar parodies in this section of the *Birds*, and like the others, it can be located nowhere else but in Athens itself. It can be none other than the one swamp in Athens of which we have knowledge, the sacred Swamp near the base of the Acropolis, the so-called Swamp of Dionysus. It was precisely there that one could expect to summon up spirits, as, in fact, another comedian, the poet Eupolis, appears to have done in a play produced about this same time, the *Demes*, which involved the resurrection of the departed localities or parishes of an ealier Athens (*cf.* Edmond's reconstruction, fr. 90-135). This Swamp was the Athenian entrance to Hades, for such noisome places suggested to the folk imagination the putrefaction that lay beyond the grave. The god Dionysus himself was shown in a later comedy of Aristophanes, the *Frogs*, rowing across this very place to get to the other world, where he is met by a chorus of initiates from the Eleusinian Mysteries. One might well expect to find them there, for this Swamp was also the scene for a secret annual event that apparently was part of the Eleusinian rituals. There was a temple in this Swamp of Dionysus that was opened just twenty-four hours each year, from the evening of the second day of the Anthesteria Festival until the evening of the third and final day, at which time the spirits of the city's dear departed, who had returned to visit their families, were lovingly reescorted back to their proper abode in the otherworld. These spirits had wandered abroad through the city for the three days of the festival, resurrected to celebrate a drunken revel with the living, who had summoned them at the start of the feast by drinking the intoxicating spirit of the new wine that had at last completed its subterranean fermentation. There was just one event that occurred in this temple in the Swamp of Dionysus during the Anthesteria. The so-called Queen of Athens, who was the wife of the king archon or inheritor of the sacral functions of kingship that went back to more ancient times before the secularization of the Athenian government, was prepared in this temple for her ritual union with the god Dionysus in an annual reenactment of the primal sacred marriage that magically reassured the yearly refounding of the city and reaffirmation of its fertile accord with the sources of life stemming from the other world (pseudo-Demosthenes 59.117).

This sacred marriage had some relation to the so-called Lesser Eleusinian Mystery,[1] a ceremony that was a preliminary to the Greater Mystery that would be performed in the autumn of the year at the neighboring village of Eleusis. Socrates' rite of necromancy, therefore, in this Swamp with a person like Peisander and at this particular date would seem somehow involved in the great scandal of the day, the profanation of the Mysteries.

TONGUE-IN-BELLIES AND REVEALERS

Before proceeding in our investigation into what Socrates actually is supposed to have been doing, let us gain further assurance that, whatever it was, it was a profanation of the Mysteries. The Swamp parody is part of a choreographed two-part structure in the *Birds*, for which the second part is another parody involving fabulous peoples. This time the scene is a court of law conducted by 'Tongue-in-bellies' amidst a people called 'Revealers':

> Amongst the Revealers by the Hidden Water is a naughty race of Tongue-in-bellies, who harvest and sow, gather fruit with their tongues and pick figs. Babbling like foreigners is this race, students of Gorgias and Philippus – and because of them, those Tongue-in-belies, these Philippuses, everywhere in Attica the tongue is a sacrificial victim cut apart [lines 1694-1705]

1. A fragment of a bas-relief, now in the National Archaeological Museum, Athens, originally from the sanctuary on the Ilissos River where the Lesser Mystery was celebrated, shows Heracles, holding the pitcher-shaped cup that is characteristic of the Anthesteria Festival, as he arrives for his initiation into the Lesser Mystery.
For a compilation of sources relevant to the Anthesteria, see Sir Arthur Pickard-Cambridge, *The Dramatic Festivals at Athens*, second edition revised by J. Gould and D. Lewis (Oxford, 1968). The interpretation of the 'sacred marriage' as a shamanic ritual is presented in R. Gordon Wasson, Albert Hoffmann and Carl A. P. Ruck, *The Road to Eleusis: Unveiling the Secret of the Mysteries* (Harcourt Brace Jovanovich, New York, 1978) 38ff., 85ff.

In this parody, lawyers or orators are accused of aping their teachers in the quibbling play of words that make no sense in arguments proving the worse cause the better, as Aristophanes in the *Clouds* had said of Socrates, whom he considered chief amongst such teachers. There can be no doubt that this parody is meant as a companion piece for the Shade-foot verses, for structurally it would be expected since it is danced to the same choreographed rhythms and melody. Beyond that, however, it has a clear responsion in themes, with the Swamp matched by the Hidden Water and the sacrificed camel-lamb by the tongue, as well, of course, as with the matching fabulous peoples.

Here too the subject is the Mystery profanations, the great court event of the time. The Tongue-in-belly orators are hypocrites like Peisander, the prosecutor, for the fruit that their sowing and harvesting yields is bribe money, for 'picking figs' indicates people who give evidence in court against others for bounty, the so-called sycophants or 'fig-revealers'. The Tongue-in-bellies are themselves guilty of the case they try, for the lawyers are transformed into creatures with tongues in their greedy bellies, like the mysterious dwarfish woman who was supposed to have first served the Eleusinian potion to the goddess Demeter, and the Revealers amongst whom this trial takes place implicate the accusers in the crime they prosecute, since the official charge against the guilty was that they had 'revealed' the Mystery. The Hidden Water or *klepshydra* also has a double meaning, for it puns upon the 'water-stealer' or water clock that was used for timing speeches in the court and upon the so-named fountain near the cave beneath the Acropolis where the 'Queen' Creussa conceived and bore her son Ion while gathering flowers, an event that Euripides presents in his *Ion* tragedy as a mythical version of the sacred marriage.[1] A further pun on the Revealers or *Phanai* also suggests Eleusinian connotations, for the 'revealers' are verbally indistinguishable from the 'torch processions' (*cf.* Euripides, *Rhesus* 943), such as those that took place in the cults of Dionysus; Aristophanes in the *Frogs* has Dionysus greeted by just such a torch procession of Eleusinian initiates in the Swamp when he arrives there in the otherworld (340 ff.). Even the sacrificed tongue has similar connotations, for the orators' butchering of speech recalls the prohibition of secrecy imposed upon the central events of the Eleusinian initiation.

1. Carl A. P. Ruck, On the sacred names of Iamos and Ion: Ethnobotanical referents in the hero's parentage. *The Classical Journal*, 71/3 (1976) 235-252.

SOCRATES AS PROFANER OF THE MYSTERIES

Actually, now that we recognize the Shade-foot parody and the corresponding parody of Revealers and Tongue-in-bellies as a reference to the contemporary scandal of the Mystery profanations, we might have expected that Socrates' rite of necromancy at this particular time could have been nothing else. The main political implication of the affair of the herms and the profanations was the anticipated pro-Spartan coup d'état, and it is not surprising that Socrates would have fallen under suspicion in the common mind. He was always associated with pro-Spartan sympathies and just the kind of aristocratic patrons and friends who might have been implicated in such a political coup.[1] These suspicions must have particularly centered upon him now that his disciple Alcibiades had not only been convicted of sacrilege, but was actually now living with the enemy in Sparta. It was commonly thought, moreover, that Socrates' involvement with Alcibiades was pederastic on the Laconian model (*cf* Plato, *Symposium* 215a ff.). It is, in fact precisely as a phillaconian that Socrates is labeled in the scene of necromancy in the Swamp, for he is given the epithet of 'unwashed', a characteristic of those young friends and disciples of his who earlier in the comedy had been said to ape him or 'Socratize' in a pro-Spartan mania, imitating his long hair and the hunger and filth that marked the rigorous indoctrination of young Spartans into their homoerotic warrior society (1281-1282). Already in the *Clouds*, Aristophanes had portrayed the filth of Socrates' disciples, a parody that supposedly was the beginning of the prejudice that would culminate two decades later in his own trial and execution for the crime of impiety in 399 B.C. (Plato, *Apology* 18b).

Not only were Socrates and his friends notorious Spartan sympathizers, but even before the great scandal of the profanations, he was suspected of profaning the Mysteries. In the *Clouds*, he had been shown teaching his students to disdain conventional theology in a parody of a mystery initiation, as they probed the lower world for the bulbous plants that in the Eleusinian myth were associated with Persephone's abduction to Hades (188 ff.). He had, in fact, even been labeled a Melian in that comedy (830), on the model either of Diagoras of Melos or Aristagoras of that same island, both of whom had profaned the Mysteries on some occasion before the great scandal of 415 (scholia to *Clouds* 830 and *Birds*

1. In addition to the documentation from Aristophanes cited in the text, note also that Socrates is portrayed by both Plato and Xenophon, himself an ardent admirer of Sparta, as praising the Dorian institutions of Crete and Lacedaemon (Plato, *Crito* 52e, *Republic* 544c, *Laws* 634; Xenophon, *Memorabilia* 3.5, 4.4).

1072). If one could accuse Socrates of profaning the Mysteries in 422, the date of the *Clouds*, certainly the proven guilt of Alcibiades seven years later would have implicated his unconventional and pro-Spartan teacher as well, and, in fact, the infamy of Diagoras is recalled in the *Birds* when the chorus of birds cites the reward that had been posted for the capture and death of that earlier profaner of the Lesser Mystery (1072-1073). It would have been inevitable, in any case, that suspicion would fall upon Socrates since it was apparently well known that he was subject to mystical trances that were so similar to the experience of the Eleusinian vision that Plato adapts the language of the Mystery to describe them (Plato, *Symposium* 174d ff., 220b ff., *Phaedrus* 250c).

MUSHROOMS

To return, then, to our original question about what Socrates was really doing in the Swamp, it would appear that he was profaning the Mysteries. The scene of necromancy, therefore, is vital evidence about what was involved in the Eleusinian Mysteries, and evidence that hitherto has not been detected.[1] It remains to see whether the identity of the Shade-foots will allow us to be more precise about what happened at the Mysteries and about what Socrates is accused of doing in the company of that fabulous tribe of one-legged people from India.

I should like to show that the Shade-foot parody confirms a suggestion I made about the nature of the Eleusinian Mysteries in *The Road to Eleusis*. In that book, I and my colleagues interpreted the Eleusinian Mysteries as communal shamanic ceremonies involving the ingestion of drugs. The Shade-foots will confirm what we suspected to have been the drug involved at the Lesser Mystery.

It is appropriate first to give some background about the studies from which our theory evolved. The collaboration was organized by R. Gordon Wasson, an amateur mycologist, who brought me together with the Swiss chemist, Dr. Albert Hofmann, to investigate the subject of the Eleusinian Mysteries.

In 1968, Wasson first proposed the cautious supposition that nothing in the *Ṛg Veda*, a collection of religious hymns assembled in definitive form about

1. It is surprising that this reference to the recent profanations has apparently gone unnoticed, despite the fact that Socrates is labelled as a pro-Spartan in this very comedy. Previous readers of the Shade-foot ode have been misled into thinking that the Swamp must be a foreign place since the fabulous one-footed creatures are in it, although so are three Athenians; it has also not been noticed that the Tongue-in-bellies are equally fabulous, but this ode, which is clearly a complement to the former, describes an Athenian court of law.

1000 B.C. or a little later, after a previous long tradition of oral transmission, was inconsistent with the idea that the plant and god Soma and his reputedly inebriating drink, the focus of a very ancient ritual, were to be identified as being originally a particular species of psychotropic mushroom or entheogen, *Amanita muscaria* or, as it has sometimes been called in English, the 'fly-agaric', a mushroom that has been employed until lately both in shamanic rites and as an inebriant in the forest belt of Siberia.[1] Since the initial publication of that hypothesis, Wasson's theory has received significant acceptance and corroboration.

Various surrogates, usually not psychoactive, replaced the original inebriant in the later performances of the ancient ritual, perhaps because the true Soma was no longer easily obtainable in the lands to which the Indo-Iranian peoples migrated and had perhaps even been forgotten with the passage of time. These substitutes perpetuated certain symbolic or physical attributes of the original as remembered in the ancient poetic phrases that went back to a time before the poems were recorded in writing. It has recently been shown that the earliest surrogate for Soma in India was fungoid, hence adding strong confirmation for Wasson's theory.[2]

This emergence of the lowly and often despised mushroom at the center of one of the major ancient religions validates what Wasson and his wife Valentina Pavlovna had first surmised during the years they spent together investigating the rich European folklore about fungi, for the widely dichotomous attitudes of the Indo-European peoples today seemed to suggest derivation from a still living and powerful taboo protecting the usage of a sacred plant.[3] It was just such a religious usage that Wasson was to discover and elaborately document amongst Amerindian shamans in his study of the Mazatec María Sabina.[4]

If, however, the Soma theory were justified, one should also expect to detect analogues to the shamanic rite amongst other Indo-European peoples. Recently, Wasson has discovered an Ojibway shaman and herbalist, Keewaydinoquay,

1. R. Gordon Wasson, *Soma: Divine Mushroom of Immortality* (Harcourt Brace Jovanovich, New York, 1968).

2. Wasson summarizes the developments since the initial publication of *Soma* in the introduction to the new French translation. The original English text of this introduction appeared as: Soma Brought Up-to-date. *Botanical Museum Leaflets, Harvard University* 26/6 (June 30, 1978) 211-223, published also in the *Journal of the American Oriental Society*, 99/1 (1979).

3. The Wassons privately shared this idea with each other, although it does not appear in their massive compilation of mushroom lore: Valentina Pavlovna and R. Gordon Wasson, *Mushrooms, Russia, and History* (Pantheon Books, New York, 1957). Documentation for the theory was first forthcoming in Wasson's ensuing North American and Meso-American researches.

4. R. Gordon Wasson, George and Florence Cowan and Willard Rhodes, *María Sabina and her Mazatec Mushroom Velada* (Harcourt Brace Jovanovich, New York, 1974).

who belongs to one of the tribes of the Algonkian Nation and who has confided to him her people's traditions about the ritual usage of *Amanita muscaria*.[1] The likelihood of continuity with the Siberian rites presents itself forcibly, and doubly so now if the language of the Wintun tribe of California has a close genetic relationship to the Ob-Ugrian languages of north-western Siberia.[2]

Could the rite be detected not only in the ancient Aryan traditions, but also, as Wasson suspected, amongst the classical cultures of Greece and Rome? It was this question that Wasson proposed to me at the beginning of our collaboration on the ancient mystery religions, which he had long suspected of centering upon drug-induced visions.[3] There could be no doubt that the drinking of a specific potion was part of the ceremony at Eleusis, where the culmination of the Mystery was consistently described as an overwhelming vision of spiritual presences demonstrating the relationship of the living to the dead. Drinking or drunkenness, moreover, seems to have been an element in the other, less known mysteries, such as those of the Kabeiroi at Thebes or the one celebrated at Samothrace. That the Eleusinian ceremony had been illegally performed for the enjoyment of dinner guests in private homes toward the end of the fifth century, moreover, suggested obvious parallels to the profane use of entheogens in modern times.

The ingredients of the Eleusinian potion are given as water, mint, and barley in the Homeric hymn to Demeter, our earliest literary source about the Mystery. Since the mint or *blechon* (*Mentha pulegium*) is hardly (or not at all) psychoactive,[4] our attention was directed to the barley. Here our third collaborator, Dr. Albert Hofmann, the discoverer of LSD, was able to supply us with the information that ergot or 'rust', a common fungal parasite on grain, contains a powerful water-soluble drug. Ergot, moreover, like other higher fungi, pro-

1. Keewaydinoquay, *Puhpohwee for the People: A Narrative Account of Some Uses of Fungi Amongst the Ahnishinaubeg* (Botanical Museum of Harvard University, Cambridge, MA, February, 1978). Keewaydinoquay is also collaborating on a further study with Wasson.

2. Otto J. Sadovszky, *Demonstration of a Close Genetic Relationship, Preliminary Report* (Fullerton, CA, July 3, 1978).

3. R. Gordon Wasson, The divine mushroom: Primitive religion and hallucinatory agents. *Proceedings of the American Philosophical Society*, 102 (1956) 221-223.

4. C. Kerenyi, working with Dr. Albert Hofmann, suggested that *Mentha pulegium* may have been responsible for the Eleusinian vision: *Eleusis: Archetypal Image of Mother and Daughter* (Pantheon, New York, 1967, translated from the German manuscript revised by the author from publications in 1960 and 1962) appendix 1. Dr. Hofmann, however, now claims that Kerenyi overstated the psychoactive properties of *Mentha pulegium*, and, in any case, this mint is clearly not strong enough to have warranted those instances of profane use and attendant severe penalties that were occasioned during the great scandal of 415 B.C. The inclusion of *blechon* in the Eleusinian potion had a symbolic significance, as explained below.

duces fruiting bodies of the characteristic mushroom shape. Did ergot figure in Greek botanic traditions in a way that might suggest its involvement in the Eleusinian Mystery?

The Greeks believed, as is to some extent actually true, that edible plants were evolved forms of more primitive, wild, and in some cases actually inedible avatars, and that agriculture, as opposed to the mere gathering of plants, was a triumph of civilization or culture. In particular, *aira* or *Lolium temulentum*, commonly called 'darnel', 'cockle', or 'tares' in English, an inedible grass that grows as a weed in fields of grain and is usually (like grain itself) infested with ergot, seems to have been thought to be a primitive form of barley, which would revert to the weedy growth if not properly tended. A similar opposition between gathered and cultivated plants involved the god Dionysus: poisonous and intoxicating wild ivy with its diminutive clusters of berries was apparently related to a cultivated plant that it resembled, the vine with its bunches of juicy grapes. This opposition is often depicted in vase paintings, where the elder Dionysus is shown confronting the younger manifestation of himself in a new generation as his own son, the boy named 'Bunch of Grapes', who carries the vine plant, while his father holds the wild ivy.[1] It is clear, moreover, that the winter-time mountain ceremonies of the maenads, the ecstatic female devotees of the god, involved the gathering of wild botanic versions of Dionysus, for their common implement, as shown in art and literature, was the so-called *thyrsos*, a hollow stalk stuffed with ivy leaves, a procedure that was the custom for preserving the freshness of herbs as they were gathered.[2] The fact that maenadic ceremonies did not occur in any relationship to the timing of the events involved in viticulture can now be understood, for these mountain rites centered not upon wine but upon the wild and intoxicating herbs gathered while the more civilized god was absent in the otherworld, undergoing the cultivation that would convert the juice of crushed grapes into an inebriant. Even wine, however, was felt to have an affinity to the toxins of wild plants, for, as we have shown, wine itself was flavored with various herbs that intensified its intoxicating qualities, hence requiring that it be diluted with several parts of water to tame it for civilized purposes.

1. Attic black-figured vase in the British Museum, storage-jar by Exekias, B 210, about 540 B.C., the elder Dionysus holding ivy sprigs confronts his son. Krater by the Altamura painter in the Museo Archaeologico Nazionale, Ferrara, the elder Dionysus, attended by flower-bearing maenads, seated and holding the *thyrsos*, confronts his smaller self in the form of his son standing on his lap and bearing sprigs of vine and a cup of wine. *Etc.*

2. Theophrastus, *History of Plants* 9.16.2.

In this opposition between wild and cultivated plants, the fungi played an important role, for they are seedless growths that defy cultivation and are thus paradigmatic of wildness. (The spores of mushrooms require a microscope to be seen distinctly.) Characteristic of all plants, of course, is the way they feed upon dead and putrefying matter. Here too the fungi had a special importance, for the tomb and the whole underworld were thought to be covered with mouldering growths that consumed the flesh of mortality. But even these wildest of plants could be made to function in the evolutionary botanical scheme. The Greeks realized that fermentation was a fungal process. The making of wine involved procedures and symbolism that suggested the tending of the dead and the hope for resurrection, for the blood of the harvested grape was entrusted, like any corpse, to subterranean, tomb-like containers, where the surrounding earth maintained the proper temperature for fermentation; when the process was completed, the containers were opened to release the new god, who returned together with the other spirits from the grave to celebrate a drunken revel on his birthday.

The goat also was symbolic of the more primitive god, and in the form of ithyphallic goat men, the so-called satyrs, he would lasciviously cavort and possess his ecstatic brides in the winter ceremonies on the mountains. The goat's grazing habits, however, were a danger to the cultivated vine, and the hircine representative of the god became his special surrogate, whose sacrifice was necessary to assure the continuance of more civilized manifestations of Dionysus. Amongst the religious observances of Dionysus were the great festivals of drama, where the phallic exuberance of the satyrs suggested the humorous antics of comedy, while tragedy, the song sung for the sacrificed goat, centered on the necessary fall that would reconcile man to the deeper implications of his own mortality and the healthy accord of his society with the forces of the dead.

Parallel to the Dionysian gift of liquid nature was the dry food of Demeter's grain, upon which also could be grown a transmutation of a wild fungus. The vision that resulted from the carefully programmed ingestion of the ergot potion demonstrated the continuity of life and death and reaffirmed the forward progress of Hellenic civilization. The inclusion of mint in the Eleusinian potion had a similar symbolism with regard to this evolutionary theme, for the fragrant herb had connotations of illicit sexuality; the wild herb, therefore, was appropriately bruised and crushed for the barley drink that signified the transition of Persephone from sterile concubinage to a wifedom that mediated the chthonic realm of Hades and the Olympian of Demeter and Zeus. This joining of the house of the Olympians to that of the netherworld through Persephone's matrimony is another instance of the evolutionary paradigm. The Mysteries were sacred to what was called a 'holy duo of goddesses', who need not be named specifically as Demeter and her daughter Persephone, for there was a singularity in their twoness that made their roles interchangeable. The original single Earth Mother Goddess of pre-Olympian times has become a duo at Eleusis to signify the reconciliation of more primitive traditions to the new era of gods headed by a father in the heavens: Persephone has become a daughter of Zeus entrusted to the house of Hades in the earth and barred from Olympian status, but in the form of Demeter, her mother, the Great Goddess resides on Olympus with her brother Zeus. The sacred Eleusinian reconciliation, moreover, gave mankind, who in some traditions was not deemed essential to the world order as ruled over by Zeus, an intermediary role, communicating with the chthonic powers for the fertility that would yield the continuing cycles of rebirth upon which the Olympians themselves depended for nourishment in the form of sacrifice.

Just as the goddesses, so too were the Mysteries double. Whereas the emphasis of the Greater Mystery was redemption from death by the incorporation of the underworld's putrefaction into a larger scheme where it would function as a source of fertility, or, in agrarian terms, as manure instead of pollution, the Lesser Mystery, which preceded it by half a year, occurred in the wild and involved the preliminary to reintegration, the Dionysian theme of Persephone's illegal abduction by death while gathering intoxicating uncultivated flowers. In view of the role played by cultivated fungal parasites in the fermentation process and in the Eleusinian potion, we suggested in *The Road to Eleusis* that a wild mushroom may have figured in the Lesser Mystery, for such a fungus would both complete the pattern and explain certain aspects of Dionysian symbolism, such as, for example, the fact that a mushroom itself could be viewed as a miniature *thyrsos*, with the intoxicating cap replacing the ivy leaves stuffed into the stalk-like stipe.[1]

AJA EKAPĀD

The Shade-foots, in whose company, as we have seen, Socrates appears to have communed with spirits in profanation of the Lesser Mystery, can be found also in Vedic traditions. The Hellenic migration into the Greek lands in the second millennium before Christ was only one branch of widespread migrations of

1. Apicius 7.15.6.

Indo-European peoples, another group of which moved down from the northwest into what is now Afghanistan and the valley of the Indus. This latter group was the so-called Aryans, whose language was Vedic, a parent of classical Sanskrit. The canonical collection of 1028 hymns called the *Ṛg Veda* preserves the ancient oral traditions of these people dating back to a time before the migrations when presumably they shared a common homeland with the other Indo-Europeans. We should expect to detect common elements and parallels between the Greek-speaking Indo-Europeans and the Vedic Aryans, as, in fact, we can in their languages, poetic metaphors, and customs.

In the *Ṛg Veda*, amidst a complex pantheon, headed by Indra, appears the god Soma, a plant that was pounded to extract a divine inebriant. This drink is described with symbolic components that, as has been recently shown,[1] are traceable back to an Indo-European original from which it apparently derived, for similar components occur also in the descriptions of magical drinks or potions in Greek traditions. Soma is often accompanied by Agni, the god of fire, and is richly described with formulaic epithets that note his color and metaphorically associate him with the bellowing of bulls, the pillar of the sky, the single eye, the navel, and so forth, although (remarkable for a plant) no mention is ever made of roots, leaves, blossoms, or seeds. It was this omission that attracted Wasson's notice. He demonstrated that a mushroom was the only botanic specimen that would fit such a description and that similar metaphors could be traced in later traditions about fungi.

Through oversight, however, Wasson did not mention 'Aja Ekapād' in the original edition of Soma, an omission that is repaired in his new introduction to the French edition.[2] Aja Ekapād, as his name implies, is the 'Not-born Singlefoot', a deity mentioned six times in the *Ṛg Veda* and apparently an archaic name for Soma himself, for he shares epithets with him, is often accompanied by the chthonic serpent who invariably is the guardian of the holy plant, and once even has only the first of his names linked to a common epithet of Soma as Aja Nābhi, the 'not-born Navel'. As Wasson observes, 'Aja Ekapād' is the perfect binomial nomenclature for a mushroom, for mushrooms are 'not-born' since, as already mentioned, their seedless propagation by microscopic spores was not understood in antiquity, for which reason in India as in Greece (as well

1. Calvert Watkins, Let us now praise famous grains, *Indo-European Studies III* (Cambridge, MA, 1977) 468-498.

2. The oversight was first corrected in Wasson's *Soma and the Fly-agaric: Mr. Wasson's Rejoinder to Professor Brough* (Botanical Museum of Harvard University, Cambridge, MA, November, 1971) 37-38, and repeated in Soma Brought Up-to-date.

as elsewhere) they were thought to be engendered by the fire of the lightning bolt as they burst suddenly through the soil, expanding with the absorbed water of the rainfall, a manner of conception that the Greeks, in fact, gave to Dionysus. Similarly, although the 'single-foot' attribute is, of course, common to all plants, it appears to be particularly apposite for mushrooms, which occur in folklore as the little men with only one foot, as in the following German riddle quoted by Wasson:[1]

Sag' wer mag das Männlein sein
Das da steht auf einem Bein?

Glückpilz! Fliegenpilz!

The Shade-foots, who were also known to the Greeks with the botanical epithet of 'One-legs', and who came originally from the Indus valley, would seem, therefore, to be a Hellenic version of the deity Soma with the epithet Aja Ekapād. They survive into modern times amongst the Chukokta tribesmen in the region to the far north-east of Siberia. There, the spirits that reside in *Amanita muscaria* are said to materialize to those who become inebriated on the mushrooms as little people with a single leg; these leaping single-footed creatures, as numerous as the mushrooms that each has ingested, lead the intoxicated tribesmen on intricate and marvellous journeys to the land of the dead.[2] These tribesmen, moreover, are so impressed with the prodigious strength of the mushrooms' single leg that they often attempt to imitate them by thrusting their heads through some restraining membrane or by vigorously leaping about like the ancient jumping Shade-foots, amongst whom Socrates also communed with spirits in profanation of the Lesser Mystery.

The aptness of such a metamorphosis of mushrooms into little one-legged creatures is apparently something that suggests itself repeatedly to folk imagination, for it is thus also that they appear in the perhaps unrelated shamanic traditions of Meso-America.[3] Our ancient leaping Shade-foots are, furthermore, actually recognized as red capped mushrooms in the fabulous journey to the end of the world described in C. S. Lewis's fictional *Voyage of the 'Dawn Treader'*.[4]

In antiquity we may surmise that the Shade-foots were present by and large throughout Siberia. Although the Greeks learned of them from the Indus valley sometime after the middle of the first millennium before Christ, they were

1. Wasson, Soma Brought Up-to-date 221.
2. Wasson, *Soma* 159 and exhibits 4, 22, and 42.
3. For documentation, see R. Gordon Wasson, *The Wondrous Mushroom: Mycolatry in Meso-America* (McGraw-Hill, New York, 1980).
4. C. S. Lewis, *The Voyage of the 'Dawn Treader'* (Macmillan, New York, 1952) 141 ff.

probably present for millennia earlier in the forest belt, and other versions of them no doubt also came into the Greek lands with the arrival of the Indo-Europeans at the beginning of the Mycenaean Age. We perhaps catch a glimpse of them with another attribute of Soma as the Monophthalmoi or 'One-eyes', a fabulous people who lived on the frontier with the netherworld in the steppes north of the Black Sea and were called Arimaspeans in Scythian (Herodotus 3.116, 4.13,27; Aeschylus, *Prometheus* 803 ff.). These One-eyes engaged in combat with the monstrous guardian beasts of the otherworld and were the center of religious rites of shamanism proselytized in Greece by the priest and poet Aristeas of Proconnesus, who was said to be able to metamorphose into a raven and to travel as a spirit separate from his body (Herodotus 4.14-15). Other Monophthalmoi appear in Greek traditions as the 'Orb-eyes' or Cyclopes. They are named individually with epithets of the lightning bolt (Hesiod, *Theogony* 139) and were reputed to be workmen of Hephaestus (Callimachus, *Hymn to Artemis* 46 ff.), the god of fire in the volcanic forge. It is in this form that they may have come with the Dorians, for they figure in the epic traditions of the *Odyssey* and were said to have built the fortifications of several cities in the Argolid (scholia to Euripides' *Orestes* 965), including Mycenae, which was supposedly so-named because its founder, a son of Zeus, had picked a mushroom there (Pausanias 2.16.3).

Analogues to their name as 'Shade-foots' and 'Cover-foots' can also be found in ancient India. In classical Sanskrit, 'mushroom' is *chattra*. It is formed from the root *chad*, 'to cover' and has 'parasol' as its primary meaning. This could not have been its name before the Indo-European migrations. Since parasols were not called for in northern climes, and indeed, were unknown until recently in the regions north of India, it is probable that the Aryan invaders found the utensil in use and named it with the Indo-European root when they came south, later extending the meaning by metaphor to include mushrooms.

The metaphor, moreover, is particularly apt in Greek. The Greek parasol, like ours today, was round and ribbed with toe-like spokes that resemble the webbed foot of water fowl, which had the epithet of 'cover-footed' (*steganopodes*, Aristotle, *History of Animals* 504a7, *etc*.), as well as the gills of a mushroom. It was called the *skiadeion* (Aristophanes, *Birds* 1508), which is simply to say, the 'little shade', and was thus an appropriate term for the little *skia*, the spirit or ghost that was the 'shade' of former life to be summoned from the grave in a rite of necromancy.

PROMETHEUS AS SHADE-FOOT AND THE THEFT OF FIRE

It remains for us to consider whether Aristophanes had any special reason for choosing Prometheus to bear the parasol as his standard. In the *Birds* each of the two parodies that we have been examining, that of the Shade-foots and the matching one of the Revealers and the Tongue-in-bellies, is introduced by a scene appropriately related to it. Thus, the Tongue-in-bellies at court are introduced by a scene in which Heracles humorously discovers that as a bastard son of Zeus he does not have a clear right of inheritance to his father's Olympian estate. In the same manner, the preceding scene with Prometheus carrying the parasol to shade himself from the view of Zeus overhead is a thematic introduction to the parody of Socrates' necromancy with the Shade-foots, for Prometheus clearly is himself being presented as an impersonation of a Shade-foot, and his exit, furthermore, just before the parody, even imitates the carrying of the sacred basket beneath a parasol in a religious procession (1550 ff.).

Although Prometheus's quarrel with Zeus goes back to the time he stole fire from the gods, the traditions about that primordial theft suggest that the fire had connotations of herbalism. Prometheus was said to have hidden the stolen fire in a hollow fennel stalk or *narthex* (Hesiod, *Works and Days* 52; Aeschylus, *Prometheus* 109), thus treating fire like an herb gathered and stuffed into the Dionysian *thyrsos*; *narthex* itself, in fact, became a term for a casket of drugs, apparently because of such traditional usage in the gathering of magical and medicinal plants.[1] It is significant, therefore, that Aeschylus in his *Prometheus* tragedy refers to the stolen fire as a 'flower' or *anthos* (7) that was given to mankind as the source of that same intelligence and clairvoyance for which Prometheus or 'Forethought' is himself named, including, in particular, knowledge of drugs and the mantic art (476 ff.).

This gift of the stolen fire was involved in the mystery traditions of the Kabeiroi, for the theft took place on the island of Lemnos (Cicero, *Tusculan Disputations* 2.10.23) and had its source in the volcano there that was thought to be the forge of Hephaestus (Aeschylus, *Prometheus* 7).[2] It was to the primordial men of that island that Prometheus gave the fire. These men were called the Kabeiroi,

1. Thus *Narthex* was used as the title for medical works by Heras, Cratippus, and Soranus (Galen 12.398, 959; Aëtius 8.45).

2. C. Kerenyi, *Prometheus: Archetypal Image of Human Experience* (Pantheon, New York, 1963, translated from the German versions of 1946 and 1959) 80 ff.

the eldest of whom was supposed to have been born there from the earth itself.[1] In art, the Kabeiroi were portrayed as dwarfish black caricatures of mythical figures. Their leader was called Kadmillos, apparently a diminutive version of Cadmus, who came from Phoenicia and founded Thebes, where there also was a mystery cult of the Kabeiroi. These traditions perhaps facilitated the transposition of the Shade-foots to a supposed homeland in the African deserts in later antiquity.

These aboriginal Kabeiroi to whom Prometheus entrusted the divine spark of intellect were in all probability originally a primitive race of botanic creatures, for autochthonous births such as theirs are suggestive of plants. Thus at Corinth, for example, the first men actually were said to have come into being by metamorphosis from mushrooms (Ovid, *Metamorphoses* 7.312-313; *cf.* Apollodorus 1.9.3); and at Thebes, Pentheus, who plays the role of the sacrificial surrogate for Dionysus in Euripides' *Bacchae*, was the son of the apparently 'serpentine' Echion, one of the autochthonous Spartoi, the men who were said to have been 'sown' by Cadmus from what is usually called in English the 'teeth' of the primordial serpent. If we translate the term more exactly for its context, it is clear that such 'teeth' must obviously be 'fangs' and hence we are dealing here with a mythical tradition about toxic botanic forms. At Athens too, we can note a similar complex of metaphors suggesting that botanic drugs were involved in the symbolism of primordial autochthony, for Erichthonius, the 'Very Chthonic' son who was born from earth out of the seed either of Hephaestus or Prometheus, was said to have bitten the nurses (Apollodorus 3.187) to whom Athena entrusted him and to have caused thereby their death in the ensuing fit of madness (Pausanias 1.38.3; Euripides, *Ion* 12 ff.).

The traditions about Hephaestus also suggest botanic paradigms for the fire that set the aboriginal creatures on the track of evolution to a higher state of being. It is no happenstance that both Prometheus and Hephaestus, as we have just seen, were said to have fathered the primordial Athenian, for they often double for each other in myth and hence it is likely that they were originally simply different aspects of the same figure, with Prometheus's so clearly transparent name merely an epithet for the other.[2]

It is Hephaestus, the god of volcanic fire, who is responsible for tormenting Prometheus and his brother Titans for their opposition to Zeus and the tyranny of his newly established rulership that at first was not reconciled to the existence

1. Hippolytus, *Refutation of All Heresies* 5.7.4. See Kerenyi, *Prometheus* 80-81.
2. Kerenyi, *Prometheus* 57-62.

of man, Prometheus's own creation. Such fiery torment that is a burden of self-inflicted sacrifice recalls the close association of Soma and the fire god Agni and is suggestive of the pattern of shamanic initiation or *askesis*.

To trace this idea, let us look first at the traditions involving the lame Hephaestus with magical plants and intoxication in his tormenting of the Titans. For example, as punishment for the giant or 'Earth-born' Typhon, Zeus was said to have confined him in the volcano of Aetna (Aeschylus, *Prometheus* 351 ff.), which, like the volcano on Lemnos, was thought to be a forge of Hephaestus (*Prometheus* 366 ff.). This punishment parallels that of Prometheus's brother Atlas, who stood as 'the pillar between heaven and earth' in the Garden of the Daughters of the West, the so-called Hesperides (*Prometheus* 347 *ff.*). The mountain with the core of fire and the special garden where magical plants grow are probably to be recognized as analogous versions of the World Axis or *axis mundi*, the place where the Tree of Life grows, allowing the shaman to ascend or descend to other realms in the torment of his *askesis*. This place is at the ends of the earth, hence, as with the Hesperides, in the place where the sun goes down. Analogous to it is the place of the dawn. Thus Hephaestus bound Prometheus in the far east, a topographical counterpoise to the torment of his brother in the land of the evening, and like the latter, it too is a place where special herbs grow. On his quest for the so-called 'apples of the Hesperides', Heracles will visit Prometheus as well as Atlas, for the two distant locales are bound by the daily journey of the sun through the darkness of the night, a trip that Heracles, who also will experience the shamanic *askesis*, was said to have taken by sailing in the fiery sun's own *depas* or 'drinking cup' (Stesichorus 8.1; Pherecydes 18a), a utensil that suggests that the voyage is one of intoxication,[1] and that Hephaestus, who fashions such metal cups in his forge (Aeschylus, fr. 69), may again be involved.

Other traditions also associate both the eastern and western locales with the shaman's fiery plant, for the word in Greek for the 'apple' that was to be found growing in the Garden of the Hesperides is verbally indistinguishable from the golden fleece of the 'sheep' (*melon*) that was hung on the tree in Medea's land in the far east. It was that fleece that had transported the children of the 'hallucinatory' Nephele to that otherworld environment. The equivalence of the two topographical extremes can also be sensed from the fact that the so-called 'Queen' Medusa, the Gorgon, was located in both places (Hesiod, *Theogony*

1. Lesley Cafarelli, *Temenos and Skene: Enclosure Motifs in Greek Poetry and Myth* (unpublished dissertation, Boston University, 1978).

274 ff.; Aeschylus, *Prometheus* 790 ff.). On a vase painting from southern Italy, we glimpse a remembrance that the fruit of the Medusa's special tree was a mushroom.[1]

Prometheus himself, in some traditions, was apparently the magical plant. A miraculous herb, parasitic on a tree and in color like the crocus, was said to grow from the blood of Prometheus in his torment. Medea picked it to anoint Jason (or Iason, in Greek, apparently so named for this anointing with the drug[2] that will protect him from the fire-breathing bulls guarding the tree with the golden fleece); when the plant was thus harvested, Prometheus himself groaned, according to the way that Apollonius Rhodius told the story, for the plant is said to grow from a double stem. In picking the Promethean herb, Medea is also in contact with the suffering Titan bound to his mountain, for which reason the root of the plant when it is plucked was said to resemble the flesh of a corpse that has just been cut (*Argonautica* 3.845 ff.).

The fiery Titanic drug found at the tree on the mountain in the lands where the sun is kindled and extinguished appears, as Wasson has shown,[3] to have had a fungal prototype in the homeland of the Indo-Europeans. In Siberia, the paradigmatic shaman's Tree is the shining white birch that is host not only to the mycorrhizal parasitic *Amanita muscaria* growing at its base, but also to the steps of shelf fungus ascending its trunk. The latter, 'punk' or *Fomes fomentarius*, provides the tinder for making fire with a fire drill, thus associating the gift of fire with the shaman's ascent to the fiery realm of his visions.

The torment of *askesis* passes from sufferer to sufferer, a labor like the sun's, forever renewed. It is upon the basis of this primitive experience in primordial times that culture is founded and continually renewed. The myth of Heracles, for example, is a case in point. He was said to have fought many poisonous monsters in order to tame the earth for mankind and to establish the reign

1. Amphora from the third quarter of the fourth century B.C., now in the Pergamon Museum, East Berlin (Staatliche Museen zu Berlin, Antiken-Sammlung, inv. no. F 3022), See Wasson *et al.*, *The Road to Eleusis* plate 8.

2. The name Iason contains the same *ia-* root that occurs in words such as *iatros* ('healer' or 'doctor') and *iasthai* ('to heal'). In addition to the anointment by Medea, Iason is associated with drugs through his education in his youth in the wilds with the centaur Chiron. See Ruck, On the sacred names of Iamos and Ion.

3. Wasson, *Soma* 216 ff. In Siberia, birch-bark containers were stuffed with punk, which deprived of air by tight packing would harbor the smouldering fire for upwards of two days. This custom invites comparison with the tradition of Prometheus's theft of fire hidden in the *thyrsos* or *narthex*, for the marrow of the giant fennel was used as tinder and even in modern times on some of the Greek islands is still the means of preserving the glowing embers or of carrying them from place to place (for references see Kerenyi, *Prometheus* 80).

of his divine father Zeus. His burning torment came upon him when his wife Dejanira anointed his robe with the drops of poison that came originally from one of the monstrous beasts he had killed (Sophocles, *Women of Trachis* 831 ff., 1140 ff.). In another tragedy, he was shown in a mad state, poisoned by this same primordial source (Euripides, *Heracles* 1189 ff.). This intoxication represents his regression to a primitive state, to a time before the world was civilized, when he, who would eventually pacify the earth and show the way to reconciliation with the heavens, was still a dwarfish creature called a Daktyl or 'finger man'.[1] The dichotomy between primitivism and culture at the Eleusinian Mysteries can be detected in the tradition that claimed that this poisoned and primitive Heracles underwent purification at the Lesser Mystery (Apollodorus 2.5.12; Diodorus Siculus 4.14; Scholia to Aristophanes' *Plutus* 1013) in order to prepare him for his initiation into the Greater. Heracles, however, can be freed from his poisoned state and restored to his Olympian destiny only by passing the venom to another who will play the role of the primitive sufferer. Thus, on the pyre that was eventually lit on the mountaintop of Oeta, Heracles escaped from his mad torment, giving his venomed arrows and bow to a member of the family of Poeas, whose name suggests that he had a botanic identity.[2] The words for 'poison' and 'arrow' (*ios*) are identical in Greek, and the transference of the bow apparently entails also the contamination by its metaphoric complex of primitivism and toxicity. Thus when we hear of this bow again, it is in the hands of Philoctetes, a son of Poeas. He was shown in Sophocles' tragedy yearning to be burnt in the Lemnian volcano of Hephaestus (*Philoctetes* 800, 986 ff.), a release from torment analogous, as he claims, to the fiery consummation that he once afforded Heracles on Oeta (801 ff.). Instead, cursed by his inheritance, he must live a primitive existence, dragging his poisoned foot in a track like the primordial serpent's (163, 291) and hunting for food that necessarily is tainted with the arrow's toxin (105, 166). Periodically he falls into fits of madness that are described as a wild kind of intoxication, ungraced by the evolution of the custom of communal drinking of tempered wine (213, 712 ff.). Eventually, he too, it was said, passed the role of sufferer to another, when he shot Paris at Troy on his foot with an arrow, while he himself was reintegrated with society and his own foot healed with curative herbs and wine (Apollodorus, *Epitome* 8; Tzetzes, *On Lycophron* 911).

1. For a discussion of the tragic hero as reversion from Olympian to chthonic or Dionysian symbolism, see Ruck, Duality and the madness of Herakles. *Arethusa*, 9/1 (1976) 53-75.

2. Poeas (or more exactly Poias) is perhaps to be related to the word for 'herb', *poie*.

Prometheus too could be freed from his torment on the mountain to which Hephaestus unwillingly had bound him only by passing his role to another. Thus it was said that the centaur Chiron was poisoned when Heracles accidentally shot him on his foot as the other centaurs fought in their typically uncivilized way to drink from a newly opened jar of wine. Despite Chiron's vast knowledge of drugs and herbs, a lore he was said to have taught many heroes in their youth spent with him in the wilderness, he was unable to heal himself. Heracles at last freed Prometheus by offering Chiron as a substitute (Apollodorus 2.5.11).

We cannot expect that Aristophanes reacted consciously to the full implication of presenting Prometheus as a Shade-foot, although it is perhaps possible that in the Kabeiric mystery traditions something was known that is now lost. Much, however, of what we have been discussing in the patterns of myth probably represents the inheritance of traditions from very ancient times whose meaning the classical writers did not question. Embedded in those traditions was a special value placed on lameness, like that of Hephaestus, Oedipus, and Philoctetes, or on single-footedness, as in the case of the 'one-shoed' (Apollodorus 1.9.16) Jason. The obvious psychological aptness of such an attribute of heroism no doubt facilitated its perpetuation, but the consistent way that it is incorporated as a detail in a larger complex involving the young hero's exposure to a mountainous wilderness of toxic plants as a preliminary to his reintegration with the civilized world suggests that the 'one-leg' paradigm, with its botanic manifestations, derives from the same ancient metaphor that in a more bizarre form was preserved as the Shade-foots.

Part of that ancient inheritance of heroic paradigms clearly derives from tales of shamans in primordial times. The torment of Prometheus and his brother Titans represents the toil imposed upon them by the new race of gods ruled by Zeus. The eagle that once was symbolic of Prometheus's flight toward the celestial realm has been expropriated as an emblem for Zeus. Prometheus no longer flies. Instead, chained to the eastern mountains that in the Iranian traditions were the home of the magical herb, he is tormented by the eagle who feasts repeatedly on the liver that was the seat of the Titan's power of divination.[1] The mountain itself, with its volcanic core, provides a passageway down to the netherworld (Aeschylus, *Prometheus* 1080 ff.), just as the holy plant found on its

1. On hepatoscopy and the wounding of Prometheus, see Kerenyi, *Prometheus* 39-40. For an interpretation of Prometheus's torment by the eagle as shamanic *askesis*, see E. A. S. Butterworth, *The Tree at the Navel of the Earth* (Walter de Gruyter, Berlin, 1970) 201 ff.

slopes afforded transport to the fiery heavens. His eventual release is symptomatic of the great reconciliation that reapportioned the world amongst the earlier and later races of gods and found room as well for the humans that were his creation. With the stolen fire, at a place called Mekone, apparently named for the 'Poppy' and sacred to Demeter and Persephone,[1] he taught mankind how to sacrifice, cooking the edible parts of the butchered victim and burning the rest for the gods. In doing this, his shamanism, for so the name of the place would suggest, set man in his vital role in the cosmos and began the arduous evolution toward the civilized arts, for in every repetition of such sacrificial eating, the Greeks retraced, in culinary symbolism, the steps of their long progress toward culture.[2] Without the ritual, mankind could not come to terms with the horrible realization that life is nourished, just like plants, by what is dead, and that primitivism, as in the maenadic ceremonies, must be tended as the fertile foundations of civilization.

In addition to the common Indo-European heritage of traditional metaphors and religious ideas, however, the close proximity of the Greeks to their eastern neighbors no doubt also added to the storehouse of myth. Thus, the hero's Promethean flight with the eagle in search of Soma or the magical potion can be found in the traditions of the Indo-Iranian peoples.[3] Its earliest written account appears in *Ṛg Veda* 4.26 and 27, with parallels in the *Avesta* and later texts, as well as in the literature and art of Mesopotamia. In addition to the similarity to the Prometheus myth, the same story seems to underlie the traditions about the eagle who brings nectar to Zeus[4] and the myth of Ganymedes' abduction from a mountain by Zeus in the guise of an eagle so that the handsome youth might serve nectar on Olympus as cupbearer to the gods (Homer, *Iliad* 20.133-335; Vergil, *Aeneid* 5.252 ff.; Ovid, *Metamorphoses* 10.155-161). The eagle traditionally sits in the branches of the shaman's tree. Perhaps this image too is detected in Greek, in Nonnus's description of a blazing olive tree off the coast of Tyre with an eagle at its top holding a libation cup (*Dionysiaca* 40.467 ff.).[5]

1. Kerenyi, *Prometheus* 42 ff. Mekone was supposed to be located in the vicinity of the Peloponnesian city of Sicyon, near Corinth.

2. Marcel Detienne, *Dionysos Slain* (Johns Hopkins University Press, Baltimore, 1979, translated from the French edition of 1977) 68-94.

3. David M. Knipe, The heroic theft: Myths from *Rg Veda* IV and ancient near east. *History of Religions*, 6/4 (1967) 328-360. See also the discussion of Greek and Eastern traditions associating heat with the light of mystical vision and with shamanic *askesis* in Butterworth, *Tree at the Navel of the Earth* 133 ff.

4. D'Arcy W. Thompson, *Glossary of Greek Birds* (Oxford, 1936 2nd edn.) 180-184.

5. Butterworth, *Tree at the Navel of the Earth* 85 ff.

Of particular interest for our interpretation of Prometheus's impersonation of a Shade-foot in the *Birds* are three reliefs from the temples at Sanchi and Amarāvati in India built in the first and third centuries A.D., but employing traditional symbolism that is certainly much older and which is essentially not different from that found in the eastern Mediterranean.[1] On these reliefs, the Tree of Life is shown as a pillar between earth and sky, resting on an *omphalos* or Navel Stone and surmounted by sunshades, apparently as indication of the fiery brilliance of the higher realm.

PHILOSOPHERS

Aristophanes' parody of Socrates' necromancy in the Swamp makes clear that the symbolism of the Aryan fungus played an essential role in the Lesser Eleusinian Mystery. As with Soma, of course, it is possible that surrogates or substitutes were actually employed by the classical period, although the attributes of the original were in some form retained. Thus, the color of Medea's Prometheus herb is roughly consistent with the Vedic traditions, as is that also of the ergot fungus of the Greater Mystery. A similar spectrum of sacred color is described in Pindar's *Sixth Olympian Ode* as characteristic of the magical herb that was responsible for the primordial source of inspiration for the mythical ancestor of the Iamidai, the prophets who continued to practice divination at the sanctuary of Zeus at Olympia.[2] We should not conclude, moreover, that the *Amanitas* were not to be found in ancient Attica, for it was doubtless a deadly species of that genus that was responsible for the accidental deaths commemorated by Euripides in a famous epigram (Eparchides, quoted in Athenaeus 2.61a-b). And in the forested regions of modern-day Greece, the country people retain a knowledge of edible and inedible species.

By sending Peisander into the Swamp to consult Socrates amongst the Shade-foots, Aristophanes was cutting through appearances and showing up the vigorous prosecutor of the investigation into the scandal of the recent profanations as basically no other than he would soon turn out to be, an aristocrat like the now infamous Alcibiades, whose democratic demagoguery would last only so long as it suited his own political ascendency. Like the other students at what Aristophanes in the *Clouds* had called Socrates' *phrontisterion* or 'thinkshop', Al-

1. Butterworth, *Tree at the Navel of the Earth* 49 ff. and plates 11-13.

2. Ruck, On the sacred names of Iamos and Ion.

cibiades and Peisander both could be expected to have learned from the philosopher to despise convention and speak with the deceitful rhetoric of the Tongue-in-bellies.

It would appear, therefore, from our discussion of the scene of necromancy that the common suspicion about people like Socrates was that they were apt to have derived their ideas about other realities and about the relativity of everything to be found in this present world from drug-induced visions. In rehabilitating the reputation of his teacher, a man who had been put to death for impiety, Plato chose precisely a time just before the scandal of the profanations to portray Socrates at Agathon's symposium as a person subject to spontaneously generated periods of mystical trance and to emphasize the non-erotic involvement and growing separation between the philosopher and his drunken disciple Alcibiades. That, however, was not what was commonly believed by Socrates' contemporaries. To them, he seemed to speak of experiences that resembled those of a shaman, and his unconventional manner of life and his novel deities made it likely that he acted as a mystagogue for the young men devoted to him.

He was, in fact, not unlike other early philosophers whose lives and ideas have been recognized as shamanistic.[1] Amongst them, let us recall only Empedocles, who was said to have attempted to prove his divinity by jumping into a volcano, leaving behind only a single sandal (Heraclides 77 Voss). In his life he had a great reputation as a healer and, as he himself says, he was sought in his native Sicily by many who wanted prophecies or drugs (111, 112 Diels). He died when Socrates was in middle age, but the characteristic life of such men, as the necromancy parody shows, still set the expected pattern for wise men in Athens at the end of the century. Even Plato in the following decades would describe his master's devotion to wisdom by the metaphor of the inspiring god of Love, the child of ragged poverty, who spent his whole life in philosophic quest, an enchanter and herbalist and sophist (*Symposium* 203d).

1. E. R. Dodds, The Greek shamans and the origin of puritanism, *The Greeks and the Irrational* (University of California Press, Berkeley and Los Angeles, 1951) 135-178.

CHAPTER SEVEN

THE WILD AND THE CULTIVATED: WINE IN EURIPIDES' *BACCHAE*

In the *Bacchae*, the cultivation of grapes for the making of wine is presented as a novel advance in the science of agriculture. The prophet Teiresias compares it to the cultivation of grain as mankind's basic food. The latter is the dry nourishment that Demeter offers, whereas wine is its liquid complement, the new gift that the god Dionysus 'discovered and introduced' (ηὗρε κεἰσηνέγκατο 279). It is something as yet unknown in Thebes. Hence, he explains that it is a potion prepared from the clusters of grapes from the vine. As a 'drug', it is the supreme anodyne (οὐδ' ἔστ' ἄλλο φάρμακον πόνων 283), granting sleep and surcease from pain and daily cares (280-283), and it is a divine inspirative of wisdom and courage (298 ff.).

Others also have heard about wine in Thebes. The herdsman too claims that the vine is apparently an anodyne (παυσίλυπον ἄμπελον 772), without which there can be no love or pleasure for mankind (773-774). If such are the characteristics of this new drug, however, his praise of wine would seem an inappropriate conclusion to his narrative of the wild events he has just witnessed on Mount Cithaeron, for he barely escaped with his life from the god's maddened devotees. Clearly, we are not to assume that the revel on the mountain was caused by this new gift of the vine's potion. In fact, he had begun his narrative by stressing that there was no amorous dalliance amongst the women, nor were they drunk on wine, as the king who opposes this new god has suspected (686-688).

Pentheus, as will be shown, is king of a pre-viticultural city, and his persona in the drama is characterized by the antithetical properties to the wine whose introduction he opposes. In such a city, it cannot be the fermented juice from the cultivated vine that is responsible for the maenadic revels on the mountain, but wild and hunted growths instead, more primitive versions of the god, predating his Asian journey of discovery. This contrast of the wild and the cultivated will establish the basis for a new understanding of Euripides' meaning in this drama and of the tragic genre in general as a religious celebration of Dionysus.

THE DISCOVERY OF WINE

At the beginning of the *Bacchae*, Dionysus announces that he has come to Thebes from Asia Minor bringing with him the cult of his new religion and that he has planted what must be the first grape-bearing vine in this land where he was born (11 ff.), for Thebes is a country that has yet to learn the art of viticulture and experience the blessings of wine. The herdsman, for example, can praise wine later only from hearsay evidence (ὡς ἐγὼ κλύω 771), and Teiresias introduces his explanation about the parallel advances in agriculture by predicting the god's future greatness in Greece. Pentheus too knows of wine only by rumour (λέγουσι δ' ὥς τις εἰσελήλυθε ξένος 233 ff.) and he suspects that the experience that the god is introducing from Asia is merely a 'fiction' (πλασταῖσι βακχείαισιν 218) that the women use as a 'pretext' (πρόφασιν 224) for illicit love-making in the wilderness.

The situation in Thebes at the beginning of the play corresponds with other Greek traditions about the importation of viticulture, as well as with historical fact, for the growing of grapes for the production of wine apparently did originate in Asia Minor as a parallel development to other advances there in the cultivation of human foods. The art of viticulture spread westward from there via Crete and the Aegean islands to Thrace and mainland Greece.[1] With wine came also the cult of its ecstatic religion, undergoing accretions and developments, notably from Egyptian and Minoan influences. Dionysus himself traditionally landed in Attica around the fifteenth century before the Christian era,[2] and the names of his first proselytizing priests suggest Semitic, eastern Mediterranean and Egyptian origins.[3] His name has been read in Mycenaean-

1. Kerenyi, *Dionysos: Archetypal Image of Indestructible Life* (Princeton University Press 1976) 50 ff.

2. Hieronymus's Latin translation of Eusebius records 1497 B.C. as the date of the god's arrival in Attica and 1387 B.C. as the date of his birth from Semele at Thebes. The date of arrival derives from Athenian traditions preserved in the Atthidographers. See Kerenyi 143, note 32.

3. Dionysus was first received as a guest in Attica by Semachus, the founding hero of the deme of Semachidae, whose name appears to be West-Semitic, meaning 'made to rejoice'. Another tradition placed the god's landfall similarly on the west coast of Attica at Ikarion, where he was received by Icarius, whose name suggests that he came originally from Icaria, the island off the coast of Asia Minor, where the god was supposed to have been born. Icarius can be related to Caria and to the 'light-bearer' names of Ikar (the star Sirius) and Iacchus (a name of Dionysus at the Eleusinian Mysteries), as well as the Egyptian Iachim, a man who was supposed to have lived in the time of the otherwise unknown King Senes. A third route of arrival was through the mountain village of Eleutherae on the Boeotian border, a place associated with Eleuther and an apparition of the chthonic aspect of the god under the name of Melanaigis, the 'black goatskin', and with the proselytizing seers Pegasus and Melampous, the

Minoan documents, as well as the name of his arch-opponent Pentheus, indicating that the antagonism between the two belongs to a very early stratum of the religion as it developed in the Greek lands.[1]

As would be expected, the name for the newly cultivated plant, the 'vine' or *ampelos* (ἄμπελος), appears to be a word assimilated into Greek from a non-Indo-European language of the Mediterranean substratum, like other words for things that were novel to the experience of the immigrating Indo-Europeans.[2] The same is probably the case for the intoxicant fermented from the vine's grapes, 'wine' or *oenos* (οἶνος), and for the 'cluster of grapes' or *botrys* (βότρυς).[3] It is also possible, however, that *oenos* is derived from a very ancient Indo-European word, ultimately related to the Latin word for 'grape-vine' (*vitis*) and the Greek *itys* (ἴτυς), 'circular rim', as of a wheel supported by its spokes.[4] If the latter is the case, *oenos* presumably referred originally to some intoxicant other than wine, perhaps to a plant appropriately designated with the metaphor of *itys*. In Greek mythical traditions, Itys appears with Dionysian connotations as the butchered son of the maenadic sisters, Procne and Philomela, whose story involves the pattern of possession and abduction by a chthonic spirit, as in the myth of Persephone.[5]

The name of Dionysus himself contains the Indo-Europeans' word for their chief god, Zeus/Dios, and testifies to an attempt to incorporate the alien deity into Indo-European mythology as a son of Zeus, the so-called 'Nysian Zeus'. A similar assimilation occurs in the traditions about Zeus's birth on Crete, which clearly must be a rebirth since the god existed before the Indo-Europeans made contact with the Minoan culture of Crete. This Minoan 'Zeus' was one of the so-called 'divine-child' deities of botanic nature.[6] One of the names for him may have been retained in classical Greek as Bacchus, another name for Dionysus

latter being the one who supposedly introduced the phallic worship of Dionysus from Egypt by way of the Peloponnesus. See Kerenyi 73 ff., 146 ff., 160 ff.

1. Juan Puhvel, Eleuther and Oinoatis: Dionysiac Data from Mycenaean Greece, in *Mycenaean Studies, Wingspread, 1961: Proceedings of the Third International Colloquium for Mycenaean Studies held at 'Wingspread', 4-8 September 1961*, edited by E. L. Bennett, Jr. (Madison 1964) 164-168. The tablets in question are as follows: Pentheus on Knossos As 603; Dionysus on Pylos Xa 102 and Pylos Xb 1419; Eleuther on Pylos Cn 3.1-2.

2. P. Chantraine, *Dictionnaire etymologique de la langue grecque* (Paris 1968) *s.v. ampelos*; H. Frisk, *Griechisches etymologisches Wörterbuch* (Heidelberg 1954-1970) *s. v. ampelos*.

3. Chantraine and Frisk *s. v. oinos* and *botrys*.

4. Chantraine *s. v. oinos*.

5. C. Kerenyi, *The Heroes of the Greeks* (Thames and Hudson, Southampton 1959, 1974, 1978) 287-289.

6. On the 'divine child' figure in Greek religion, see M. P. Nilsson, *The Minoan-Mycenaean Religion and its Survival in Greek Religion* (Lund 1949) 531-583; and B. C. Dietrich, *The Origins of Greek Religion* (De Gruyter, Berlin 1974) 14 ff., 88 ff.

and for a 'sacred branch' or *bakkhos* (βάκχος), which, according to Hesychius, is a Phoenician word for 'lamentation', such as might be expected to attend the death of such divine children, as in the classical rites of Adonis.

The myths recounting the story of the god's arrival in Greece attest to the pattern involved in the assimilation of his cult. Traditionally, he is met by a king and his daughters, who are initiated into his new religion.[1] This initiation, as we shall see, was apparently some form of 'sacred marriage' between the princess and the god, a shamanic rite of spiritual possession whereby the alien deity was reborn in his Hellenic form, for, as the poet of the Homeric hymn to Dionysus claimed, the god's mother was said to have borne him in many places along his route to Thebes, although actually the true account was that he was born far off in Phoenicia near the streams of Egypt on a mountain called Nysa (1.1-9), the sacred place after which he is named as the 'Nysian Zeus'. The paradox of a foreign as well as native births was reconciled in later traditions by assuming that the Dionysus who arrived in Greece as the bringer of his cult was different from the one born at Thebes, but the two must originally have been the same god,[2] and, in the *Bacchae*, Euripides is closer to the truth in disguising the Theban-born Dionysus as the prophet arriving from the East with the rites of his foreign religion of viticulture, which his mother's people do not yet know.

As the god was repeatedly born anew as Zeus's son, the sacred place of his birth also was multiplied, so that there were many places called Nysa, and women other than Semele who were his mother. Even in antiquity it was recognized that the supposedly Theban Semele, whose family had migrated from Phoenicia, was no other than the Earth Mother (*F. Gr. H.* 244 F 131 Jacoby) imported from Anatolia. Thus Persephone, the great queen of the netherworld, was his mother too, and she also experienced the sacred marriage at Nysa, according to the Homeric hymn to Demeter (2.17).

The latter tradition gives us valuable insight into what was involved in these sacred marriages, for Persephone was said to have been gathering wild flowers with a group of maiden women when she was possessed by the spirit of death, the lord of the otherworld, who was synonymous in such experiences of spiritual possession with Dionysus himself (Heraclitus 15 Diels). By that abduction, she eventually gave birth to a new form of Dionysus.[3] The ecstatic devotees in the

1. Kerenyi, *Dionysos* 139-188.
2. Kerenyi, *Ibid.* 143-144.
3. Kerenyi, *Ibid.* 83, 110 ff. The birth of Dionysus by Zeus from Persephone was specifically a Cretan tradition (Diodorus Siculus 5.75.4) and is parallel to the traditions of the Cretan assimilation of Zeus by a similar rebirth.

cults of Dionysus similarly performed some secret ritual that apparently symbolized the gathering of wild plants, for the recurrent indication of their maenadic occupation is a strange implement, the so-called *thyrsos* (θύρσος), apparently another non-Indo-European loan-word in Greek that designated a stylized 'sacred branch' or 'wand' in the form of a hollow giant fennel stalk crowned with leaves of wild ivy. As I have shown in a recent study of the Eleusinian Mysteries,[1] this sceptre of Dionysus takes on particular meaning when we consider that such hollow stalks were customarily employed by herbalists in Greece to preserve the freshness of the wild plants they gathered (Theophrastus, *H. P.* 9.16.2) and that 'ivy' or *kissos* (κίσσος), a plant sacred to Dionysus, was the sort of magical wild plant that would have been gathered in this manner, for it was reputed to be poisonous, with a deranging effect upon the mind (Pliny, *H. N.* 24.75; Dioscorides, *Alex.* 2.176). The plant that Persephone gathered was also reputed to be a drug, for the flower that she picked was the *narkissos* (νάρκισσος), like *kissos*, another loan-word in Greek from a non-Indo-European language,[2] but a plant that was thought in classical times to have been so named because of the 'narcotic' stupor that it induced (Plutarch 2.647b; Dioscorides 4.161). A further similarity between Persephone's Nysian abduction and the activities of the Dionysian maenads in the sacred places called Nysa is indicated by the generic titles of the god's devotees in their mountain rites, for they too, like Persephone, were his nymphs or 'brides', as well as the women who 'nursed' him in his infancy (Homeric hymn 26). These women who nursed another's child are, more exactly, 'wet-nurses', and their affinity with Persephone's realm was symbolized by their patronage by Hecate (Hesiod, *Theogony* 450-452), another manifestation of Persephone as the chthonic queen.

Other traditions confirm that the Dionysian sacred marriage and ecstatic madness are to be understood as symbolic of what, originally at least, was a drug-induced shamanic possession, for Semele was sometimes said to have conceived Dionysus, not by means of the destroying thunderbolt of Zeus, but actually by ingesting a potion containing the heart of Dionysus himself (Hyginus, *F.* 167), and, in addition to the *thyrsos*, maenads are sometimes depicted wielding gigantic pestles, an obvious implement for herbalist activities.[3] In the *Bacchae*,

1. R. Gordon Wasson, Carl A. P. Ruck and Albert Hofmann, *The Road to Eleusis: Unveiling the Secret of the Mysteries* (Harcourt Brace Jovanovich, New York 1978) 88.

2. Words ending in *-issos*, like those in *-inthos*, are not Indo-European.

3. *Hydria* from Nola, *Archäologische Zeitung* 26 (1888) 3-5, pl. 3 (=illustration 5 in W. H. Roscher, *Ausführliches Lexicon der griechischen und römischen Mythologie* (Olms, Hildesheim 1884-1937, 1965²) *s. v.* Orpheus): Orpheus attacked by a Thracian maenad with a mortar in the presence of a satyr.

moreover, *narthex*, the word for the 'giant fennel', is apparently synonymous with the *thyrsos*; metaphorically, *narthex* could be used to describe a container for drugs and was thus employed as the title for medical treatises by several ancient doctors (Galen 12.398, 959; Aëtius 8.45), and in Euripides' play it seems to contain Syrian frankincense (144), an incense that was reputed to affect the mind (Dioscorides 1.81).

Even more explicit, however, is the tradition about the abduction of Oreithyia, which Plato rationalizes in the *Phaedrus* (229c). She was said to have been ravished by the wind Boreas. Her name describes her as an ecstatic woman on a mountain, and in the rationalized version of her myth, she was playing on the mountain with her friend Pharmakeia, the 'use of drugs', when she fell to her death in a gust of wind. Oreithyia, furthermore, was one of the Hyakinthidai or Daughters of Hyakinthos, a vegetative deity who changed upon his death into the *hyakinthos*, another pre-Indo-European plant name assimilated into Greek. Like Itys, whose name is supposed to be the nightingale's eternal lament (Sophocles, *Electra* 148), and perhaps also like the Phoenician Bakkhos, Hyakinthos has connotations of mourning, for his flower was supposed to imitate the letters that spelled the sound of lamentation (Moschus 3.6-7; Euphorion, frg. 36M Powell; Ovid, *Metamorphoses* 10.215). Hyakinthos appears to have been an aboriginal deity at Sparta, later supplanted by Apollo,[1] who, like Dionysus, as a son of Zeus represents another assimilation of a pre-Greek god into Indo-European traditions. Oreithyia's abduction by the wind, moreover, is a rather transparent metaphor for 'inspiration' and chthonic possession, especially in view of the wind's direction from the wintry north.[2] Hyakinthos himself was destroyed by the

1. J. D. Mikalson, Erectheus and the Panathenaia. *American Journal of Philology*, 97 (1976) 141-153.

2. 'To blow or breathe upon' (ἐμπνέω, καταπνέω) is the Greek equivalent of the Latin *inspirare* and commonly means 'inspire': for example, Hesiod, *Theogony* 31; *Plutarch* 2.421b; Homeric hymn to Demeter 238; Aristophanes, *Lysistrata* 552; *etc.* All winds were thought to blow to and from caverns within the earth: Elmer G. Suhr, *Before Olympus: A Study of the Aniconic Origins of Poseidon, Hermes and Eros* (Helios, New York 1967) 30 ff. The destructive Boreas was an apt figure for a deadly ravisher of vegetation.
Oreithyia was a daughter of the primordial Athenian king Erechtheus. Her sister Creusa was similarly ravished in a sacred marriage while picking flowers (Euripides, *Ion* 889) in a spot exposed to the north wind (11). Creusa herself was married later to a son of Aeolus, the lord of the winds (63). Since it was apparently Erechtheus himself who originally enacted such deadly abductions upon his own daughters (260 ff.), these unions with foreigners are probably to be understood as displacements of his role upon outside forces, who are merely aspects of his own persona, as in the traditions about the immigrant and indigenous Cadmus, on which see 'The Regression of Cadmean Thebes', below. By such sacred unions, moreover, the sinister alien forces become incorporated into the sustaining beneficent metaphysical alliances of the city, on which see 'The Reconciliation with Primitivism', below. In actual fact, the Athe-

equally sinister wind from the west, the lands where the sun goes down. The abduction of Oreithyia by Boreas is depicted on a fifth-century Attic *hydria* in the Vatican Museum; she is shown with Pharmakeia and holds the wild flower that she has apparently just picked, as the winged Boreas abducts her.

It would be expected that with the advent of viticulture, the wine god would be assimilated to the prevailing patterns of shamanic religions, for the fermented juice of the cultivated grape, as well as the pre-viticultural magical plants, induces a kind of spiritual communion with deity. Some aspects of this assimilation must have occurred before Dionysus arrived in the Greek lands with his gift of the vine, and still others after the coming of the Indo-Europeans. There is, however, a basic pattern to be discerned in these assimilations. Dionysus is represented both by the grape-bearing vine and by wild plants reputed to be intoxicating or poisonous. The mountain revels did not occur in the vineyards or during the time of year suitable for agriculture, but in the winter months, when the Greek mountains bloom with untended flowers, and in the wilderness. They are characterized by the symbolism, not of the harvest, but of the hunt, a search both for wild plants and for animals, that were wrenched brutally to pieces and eaten raw in a primitive manner, predating the civilizing advent of the arts of cooking. The brutality of this primitive experience was clearly meant as regression to a primordial existence. The women were said on occasion actually to have eaten their own children (Plutarch 299e; Aelian, *Varia Historia* 3.42; Apollodorus 2.2.2, 3.4.3, 3.5.2; Nonnus 9.49 ff., 47.484 ff., 48.917 ff.). In the *Bacchae*, they attack village agricultural settlements and their tilled fields of grain (748 ff.) and invert the normal order of society, for they are females performing the hunt, an occupation more appropriate for males,[1] and, thereby, they regress to the role of male-dominating women who seemed to prevail in the mythical traditions about primordial times.

The prime botanic symbol of this Dionysian inversion of the civilized order was the ivy or *kissos*, by one account, the actual meaning of Nysa (Pseudo-Dioscorides, *de Mat. Med.* 2.179). Its leaves and manner of growth bear an uncanny resemblance to the vine, but it is a wild plant and its diminutive berries are like primitive versions of the clustered grape. The ivy, moreover, reputedly is intoxicating in itself, whereas the grape must be harvested and tended

nians believed that their marital alliance with Boreas was responsible for the destruction of Xerxes' fleet off Mount Athos as he came against Greece, and they commemorated the natural disaster by building a temple to Boreas on the supposed site of his union with Oreithyia (Herodotus 7.189).

1. Marcel Detienne, *Dionysos Slain* (Johns Hopkins University Press, Baltimore 1979, translated from the French edition of 1977) 20-52.

through the long fermentation process. In the winter when the vine is leafless and dormant, the ivy grows like the vine on upright stems, blooming at the time of the autumn grape harvest and producing its fruit in the spring as the vine comes back to life, a return that seems markedly reluctant, compared to the spring-time growth of other plants. During the summer, while the vine grows upright, the ivy now enters into a second stage of growth, with trailing tendrils of leaves of the more familiar shape. It is a plant of dual nature, like the twice-born god it represents, and was thought capable of hybridizing from one variety to another. As Walter Otto has observed, 'The vine and the ivy are like siblings who have developed in opposite directions and yet cannot deny the relationship.'[1] Ivy, moreover, was thought to be parasitic, wildly sending out roots all along its stem and capable of sustaining its own life from the nourishment extracted from the host trees upon which it climbs, eventually destroying them, and even continuing to grow when its contact with the ground is severed (Theophrastus, *H. P.* 3.18.9). Ivy was related to the vine apparently as the weed to the cultivated hybrid.

Ivy was the vine's avatar. It belonged mythologically to a previous generation. Dionysus himself was called Kissos (Pausanias 1.31.6), but never Ampelos or 'vine'. It was only after his own sacred marriage with his maenadic bride Ariadne that he produces sons named Staphylos or the 'clustered grape' and Oinopion, 'vinous', whom Dionysus first taught how to make wine (schol. in Apollonium Rhodium 3.997). This evolution is often a theme in vase paintings, as, for example, on the *krater* by the Altamura painter, where Dionysus is shown confronting the younger image of himself standing on his lap: Staphylos holds a wine cup and sprigs of vine, while his seated father, attended by flower-bearing maenads, holds the ivy-crowned *thyrsos*.[2]

Other pre-viticultural magical plants are also associated with Dionysus as his primordial avatar. Amongst these are to be counted the opium poppy,[3] whose role in Minoan religion is attested by the female 'sleeping' idol from Isopata in the Iraklion Museum, who wears a diadem of the plant's seed capsules, each painted with the slit that would be cut to extract the drug. Dionysus

1. Walter F. Otto, *Dionysos: Myth and Cult* (Bloomington, Indiana 1965, translated from the German edition of 1933) 153 ff.

2. Museo Archeologico Nazionale, Ferrara. The confrontation of the seated god and his diminutive son is reminiscent of similar scenes depicting the birth of Dionysus, the younger Zeus, out of the thigh of his Olympian father.

3. On the role of opium in early Mediterranean culture, see P. G. Kritikos and S. P. Papadaki, The History of the Poppy and of Opium and their Expansion in Antiquity in the Eastern Mediterranean Area, *Bulletin on Narcotics* (United Nations, New York), 19 (3) (1967).

himself is seen wearing such a crown on a volute *krater* in the National Archaeological Museum of Taranto: he is depicted as a youthful hunter amidst ecstatic maenads, one of whom holds the *thyrsos*. In a similar manner, Dionysus assimilated the role of honey and its ferment, mead, from the Minoan culture.[1] The latter intoxicant involves the symbolism of the bee, who, like the herb-gathering maenadic women in the wilds, goes from flower to flower, extracting their essence, which is a drug related to the venom of serpents, but its beneficial antithesis, instead of a poison.[2] Such a ritual is apparently depicted on a gold signet ring from a tomb near Knossos, now in the Iraklion Museum: women with the heads of insects are seen dancing amidst flowers as they experience the mystical apotheosis of a deity.

The association of Dionysus with certain trees, in particular the resin-bearing firs and pines, is also testimony to such an assimilation of pre-viticultural intoxicants into Dionysian religion. Primitive man cut the bark of such trees to extract the sap, which would ferment to produce an intoxicant (Pliny, *N. H.* 12.2).[3] Thus Dionysus maintains several 'arboreal' epithets, such as Dendreus, Endendros, and Dendrites, and he is called Phleus as the god of the 'abounding sap'.[4] Thus too, the maenads carried sacral branches or *bakkhoi* for the mountain revels (*Bacchae* 109-110), and, as we shall see, the final consecration of Pentheus as the Dionysian sacrifice will take place in the god's sacred tree. Greek wine, moreover, assimilated the taste of such more primitive intoxicants, for it was resinated (Aristophanes, *Acharnians* 190 *cum schol.*) in the manner of modern retsina.

We should expect that whatever pre-viticultural intoxicant figured in the shamanic religions of the Indo-Europeans would similarly be assimilated to the cult of wine as an avatar of the evolved and cultivated god. The Aryan branch of the migrations of these northern peoples into Iran and India in the second millennium before Christ preserved a shamanic cult from their homeland. This religion is recorded in the collection of Sanskrit hymns known as the *Ṛg Veda*, which is the written form of what was originally oral and formulaic material dating back to a period before the migrations. Amongst the deities of a complex

1. Kerenyi, *Dionysos* 29-51.

2. Pindar (*Olympia* 6.43 ff.) describes the primordial inspiration of a divinely born child as his nourishment in the wilderness by serpents who feed him with honey, a beneficent transmutation of their venom. See Ruck, On the Sacred Names of Iamos and Ion: Ethnobotanical Referents in the Hero's Parentage, *Classical Journal*, 71 (3) (1976) 235-252. Dionysus himself was first fed with honey from his nurse at Nysa (Apollonius Rhodius 4.1134-1136).

3. Gaetano Forni, The Origin of Grape Wine: A Problem of Historical-Ecological Anthropology, *Gastronomy: The Anthropology of Food and Food Habits* (Margaret Arnott, ed.) (Mouton, The Hague 1975) 67-78.

4. E. Werth, *Grabstock, Acker und Pflug* (Ulmer, Ludwigsburg 1954) 229.

pantheon appears the god Soma, a god who was a plant that was sacrificed to extract its inebriating drug for a sacred potion. The physical properties of this plant are recorded in its formulaic epithets and descriptions in the hymns. Although Soma is a plant, surprisingly no mention is ever made of its flower, leaves, or roots. R. Gordon Wasson has demonstrated, to the satisfaction now of most Indo-Iranologists, that the original Soma, for which substitutions were made in the later performances of the rite, was a particular mushroom, the *Amanita muscaria* or 'fly-agaric', a plant that still figures in Siberian shamanism today. This mushroom grows in northern latitudes only in association with the roots of certain trees, in particular, pines, firs, and birches. The birch, because of this association, figures symbolically as the shaman's Tree of Life, the axis by which he ascends to the realm of the gods.

The Hellenic branch of these Indo-European peoples can be expected to have brought some knowledge of the traditions of this shamanic cult with them on their migrations into the Greek lands. This indeed seems to be indicated by the fact that Greek epic preserves a pattern for the mixing of magical potions that has formulaic analogues in the Vedic material. Working with Wasson and the Swiss chemist, Dr. Albert Hofmann, I have attempted to show that the Eleusinian Mysteries, and probably the other mystery religions of classical Greece, can be interpreted as communal shamanic seances, in which mystical visionary experience was induced by the ingestion of drugs. For the Greater Eleusinian Mystery, the drug was a water-soluble extract of ergot, either expressly cultivated on barley or gathered from other, weedy grasses, such as *Lolium temulentum*. This fungus, which produces fruiting bodies of the characteristic mushroom shape, is a natural source of psychoactive alkaloids commonly referred to as LSD.

The paired Eleusinian Mysteries, which centered upon the art of cultivating grain, were, like the Dionysian art of viticulture, an assimilation of the religious traditions of the pre-Greek agrarian peoples into Indo-European mythology. Thus the original solitary Mother Goddess becomes split into the sacred duo of the Mysteries, Demeter, an Olympian as sister of Zeus, and the chthonic Persephone, who, like Dionysus, has been reborn as a child of Zeus. *Lolium*, which in Greek was called *aira* (αἶρα), was thought to be the inedible avatar from which the cultivated barley had been evolved by the agricultural arts and into which it would again revert if not properly tended. The Greater Mystery celebrated this successful hybridization and reconfirmed the forward evolutionary progress of Hellenic culture, a civilization nourished like the barley itself by its healthy accord with its roots in the chthonic realm.

The cultivation of grain is the culmination of an event that began in more primitive times, namely, the abduction of Persephone while gathering wild flowers. This illicit stealing of her as a concubine eventually is legitimized in a more civilized age as she becomes a wife related by law to the powers of death. The primitive precedent for the Greater Mystery was imitated as the Lesser Mystery. By investigating the traditions about a fabulous Indian tribe of single-footed, parasol-like creatures who were supposedly implicated in a profane performance of the Lesser Mystery, I have demonstrated that the symbolism of the Indo-European wild mushroom, with analogues to the Vedic material, was preserved at this rite that was considered the prelude to the revelation of the Greater Mystery. In view of the parasol metaphor, moreover, it seems possible that if *oenos* and *itys* did indeed refer originally to a pre-viticultural intoxicant of the Indo-European people before their migration into Greece, the identity of that intoxicant was fungal, for the metaphor of a 'circular rim' is singularly apposite for a mushroom. Apparently by coincidence, it is actually as such that the sacred mushroom of Mesoamerica is indicated pictographically.[1]

It is appropriate that the fungi should have figured in the symbolism of the hunt, as opposed to cultivation, for they are the prototypic wild plant. Their propagation by microscopic spores instead of seeds made their manner of growth a mystery in antiquity, and, even today, certain species resist cultivation. For this reason, in Greece, as well as in India, they were thought to be planted by the lightning bolt, as they burst suddenly from the ground, swollen with the water absorbed from the rainfall. Dionysus, himself, had such an engendering by his Indo-European father, whose bolt of lightning can be traced as a symbol of enlightenment in Asiatic shamanism.[2] The assimilation of the fungi to the Dionysian complex of symbolism as the wild avatar of the cultivated god can be noted in the metaphoric description of a mushroom as a miniature *thyrsos* (Apicius 7.15.6), with the intoxicating cap atop its stipe substituting for the crown of gathered ivy leaves.

1. R. Gordon Wasson, *The Wondrous Mushroom: Mycolatry in Mesoamerica* (McGraw Hill, New York 1980) 64. Wasson identifies the flower glyphs that decorate the effigy of the Aztec deity know as Xochipilli or the 'Prince of Flowers' as all indicating various magical plants or 'entheogens' that figured in shamanism. By another amazing coincidence of iconography, the butterfly in both Mesoamerican and Hellenic cultures indicates the soul. A common word in Greek for 'butterfly' is *psyche* or 'soul', and Psyche is actually depicted as a butterfly on a neo-Attic marble pedestal in the Vatican, probably copied from an original work of the second century B.C.: the soul is being burnt by two weeping Erotes as a Dionysian sacrifice, a parallel event to the visit of the drunken god to a poet, and the preparations for the dismemberment of a sacrificial animal and its boiling in milk. See Kerenyi, *Dionysos* plate 64 B.

2. E. A. S. Butterworth, *The Tree at the Navel of the Earth* (De Gruyter, Berlin 1970) 129 ff.

Other characteristics of fungi would have facilitated the assimilation of the viticultural deity to Indo-European traditions. Each year in Greece, the three winter months belonged to a primitive, maenadic aspect of Dionysus. These were the months that the harvested and presumably dead viticultural deity spent in the otherworld, and, even at Delphi, the Olympian sanctuary regressed to more primitive Dionysian rites in honor of chthonic powers. In the absence of his cultured self, Dionysus was represented by the *phallos*.[1] The phalloid shape of mushrooms, which fruit in the non-viticultural season, made them an apposite metaphor for the male organ (Archilochus, frg. 34 Diehl). The *phallos* itself, as a symbol of Dionysus, was an importation from Egypt by the seer Melampous (Herodotus 2.49) in the Mycenaean age,[2] although it was a Greek innovation to represent the god by the *phallos* alone, instead of a movable one, in the Egyptian manner, attached to the god's effigy. Melampous belongs to a tradition similar to that of the confrontation between Pentheus and the Dionysian prophet, for it was he who cured the daughters of Proetus of the madness that afflicted them when their brother Megapenthes opposed the rites of Dionysus. Since their madness took the form of bovine rutting, the Egyptian import suggests that their cure comprised sexual gratification.

The metaphor of the bovine oestrual madness also involves the pre-viticultural aspect of Dionysus in taurine symbolism. Amongst the Indo-Aryans, the bull was the commonest metaphor for Soma,[3] and the sacral function of the bull amongst the Minoans obviously reinforced Indo-European traditions. It was apparently as a bull that Dionysus united with the sacral queen of Athens in her annual, ancient, winter rite of marriage, which took place in what was called the 'bull stable' (Aristotle, *Ath. Pol.* 3.5). The 'bellowing' or *mykema* of a bull seems to have been a metaphor for the imagined cry of the fruiting bodies of the mushroom as they burst from the earth or are harvested.[4] The metaphor perhaps derives from a pun on *mykema* and *mykes* or 'mushroom', words whose initial sounds would both have been written in the Mycenaean syllabary with the pictogram of a bull's head.

In addition to the supposed successful hybridization of the vine from primitive avatars, the art of viticulture also was symbolic of the taming and cultivation of the wild mushroom. The Greeks suspected that there was a similarity between the growth of mushrooms and the fermentation that transformed the juice of the vine's grapes into wine, a process that actually is caused by the

1. Kerenyi, *Dionysos* 285 ff.
2. *Ibid.* 72.
3. Wasson, *Soma* 42.
4. Wasson, Ruck and Hofmann 118-121.

growth of microscopic lower fungi, the yeast. Thus a mushroom itself could be called metaphorically a 'ferment' or *zumoma* of the earth (ζύμωμα χθονός Nicander, *Alexipharmaca* 521), a word that implies an effervescing or boiling of corrupting digested matter. A similar corruption occurred in the tomb, which traditionally in Greek, as in modern languages, was a mouldy place (Homeric hymn 2.482; Sophocles, *Ajax* 1167). 'Mushroom', in fact, was apparently a metaphor for the 'burial coffin' or 'tomb' itself (Suidas *s.v.* μύκη). Thus, upon the body of the harvested grape could be grown the regeneration of the primitive god into his evolved form as the cultivated and refined intoxicant of civilized times, a rebirth that was clearly observable in the effervescing movement of the rotting ferment, as well as in the perceptible warmth generated by the process.

Here too, the art of viticulture was parallel to Demeter's gift of edible grains. Fungi are also responsible for 'leavened bread' or *zumites artos* (ζυμίτης ἄρτος), which in Greek is designated by the same metaphor of fermentation. The harvested grain similarly was host for the wild corruption. The association with the tomb would have been particularly obvious since the ancient method of cultivating the leaven would have corresponded to modern 'sourdough', a process of apparent rotting marked by a distinctive unpleasant smell. By comparison to the reddening corruption that overspreads iron, the dry grain too was host to a fungal 'rust' or ergot, *erysibe* (ἐρυσίβη), from which Demeter's analogue to wine was extracted for the Greater Eleusinian Mystery.

THE RECONCILIATION WITH PRIMITIVISM

For the Greeks, evolution was not a stable process. Civilization and the arts of cultivation were continually in need of renewal, to found them again upon the healthy accord and reconciliation with their more primitive origins, the fertilizing source in the chthonic realm from which they grew into the Olympian age. If the primitive were not given its proper role in the evolving order of the world, there would be no place for mankind, which, by virtue of its mortality, participates in the non-Olympian contamination of the tomb. The dishonored earth, instead of supporting the foods of life, would yield only poisons and sterility from the rotting dead, whose angry spirits would hound the living with wild delusions. Such is the threat made by the loathsome and despised Erinyes of Aeschylus's *Oresteia*, the maddening, female Hell-hounds, whose presence pollutes Apollo's Delphic temple. The priestess likens them to the Harpies who defiled Phineus's food with their rotting excrement (*Eumenides* 50 ff.). When at first they are dishonored in the civilized institution of the court at Athens, they threaten to drip tears of poison from their wounded hearts, polluting the earth with a stoppage of growth of both crops and mankind (780 ff.). Athena, however, cajoles them into accepting an honored place beneath the earth, and the threatened curse becomes a joyous benediction of fertility for the city.

Even the Olympians, moreover, would starve if mankind were not to fulfill its essential role of mediation between the two realms, converting the foods of the earth into the pure fragrance of burnt sacrifice rising to the heavens. Zeus himself, as in Aeschylus's *Prometheus*, would fall into mortality if he were not to cooperate with mankind's earth-born creator. Similarly it was a conspiracy of Zeus and earth, as announced in the Homeric hymn to Demeter, that led to the separation of the Olympian mother from her chthonic daughter and the eventual institution of the Mystery, whereby death itself was transmuted into a friendly visitor amongst mortals, the lord of riches, personified in his subterranean temple at Eleusis as the handsome youth who represented that very conspiracy, the primordial plan of Zeus.[1] Thus Demeter's first two reactions to her daughter's loss are to feed a child, not with food, but by anointing him with ambrosia and by inspiration, keeping him from the grievous witchcraft of worms burrowing in his flesh, and when that attempt to purify from mortality fails, similarly to deny all growth of mortal foods from the earth, until at last her own mother, who bore her into the Olympian realm, induces her to save the Olympians from starvation and accept back a chthonic Persephone, now pregnant and contaminated with the seminal foods of earth eaten in the tomb.

Reconciliation between the gods of the older and newer orders is, in fact, a common theme in Greek mythology, and the iconography of the deities themselves, as well as the rites of their worship, testifies to the conservative retention of very ancient, pre-Olympian aspects preserved and honored in their classical cults. Thus, for example, the pre-Indo-European goddess Athena, although reborn as an Olympian daughter of Zeus, still was associated with the transmuted symbols of her primordial identity. The Gorgon's head has been displaced, but is still worn, as indication of her role in triumphing over the chthonic queen, and the owl, her predatory night bird, has lost its meaning as the spirit responsible for her ecstatic possession, but persists as indication of the rational wisdom of the cultivated arts that she inspires. Amongst these was that of weaving, whose sinister, fateful symbolism was displaced upon the spider in the myth

1. C. Kerenyi, *Eleusis: Archetypal Image of Mother and Daughter* (Princeton University Press 1967) 169-174.

of her contest with Arachne, and ritually placated in the quadrennial presentation of a tapestry at the Panathenaic Festival, specially woven by a group of pre-nubile girls. Even the serpent, symbolic of the toxins of the earth, persists, but as her foster-child, responsible for the maddened deaths of others, maidens of the autochthonous dynasty at Athens.[1] In a similar manner, Demeter had non-Olympian manifestations, more akin to Persephone, as an Erinys, the Black One, and, like the Gorgon Medusa, a centauress.[2] Often the pre-Olympian identity persists and is assimilated as an epithet, supposedly indicative of a beloved companion whom the deity inadvertently destroyed. Thus Athena murdered Pallas when distracted at play by a sign from her Olympian father, the aegis or serpent-fringed goatskin, which is part of Athena's attire. Similarly, Apollo was once Hyakinthos, the beloved pre-Olympian plant-god whom he displaced.

Such reconciliation indicates the essential participation of primitivism in an evolving world where humans are to have a role. In terms of agrarian realities, mankind, by virtue of its mortality, is contaminated with the rotting dead matter it must slaughter or harvest for food, a putrefaction that is both the potential cause of pestilence and yet the honored, stinking nutriment that sustains the generations rooted upon the earth. The affinity of the dead and their living counterpart can also be sensed in the culinary arts, another evolutionary sign of civilized mankind's progress from primitivism. The 'ripening' of fruits, by which they softened toward rottenness, was a kind of 'digestion', a process that was hastened, in its refined way, by 'cooking' or 'baking' (πέσσω). The meat of the sacrificial animal, moreover, was prepared in a manner that recapitulated the supposed ontogeny of both the beast and the cultivated arts, the primordial organs grilled first, in primitive fashion, before the parts that grew later were boiled as stew. In Orphic doctrine, mankind inherited original sin from the Titans, who opposed the evolution of Dionysus into the assimilated son of Zeus and feasted atavistically upon his flesh, cooked in perversion of the culinary arts. Zeus rescued the primordial organs and regenerated his son in an Olympian identity.

1. Robert Lyster, Symbolic Elements in the Cult of Athena, *History of Religions*, 5 (1) (Summer 1965) 133-163.
2. Kerenyi, *Eleusis* 30-33.

THE MAKING OF WINE

In the making of wine, the god's experience was analogous to mankind's journey toward redemption through the mouldering tomb. As in the scene depicted on Homer's shield of Achilles (*Iliad* 18.561-572), the cultivated fruit of the vine was harvested to the music of lamentation, for the god had died. His slaughtered body was then dismembered in the wine press, a crime that the harvesters sought to ascribe to agents other than themselves. In art, it was traditionally satyrs who trod upon the grapes, and, in actual practice, the treaders seem to have worn masks.[1] The juice, that was the god's blood, flowed into urns placed like burial chambers beneath the earth, where the subterranean environment maintained the proper temperature for the fungal growth of fermentation.

While the spirit of the god was being cultivated in the otherworld, he was absent from the living. The months of his sojourn in the tomb are marked in the Greek lands by a winter-time profusion of wild flowers upon the mountains, although the cold is too intense to favor the growth of garden varieties or vegetables. This was the time when the atavistic Dionysus prevailed. It was the time for the phallic processions of the rural Dionysia celebrated in the villages, primitive rites dating back to the period before the incorporation of the god's worship in the civic calendar under the popular tyrant Peisistratus. This was the time too for the enactment of the primordial sacred marriage and for the ecstatic ceremonies of the 'maenadic' *lenai* at Athens, when the women urged the god through his winter sleep, worshipping him at his effigy composed of the empty robes and mask that awaited his return.[2] Comedy, the 'revel song', originally was the only drama performed at this period, and appropriately so, for the phallic dancers described an inverted world, given over to libidinous desires that satirized the mighty and reshaped society according to the whims of baser fantasies.

When the wine was at last ready at the February festival of the Anthesteria, the urns were opened, and the god's spirit was reborn as an infant. The graves of the dead released their spirits as well at this time, and for the three days of the festival, ghosts roamed abroad in Athens. The Anthesteria was the time of reconciliation between the two realms of the living and the dead. It was then

1. Goffredo Bendinelli, *La vite e il vino: Monumenti antichi in Italia* (Milan 1931) fig. 86, 172-173, 251-253, 264. See also Kerenyi, *Dionysos* 65 ff. Satyrs are sometimes replaced by Erotes in late antiquity (as in the sacrifice of Psyche mentioned above, note 1, p 189).

2. Kerenyi, *Dionysos* 281 ff.

that the maddened Orestes was supposed to have arrived at Athens and been offered hospitality, despite his polluted condition. That event was recalled in the special arrangements at the festival for drinking from separate pitchers and eating at small private tables, so that the hospitality that was extended to the visiting ghosts thereafter would not contaminate the food of the living by the putrefaction that clings to those who come from the grave. This was the time too when the hounding Erinyes were placated and honored as the Eumenides, the Blessed Ones. In preparation for the encounter with the dead at this festival, the Athenians purified themselves symbolically of the contamination they shared with the other realm by chewing upon pieces of *rhamnos*, a shrub whose laxative properties purged their bodies of chthonic pollutants.

This was a time also for honoring an earlier age of mankind, for the Anthesteria commemorated those who died in the Great Flood that Zeus sent against the evil primitive race, after which the sole surviving couple, descendants of the first creator, repopulated the world with its present people by throwing the stones of earth behind them. Amongst the sons of that couple was Orestheus, who discovered and planted the first vine, and Amphictyon, who first received Dionysus and learned from him how to tame the toxins of wine, and Hellen, the eldest, after whom the Hellenic race took its name. The primordial race that the Hellenes replaced was the Pelasgian, a pre-Indo-European people of whom remnants survived into classical times. Their sin, for which Zeus sent the Flood, was to have attempted to contaminate the Olympian by feeding him the flesh of a boy, Nyctimus, a creature of the night, as though Zeus were the lord of the other world. Zeus changed them all into wolves and assimilated that more sinister identity, as in the case of the other deities we have mentioned, by assuming the epithet *Lykaios*, the 'wolfish'.

An earlier age at Athens itself was also placated at the Anthesteria by a curious rite of swinging in swings, supposedly in commemoration of Erigone. It was her father who first received Dionysus and his gift of wine in Attica, but when he shared it with his fellow men, they saw double and thought themselves poisoned, for which they killed and buried him beneath a pine tree. Erigone found his body and hanged herself from the tree in grief. The swinging thereafter at the festival recalled that initial misunderstanding about the civilized nature of wine.

Reconciliation with the dead and the past at the Anthesteria also took the form of an initiation into the experience of wine for the very young, the children of three or four years of age. They were the personification of the young god, and as they cavorted among the revellers and the ghosts, the continuity of mortal lineage through the transformations of the tomb was sensed as analogous to the god's fermenting gestation and rebirth out of death.

The birth of the wine, moreover, was symbolic of the god's triumph over his own more primitive identity. The satyrs, who had presided at the treading of the harvested grapes and who had inverted the norms of civilized behaviour in the maenadic revels of the winter, were the natural enemies of the cultivated god, for goats, whose hircine nature they shared,[1] were thought to be particularly invidious to the vine because of their dangerous tendency to graze on its young shoots (Vergil, *Georgics* 2.380).[2] Now the goat yielded to Dionysus. The goatskin was filled with wine, and as a test of the triumph of sobriety over drunkenness, the revellers at the Anthesteria competed in a contest, attempting to balance themselves upon a greased wineskin (Pollux 9.21). There was also a contest of drinking, for which the prize was a goatskin (Aristophanes, *Acharnians* 1224 *cum schol.*). It was the goat too that was the special sacrificial victim for Dionysus. The song for its slaughter, the *tragoidia*, was perhaps the origin of tragedy.[3] In the next month the Athenians would celebrate the Great Dionysia, a drama festival that originally involved only the tragic poets, without the comedy later imported from the Lenaea. The Dionysia was a great celebration of Athens as a center of culture in the Greek world, and it revealed the higher inspiration of Dionysus in his civilized form.

Just as in the making of wine the two natures of Dionysus were reconciled, so too in the wine itself was the primordial deity still honored. To understand this incorporation of the pre-viticultural deity in wine, we must summarize evidence that I have presented more fully elsewhere.[4] The Greeks, as well as the Romans (Pliny *N. H.* 14.29), had the peculiar custom of diluting their wine with several parts of water before drinking it. Since they could not have fortified their wines with pure alcohol from distillation (a process not known until the alchemists discovered 'aqua vitae' around 1100 A.D.), the alcoholic content of

1. Satyrs are often confused or joined with Sileni, from whom they sometimes appear to have acquired equine characteristics, in addition to the goat-like nature that they share with Pan. All of these figures represent primitive spirits of the woodland. Like the centaurs, the Sileni were also inspired sources of knowledge and their leader was entrusted with the teaching of the child Dionysus in the wilderness of Nysa, just as Chiron was said to have educated heroes. The satyrs, on the other hand, share the centaurs' inclination toward the uninhibited satisfaction of libidinous drives, especially under the influence of wine.

2. Kerenyi, *Dionysos* 322.

3. Walter Burkert, Greek Tragedy and Sacrificial Ritual, *Greek, Roman, and Byzantine Studies*, 7 (1966) 92 ff. See also Kerenyi, *Dionysos* 333.

4. Wasson, Ruck, and Hofmann 89 ff.

their wines could have been derived only from natural fermentation, which is limited to about fourteen percent by the pickling effect of the alcohol itself upon the growing yeast which produces it as a by-product of the fungal activity upon the sugars of the juice. Greek wine, therefore, should have had only very mild intoxicating properties after the customary three- or fourfold dilution with water. Such, however, was not the case. We even hear of a wine that could stand eightfold dilution (Pliny, *H. N.* 14.53), an actual historical survival of a wine that in the mythical tradition required twenty parts of water (Homer, *Odyssey* 9.208-211) and was associated with the story of the Cyclops, a primitive one-eyed creature who figured in mystery traditions and Asiatic shamanism.[1] Undiluted wine was supposed to cause permanent brain damage. Nor should we assume that the Greeks diluted their wines so that they might safely drink excessive quantities, for just four 'little cups' of diluted wine are said to have been sufficient to induce a deep intoxication (Eubulus, fr. 94). The frequent depictions of revellers in art and literature, furthermore, should leave no doubt that the Greeks did indeed get drunk and that the purpose of drinking was, in fact, to become inebriated. Obviously, the alcoholic content of their diluted drink could not have been the sole cause.

As we have seen, the Greeks recapitulated the evolutionary history of Dionysus by incorporating the resinous taste of one of the god's pre-viticultural antecedents in their wine. It is only to be expected that they would also have assimilated other atavistic versions of the cultivated god into the fermented drink. Alcohol itself was unknown as a substance, and the affinity of the ferment to other intoxicants would have suggested itself by their similar effects upon the mind, although wine had the mark of civilization, as opposed to the wild, natural growths, and was gentler, for Dionysus had taught mankind how to tame it through dilution. Spices, unguents, and herbs were, in fact, added to Greek wines, either in the fermentation or at the ceremony of dilution before drinking. It is these additives that must account for the special inebriating properties of Greek wines, which in some cases were actually more hallucinogens than alcoholic intoxicants (Aristophanes, *Wasps* 12 ff., 213).

As sign of such an assimilation of wilder versions of the god, the quality of wine was referred to as its 'flower' or *anthos*, a metaphor that persists today,

1. The Cyclopes were apparently a Greek version of the fabulous people known as Arimaspeans, a name that designates them as Monophthalmoi or 'One-eyes' in Scythian. The Arimaspeans were involved in shamanic rites that were proselytized in Greece by the priest and poet Aristeas of Proconnesus. See E. R. Dodds, *The Greeks and the Irrational* (University of California, Berkeley 1951) 141.

without the same meaning, in our speaking of a wine's 'bouquet'. Dionysus himself was called the Flower God, Antheus and Euanthes, epithets that gave his name to the Anthesteria festival. The tradition of wine as a vinous potion persists in modern Greek, where the demotic word for wine is *krasi*, literally the 'mixture'.

THE MAD KING AND THE GOD

Pentheus, as the king of the pre-viticultural kingdom in the *Bacchae*, has a peculiar characteristic which perhaps we now can begin to understand. He is mad. Cadmus first notices it as Pentheus makes his entrance, rushing on stage to interrupt the old men's plan to join the mountain revel. He is 'all aflutter' or distraught with passion (ὡς ἐπτόηται 214), and throughout the play his violent emotions and stage presence are a visual contrast to the calm of the Asiatic deity of the vine. As the prophet Teiresias tells him, he is 'witless' (ἐν τοῖς λόγοισι δ' οὐκ ἔνεισί σοι φρένες 269), and his meaningless words have only the semblance of sense. At the close of their violent controversy, the seer sums it up: Pentheus is a babbling idiot (μῶρα γὰρ μῶρος λέγει 369); all along, he has been 'out of his mind' and now he has become 'raving mad' (ὡς οὐκ οἶσθα ποῦ ποτ' εἶ λόγων. μέμηνας ἤδη· καὶ πρὶν ἐξέστης φρενῶν 358-359).

In the context of the play, this madness is presented as a pre-viticultural state of mind. Whereas Pentheus is senseless, the mentality that wine induces, as Teiresias explains, is inspired with divine knowledge, a mania that underlies the appropriately so-called 'mantic' arts (τό γὰρ . . . μανιῶδες μαντικὴν πολλὴν ἔχει, 298-299), as well as the panic 'fear that sets an army aflutter' (φόβος διεπτόησε . . . μανία δὲ καὶ τοῦτ' ἐστὶ Διονύσου πάρα 304-305) and embraves them for the conflict, whereas Pentheus's bravura as the play develops will merely demonstrate his witless state. Wine, moreover, is the superlative anodyne, as we have already noted, whereas Pentheus is the 'Sufferer' and is so lacking in the mania of clairvoyance that he cannot even see what his name so clearly warns him will be his role in his intended conflict with Dionysus (367 ff.). 'You are mad in the most painful way', Teiresias tells him (μαίνῃ γὰρ ὡς ἄλγιστα 326).

Not only, however, does Pentheus have a mentality contrary to the effects of wine, but his pain is incurable and his suffering was apparently induced by ingesting some other 'drug' (κοὔτε φαρμάκοις ἄκη λάβοις ἄν οὔτ' ἄνευ τούτων νοσεῖς 326-327). It was traditional to believe that ill humour could be traced to a maddening drug,[1] but in this context there is certainly more than convention involved.

This ill-humoured opponent of the vine, moreover, has no less a botanic identity than the god. It is repeatedly mentioned in the drama that Pentheus is the son of the 'serpent man' Echion (213, 265, *etc.*), a creature 'sown' and 'harvested' (ὅς τὸ γηγενὲς δράκοντος ἔσπειρ' Ὄφεος ἐν γαίᾳ θέρος 1025-1026; ὅς τὸ Θηβαίων γένος ἔσπειρα κἀξήμησα κάλλιστον θέρος 1314-1315) from the primordial crop that Cadmus had planted in founding the city of Thebes. The seeds for that first sowing of the Theban plain were the fangs of the deadly serpent who was the previous inhabitant of the site for the city, and the crop that sprouted from them fought amongst themselves until only five remained, the so-called Sown Men or Spartoi, of whom Echion was one. Like his grandson Pentheus, the aboriginal serpent can be expected to have derived his ill temper from toxic plants, for it was by eating evil drugs that serpents were thought to acquire their grievous bile (Homer, *Iliad* 22.94; Vergil, *Aeneid* 2.741; Pliny, *N. H.* 22.95). Serpents also contaminated other plants by their presence. Thus mushrooms were said to suck up the venom of serpents in the ground beneath them (Nicander, *Alexipharmaca* 521-525), and only after serpents had gone into hibernation was it safe to gather them (Pliny, *N. H.* 22.95). By one account, Dionysus discovered wine when he noticed a serpent eating grapes and in accordance with a prophecy improvised the first wine press (Nonnus, *Dionysiaca* 12.293-362).[2] Snakes, moreover, resemble the trailing growth of the vine and ivy. Because of their cold-blooded nature, they had a particular affinity with the latter and were twined into the ivy wreaths of the maenads (Plutarch, *Alexander* 2.6), who tore them to pieces in their winter revels.[3]

The role of the serpent in pre-Indo-European religion is well attested by the so-called snake goddesses of the Minoan culture, where it probably figured, like the predatory bird and magical plants, as representative of the possessing chthonic spirit in shamanic rites of sacred marriage. The serpentine form of Echion associates him with the symbolism of the autochthonous dynasties at other Greek cities and with the earth-born creatures whom Zeus eventually subdued in establishing his Olympian realm. The myth of Cadmus's coming to Thebes, sowing the Spartoi, and betrothal of Pentheus's mother Agave to Echion is analogous to the traditions about the advent of viticul-

1. For references, see E. R. Dodds, *Euripides' Bacchae* (Oxford 1944, 1960²) 112.

2. The myth, although recorded in a late author, seems to preserve elements of a very ancient tradition. See Kerenyi *Dionysos*, 57-60.

3. *Ibid.* 60-62.

ture, involving a sacred marriage and mediation with toxic primitivism in the establishment of culture and civilization. Matrilocality and matrilineality, which are indicative of primordial times, have been replaced by Pentheus's patrilineality and patrilocality, and the successful evolution toward the Olympian age is symbolized by Cadmus's marriage to Harmonia, the offspring of Aphrodite and Ares, who was also the parent of the primordial serpent whom Cadmus destroyed. The success of this assimilation of cultures and transmutation of symbolic forms was indicated by the attendance of the Olympians themselves at the marriage feast of the city's founder.

It is perhaps significant, however, that Cadmus in the *Bacchae* is now old, and the rejuvenation that would have come with the acceptance of Dionysus's new rites of cultivation is denied him in the play. Instead, as we shall see, the city becomes unfounded and reverts to primitivism as the pre-Olympian nature of Pentheus asserts itself.

DOUBLE BIRTH AND THE GOD'S SURROGATE

In this pre-viticultural kingdom, Dionysus has not yet been assimilated, and thus the fundamental dualism of his nature is misunderstood by everyone except the Asiatic devotees, who have come with him from the lands that have already accepted his gift of wine. The essence of this dualism involves the mystery of his double birth, by which death becomes a gestation for regeneration and evolution. The chorus of Asiatic women describes how the infant was taken from the womb of his dead mother and washed in the Theban spring of the maenadic Dirce. Zeus then took him for his thigh, calling, 'Come, Dithyrambus, enter this male womb of mine' (Ἴθι, Διθύραμβ', ἐμὰν ἄρσενα τάνδε βᾶθι νηδύν 526-527), thus giving him the sacred name which the Greeks interpreted as meaning that Dionysus had come twice to the gates of birth.[1] It is by means of this second birth that Dionysus is assimilated into Indo-European traditions, and the Asiatic wine cult became incorporated into the civilized era over which Zeus reigns. The myth is paralleled in one of the oldest of the Vedic upanishads,

1. This derivation of Dithyrambus, although well attested in antiquity and obviously implied by this passage in the *Bacchae*, is apparently false. The name may be another non-Indo-European word assimilated into Greek and can be compared to a Phrygian word for the 'tomb', thus an epithet of Dionysus as the Lord of the Tomb. See Sir Arthur Pickard-Cambridge, *Dithyramb, Tragedy, and Comedy* (Oxford 1962, second edition revised by T. B. L. Webster) 7-9.

which states that the gods took Soma and put him into the right thigh of the supreme sky-god Indra.[1]

For the Thebans, however, only the primordial half of the dualism is accepted. Pentheus, like his mother and sisters (26 ff.), ridicules Dionysus's supposed Olympian birth. They all claim that Semele's infant perished in her womb, destroyed by the thunderbolt that was her punishment for lying about an imaginary affair with Zeus in order to cover her shame for an illicit pregnancy from a mortal (242 ff.). Even Teiresias does not understand the second birth, for although he stresses that Dionysus is indeed a god and the son of Zeus, he attempts to rationalize the mystery by explaining that Dionysus was actually born only once. It was simply a confusion of words that gave rise to the idea that he was sown into the 'thigh' (*meros*) of Zeus. Instead Zeus made an illusory double of the infant out of the layer of upper air and gave it as a 'surety' (*homeros*) to the care of his jealous wife as assurance of his future fidelity, while the real Dionysus was apparently entrusted to the nurture of others (286 ff.).[2] Teiresias's explanation, however, misses the point and deprives the god of his transmutation into his civilized aspect. Instead, Hera, like a primordial great goddess, tends her delusion and seems to dominate Zeus, and the real infant, who was born only once, has yet to evolve from primitivism, for the creatures to whom he was entrusted are traditionally the satyrs and maenadic nurses and brides of Nysa, the wild place of his youth, before the discovery of wine. Even Cadmus shares the Theban doubt about the mystery, but he urges that they at least appear to accept it, for it is a noble lie that will benefit the dynasty and his dead daughter's reputation (332 ff.).

It is by means of the second birth, however, that the god acquires his special role in alleviating the sufferings of mankind, while nourishing the spirit with the superior mania of inspiration. The death of his primitive self is the essential precedent for his evolution into Olympian times, and by being born both of the mother in the earth and of the heavenly father, he is the appropriate mediator between the Olympian gods and mortals, who, like him, experience the contamination of the chthonic realm.

Teiresias attempts to explain this role of mediator in mankind's sufferings as an act of sacrifice, whereby Dionysus, although a god, offers himself in libation to the other gods so that humans, through him, can experience the bless-

1. See Dodds, *Bacchae* 78.

2. Unfortunately a lacuna in the text appears to occur after line 293. Gilbert Murray suggests the indicated completion on the basis of the myth as recorded in Apollodorus 3.4.3.

ings of wine, its ability to end pain and cause sleep and forgetfulness of daily troubles (οὗτος θεοῖσι σπένδεται θεὸς γεγώς, ὥστε διὰ τοῦτον τἀγάθ' ἀνθρώπους ἔχειν 284-285). Dionysus is identical with the 'liquid potion of the clustered grape' which he 'discovered' (279), and it is only by sacrifice of himself that he can offer his gift of wine.

Just as Dionysus came twice to the gates of birth, his act of sacrifice, therefore, must bring him doubly into death, both in the abandonment of his own atavistic precedents and in the form of his cultivated self. As we have seen, such a double sacrifice was ritualized in the actual tending of the vine's harvest through its winter fermentation. It is the mystery of this sacrifice that the god will reveal to the doubting Thebans in the *Bacchae*. The play enacts the consecration of Pentheus via a repetition of the double birth as the god's surrogate, in whose person Dionysus must, as always, die in order to free himself from his darker antithesis and grant the blessings of madness through his gift of wine.

The musical accompaniment for the dancing of the choral women in the play is a constant reminder that the story does, in fact, enact this pattern of assimilation and sacrifice, for the instrument they play is the tympanum, whose connotations they identify at the beginning of the drama in their first dance, the parodos ode. There, they describe accurately and in detail the double birth of Dionysus and present it as analogous to the Cretan birth of Zeus himself, the event whereby the Indo-European god, in like manner, assimilated the preexistent male deity of Minoan religion (89 ff.). The sound of the tympanum indicates that the evolutionary rebirth is taking place and that Dionysus brings redemption from the primitivism of the kingdom where he was first born, for it was at the Cretan birth of Zeus that the ecstatic Corybantes invented the tympanum to cover the cries of the newly born infant, and the same drum was used in Corybantic rites to cure madness (Aristophanes, *Wasps* 119 *cum schol.*). There was also a tradition, of which Euripides was apparently aware (*Cyclops* 3), that the same sound cured Dionysus himself of a madness sent upon him by Hera in his primordial state.[1]

THE FIRST BIRTH

The first birth is from the earth. It will be marked by thunder and earthquake, and symbolized by the simultaneous burst of fire upon Semele's tomb, which from the beginning of the play has been seen still smoking from the time that

1. See Dodds, *Bacchae* 83-84.

Dionysus was wrenched from his mother's womb. It is this birth that will ratify Pentheus as the primitive aspect of the Dionysian duality.

Characteristic of that role, Pentheus is first introduced as a hunter, symbolic of the pre-agrarian gathering rites of the winter revels. It was as a hunter that Dionysus manifested himself then, as Zagreus, the 'one who catches his prey alive', a chthonic child of the queen in the otherworld. In these rites, Dionysus was both the hunter and the hunted, for the maenadic women sought the wild plants and animals whose spirit would possess them in ecstatic rapture.

Thus, when Pentheus first enters on stage, he announces that he intends to 'hunt' (228) the Theban maenads on the mountain. In the ensuing choral stasimon, the Asiatic devotees of the god identify the kingdom of such a mad and senseless hunter as a land that does not know the joyous and pain-relieving festivities of the Dionysian vine and they pray to return to their eastern homelands. The next episode begins with the presentation of Pentheus's captured prey (434 ff.), and Pentheus, as hunter, taunts Dionysus, whom he has 'netted' (451) alive, as an effeminate weakling who 'hunts' (459) only those same Aphrodisian joys that the Asiatics have just extolled.

As the two opponents size each other up for the coming conflict, their uncanny similarity begins to emerge, for Pentheus, as well as the disguised god, is a Dionysus. Thus the prophet, who actually was first born in Thebes, identifies Asia as his homeland, from which place he has brought the rites of Dionysus, the son of Zeus. When Pentheus facetiously asks if they have a Zeus there who makes new gods, Dionysus replies that it was here in Thebes that the union with Semele took place. The different appearances of the prophet and Pentheus also cannot distinguish between the two, for Pentheus seeks to know what the god looks like, only to find that Dionysus apparently can look like whatever he wishes (477). He is in fact standing right there, although Pentheus cannot see him, for Dionysus is sane, and the other mad (500 ff.). Just as Pentheus had begun the episode by inquiring into the mysterious prophet's identity, Dionysus now, in structural responsion as the scene closes, claims that Pentheus himself does not know his own identity, to which the mad king unwittingly demonstrates the truth by stupidly citing his chthonic lineage from Echion and his name, whose meaning as 'Sufferer' he clearly does not comprehend.

With the two thus joined by the uncanny opposition of their dissimilar temperaments, the play proceeds to enact the consecration of the Dionysian surrogate. The first stage is the confirmation of his earth-born nature by apparently simultaneous miracles within the palace and amongst the Theban women on the mountain.

The choral dance that introduces this episode contrasts the redeeming second birth of Dionysus with the mad earth-begetting of Pentheus. The Asiatic women describe how Zeus took the infant from the flaming lightning that had blasted Semele and then quenched the fire in the Theban spring of Dirce before receiving the embryonic child into his thigh to gestate for the second birth (519 ff.). Thebes, however, refuses the 'grape-clustered joy of Dionysus' wine-vine' (τὰν βοτρυώδη Διονύσου χάριν οἴνας 534-535), and, instead, Pentheus is demonstrating the madness we have already seen – Pentheus, of chthonic lineage and begot of a serpent, the offspring that earth-born Echion once planted, no mortal child, but a wild monster, a deadly earthy creature that is the god's antagonist (537 ff.). They pray to Dionysus to come, significantly, from Olympus to rescue them from this primitive madness, and the god complies, calling to them from within the palace, where the hunter had taken his prey. The god manifests himself as Bromius, the 'Thunderer'. He shatters the foundations of the building and sets the palace afire with lightning, while, as in his own first begetting, the tomb of Semele bursts into flames.

This event has the unmistakable indications of a birth from the earth. Like the sacred marriage of the queen at Athens to the primordial Dionysus, the place where the miracle is enacted is the bull stables of the royal palace, and the thundering earthquake traditionally marks the emergence of autochthonous creatures from the ground.[1] In the theater, it would have been staged to the striking of the 'thunder gong', the same instrument that in the Mystery at Eleusis announced the birth of the divine child Brimos from the nether realm in the midst of a blinding flash of light.[2]

At the beginning of the ensuing episode, Dionysus, still disguised as the prophet, emerges from the palace to detail what has happened within. The mad Pentheus, with deluded sight, mistook a bull in the stables for the prophet, whom he thought he was roping and confining. It was at this moment that the earthquake and the fire on Semele's tomb had occurred (622 ff.). Ironically, Pentheus thinks that the house itself has caught fire and he calls for his servants to quench the flames with the same water from the spring of Dirce that had doused the burning infant Dionysus. Then, thinking that the prophet had taken

1. Thus a bellowing, as of a bull, and a shaking of the ground occur when Medea cuts the magical root with which she will anoint Jason (Apollonius Rhodius 3.864-865). The same bellowing sound occurs when Perseus 'harvested' the Medusa's head (Eustathius, on Homer, *Iliad* 2.498). The autochthonous Erichthonius/Erectheus was named the 'bellower' (cf. *erechtho*, *orechtho*).

2. See Kerenyi, *Eleusis* 84. The instrument was called the *echeion*.

advantage of the confusion to escape, he rushed into the house, where he mistook a hallucination for the prophet and entered into combat with thin air. Through all of this, the prophet emphasizes that he himself maintained his calm composure (622, 636), while Pentheus vainly struggled and rushed about. It is also clear that for the prophet too the events within the palace were only the appearance of what they seemed (ὡς ἔμοιγε φαίνεται, δόξαν λέγω 629), but unlike Pentheus, he could correctly interpret what was happening as manifestations of Bromius, whom he identifies by the primordial epithets of Bacchus and Bacchius. When Pentheus finally emerges from the palace to find the prophet still quietly waiting for him, his first words are that he has 'suffered terribly' (πέπονθα δεινά, 642), the confirmation of the role that he is too mad to understand. In contrast, the prophet claims that he himself was freed from the suffering that Pentheus had intended to inflict upon him by the 'somebody . . . who makes grow the clustered vine' (649 ff.).

The chthonic birth had been sensed also on Cithaeron. The herdsman who has just returned from there tells how Pentheus's mother Agave had heard the bellowing of bulls and waked the other Theban women. There too, as in the bull stable of the palace, the connotations are of a primordial sacred marriage, for Euripides repeatedly describes the madness that has driven them to the mountain as the oestrual heat, the poisoning sting of the 'gadfly' or *oistros* (32, 119, 665, 1229) that inflames the womb, the organ, as it was thought, that made women in particular prone to hysteria and uncontrollable longings.[1] This association of the gadfly's sting with sexual madness is a traditional metaphor in Greek. In Apollonius Rhodius (3.276 ff.), Eros himself is likened to a gadfly amidst a herd of heifers as he enters a room filled with women and shoots Medea with an arrow whose poison, like a flame, drives her madly into love for Jason. The myth of the gadfly itself involves Zeus's affair with a primordial version of Hera in the person of Io, whom Hera transformed into a cow, like her own pre-Olympian self (Ovid, *Metamorphoses* 5.330) as indicated by her ancient epithet, Boopis, the 'Bovine', still retained on Olympus. The gadfly was supposedly the ghost of the 'all-seeing' (Panoptes) herdsman who tended the cow, goading it, as in Aeschylus's *Prometheus*, into ecstatic wanderings until a Zeus of the Olympian age calmed her madness with the touch of his hand, to beget the later race of heroes. The gadfly was also known by a name that apparently is the opposite of the primordial herdsman's epithet, for it was called

1. Bennett Simon, *Mind and Madness in Ancient Greece: The Classical Roots of Modern Psychiatry* (Cornell University Press, Ithaca 1978) 238 ff.

muops, the 'close-eyed', by which name it was identified with a plant (Pseudo-Plutarch, *de Fluviis* 22.5) said to grow in a river, that itself figured as another chthonic lover of a heifer-like maiden in the myth of Deianeira (Sophocles, *Trachiniae*).

The sexual nature of the women's madness is, of course, what Pentheus has all along suspected, but, as in the case of Semele, he has mistaken the spiritual aspect of the maenadic rapture. The numerous depictions of Dionysian revels in vase paintings can leave no doubt that the Greeks of Euripides' audience were well aware that the women cavorting on the mountains were indeed engaged in sexual experience, but that Pentheus was a fool to think that it could be seen, for the eroticism was metaphysical and the lovers spiritual. Thus on vases we see the women wakened by ithyphallic satyrs and romping with them, or dancing, often nude, before the thyrsos-bearing god, or presenting hares, symbolic of sexuality, as their catch in the hunt.

What the herdsman saw, as he tells Pentheus, was not the suspected drunken orgy, but a model of decorum. The maenads had fallen asleep in three groups, apparently exhausted from their ecstatic dancing. The trifold grouping was traditional,[1] and apparently corresponded to differences in their ages, 'the young, the old, and maidens still unwed' (694), each of which is led by one of the sisters of the dead Semele (681-682). Since children do not appear in depictions of maenads on vases, and indeed would be unlikely to have experienced the oestrual madness, the age distinctions must refer to their stages of female maturity, and the 'young' are mentioned as contrast to the 'old' and would include women well into the age of child-bearing,[2] as distinct from those beyond that stage of life. Presumably, the trifold grouping pertained to the generic roles enacted by the maenads as the god's 'brides' and 'nurses' and 'hunters'.

The regressive symbolism of these women, who have been goaded into the wilderness, away from their civilized task at the loom (118), is apparent in their clothing, for they are wearing the traditional maenadic attire of animal skins, girded with serpents, a form of dress that symbolically imbues them with the

1. Tripart grouping is associated with Theban maenadism. See Albert Henrichs, Greek Maenadism from Olympias to Messalina, *Harvard Studies in Classical Philology*, 82 (1978) 137-138.

2. Dodds, who follows Bruhn, interprets the grouping thus as only twofold: 'young and old – and unmarried girls among them', *Bacchae* 163. Maenads, of course, are depicted with the Dionysian child, but not with their own. The traditions, mentioned above, about maenads who ate their children during the revels probably are not to be understood literally, but in terms of ritual impersonations, with the child either the gathered Dionysian infant or, as in the scene described by the herdsman, the wild animals and serpents that the women 'mothered' before rending limb from limb for the ritual raw meal.

animal's spirit. In this bestial transformation, they were seen cuddling animals like children or actually suckling them, apparently having abandoned in the city their own newly born babies (702).

They have evidently been gathering wild plants, for they crown themselves with wreaths of ivy, *smilax* or 'bryony', and leaves of oak (702-703). The latter two plants, like the ivy, have regressive symbolism. *Smilax* is an evergreen creeper that resembles ivy, with clusters of scarlet grape-like berries, which are said to be similar to the fruit of plants called the 'wild grape' and the 'wild vine', as well as nightshade (Theophrastus, *H. P.* 3.18.11). Like ivy, it was a wild plant, not cultivated, and thought to be parasitic, clinging even more than ivy to its host (*ibid.* 7.8.1). It was a common substitute for ivy in maenadic rites, but in some way deficient (Pliny, *N. H.* 16.155), probably because it lacked ivy's reputed effect upon the mind. The oak had similar connotations of primitivism. It was associated with a primordial Zeus, whose sacred grove at Dodona was tended by a barefooted priesthood of prophets who slept upon the ground (Homer, *Iliad* 16.233). Before the arts of agriculture evolved, mankind was supposed to have fed upon acorns, the fruit of this sacred grove (Vergil, *Georgics* 1.147-149). Acorns were also thought to be the ancient food of the Pelasgian, pre-Indo-European people of Arcadia (Adespota, fr. 67 Page; Herodotus 1.67; Hippolytus, *Refutatio Omnium Haeresium* 5.17), and the homilitic phrase, 'to be born from the legendary oak or stone' (Homer, *Odyssey* 19.163 *cum schol.*; Plato, *Apology* 34d, *Republic* 544d), seems to have implied primordial origin in pre-civilized times.

What the herdsman next saw was an apotheosis of the pre-agricultural age, a reversion to the fabled Golden Age, when the earth yielded up nourishment without mankind's toil of cultivation. Someone struck the rock with her *thyrsos*, and water flowed from the ground. Another placed the *narthex* upon the earth, and the god sent up a natural spring of 'wine', while others scratched the ground and found 'milk'. After the miraculous appearance of these three natural springs, the *thyrsoi* themselves are transfigured, with streams of honey dripping from the leaves of ivy. Thus it was in primitive times, as Vergil claims, before the streams of wine were stopped and the honey shaken from the leaves, so that mankind henceforth would have to work for his livelihood (*Georgics* 131 ff.).

The central role of the *thyrsos/narthex* in this apotheosis suggests, as one would expect, that the women in this wild place are gathering foods, instead of tending crops or herds. In the context of this play, where the gift of Dionysus is consistently designated by phrases descriptive of the clustered grape that is fruit of the tended vine, it is significant that here it is simply 'wine' that flows naturally from the earth, without the need of fermentation. *Oinos*, in fact, can be generic in Greek for any intoxicant. Thus Herodotus, for example, can speak of beer as a 'wine made from barley', as distinguished from 'vine wine' (2.77). 'Milk' too is easily metaphoric and can designate the milky sap of plants (Theophrastus, *H. P.* 6.3.4), or even wine, as the 'milk of Aphrodite' (Aristophanes, fr. 596). It is perhaps also significant that Euripides, in this description of the women's activity, speaks of 'swarms of milk' (γάλατος ἑσμοὺς 710), a strange metaphor,[1] suggestive of bees, as if what the women actually were doing was gathering the essence of flowers. Bees, moreover, have a special significance in this ethnobotanic context, for, like the gadfly, they are stinging insects and therefore poisonous, but they seem to be able to transform the poisons, which they must have derived from flowers, into honey, a nourishment akin to serpent's venom, but sweet and non-toxic.[2] Thus, in this Golden Age, even the poisonous ivy leaves gathered into the *thyrsos* yield honey. Honey, moreover, seems to have been associated with the Minoan predecessor of the viticultural Dionysus, and it is related to the common word in Greek for 'intoxicate', probably indicating the role of mead as a precedent for wine.[3]

In Pentheus's kingdom, however, the blessed age of primitivism is not allowed to express itself as a function of evolution, and thus, instead of renewing civilization, it pollutes and destroys it. The women, after the gathering ceremony, had entered into the maenadic madness, calling upon Dionysus with his mystery name as the chthonic Iacchus and as Bromius, the 'Thunderer', and the whole mountain, thereupon, had become transformed, together with its beasts, into constant motion. This is the blessed madness that the Asiatic maenads had extolled at the conclusion of their parados dance (135-169). There, they had described the god's epiphany amongst them, in the midst of the primal land flowing with milk and wine and honey, as Bromius, leading the hunt for the goat to be eaten raw and possessing their leader with a shamanic frenzy. When the repressive Pentheus intrudes upon the idyllic scene through the presence of his spying herdsmen, it is clear, to all but him, that the corollary of the blessing is the danger of dishonored primitivism, and that he and his kingdom will have a role as the tragic surrogate. When the herdsmen decide to 'hunt' (719) the maenads to please their master, they discover that there is another

1. Dodds, following Elmsley, calls the metaphor absurd and derives ἑσμός from ἵημι (instead of ἕζομαι) so that the phrase means 'springing jets' of milk: *Bacchae* 164. Thus also Liddell, Scott/Jones. In compounds, however, the word has connotations of bees and I suspect that a melissaean metaphor is appropriate to this context.

2. See Ruck, *Sacred Names*.

3. Kerenyi, *Dionysos* 36.

leader for the chase, and the women, like hounds (731), attack the hunters, using their *thyrsoi* as weapons.

Instead of the miraculous age that predated civilization, this same primordial time now is maddened to vengeance against the later agrarian age. The herdsmen themselves barely escape dismemberment, and the women fall upon their cattle instead, brutally rending them limb from limb with their hands. Then, like predatory birds, they swoop down upon the Theban farming villages beneath them, plundering and destroying them like enemies and kidnapping children, until finally they return to the miraculous springs on the mountain to cleanse their bodies of the blood.

The cultivated vine with its ferment of wine is the symbol of the world restored to balanced accord with its primitive origins, and for it to exist, its enemy must be destroyed. The primordial god must yield to Dionysus, the son of Zeus. Now that Pentheus has been ratified in his chthonic birth, both by the events within the palace and the twofold manifestation upon the mountain, the episode concludes with the presentation of Pentheus, confirmed in his coming role as victim. Once more, the dual aspects of the god are divided between him and his surrogate. Pentheus cannot, as he says, endure to 'suffer what he suffers' at the hands of women (786). Clearly, he is the sufferer, even though he had tried to make the other 'suffer' (788). In temperament, his every action demonstrates that he is the passionate one, despite the prophet's advice to calm himself (790). He is the prey for whom the net is cast (848), and the senseless confusion of his thinking is more than ever apparent. He will take pleasure in his pain (814-815). To avoid being detected in going to the mountain in stealth, he will instead go openly (816-817). And as final proof of their inverted roles, Pentheus, who had derided the prophet's effeminacy, will put on the female attire of a maenad, a stratagem that demonstrates, as Pentheus now admits, that the prophet inspired by Dionysus has been the sensible one all along (824-825). The last words of the prophet as the episode closes foretell the victim's death, which will show that the terrible god born of Zeus is most gentle to mankind.

THE SECOND BIRTH

When we next see the two, they both have a different appearance. The god no longer disguises himself as his own prophet, but he has assumed the taurine manifestation that came into being at the chthonic birth, while the passionate Pentheus is now calm, dressed in the effeminate attire that he had despised in the prophet and the maenadic Cadmus and Teiresias. From now until the completion of the sacrifice, the world apparently appears double, with two suns and two cities of Thebes.

On the mountain, Pentheus will experience the final consecration for his tragic role. Like the god himself, the primordial chthonic being will be entrusted to the celestial realm before being offered as the Dionysian victim, confirmed in his total dual identity by a second birth that mediates the schism between earth and sky, primitivism and cultivation.

The messenger who returns from the revel describes this second 'miracle' (1063). Apparently gesturing as he speaks to emphasize the symbolic nature of the event as a mediation, he says that the foreign prophet took the 'celestial, topmost branch of a pine tree and brought it, brought it, brought it down to the black earth. It curved like a bow, or like the circumference traced on a rounded wheel as it is inscribed by a compass. That's how the foreigner brought that mountain branch in his two hands and bent it to the ground, an act that no mortal could have done' (1064-1069). Then Pentheus sat on the pine bough, and the stranger let it go straight up. 'Straight up into the high up air it stood fast' (ὀρθὴ δ' ἐς ὀρθὸν αἰθέρ' ἐστηρίζεται 1073), an image again emphasized by gesture and repeated phrase.

When he is seen there by the maenads, the prophet disappears and a voice, 'apparently' (ὡς μὲν εἰκάσαι 1078) that of Dionysus himself, calls to them from the upper air, where, of course, Pentheus now is, announcing that the victim is at hand. At this moment, the lightning flash that had marked the first birth is repeated, and the earth and heavens are joined, transfixed by a light of holy fire (καὶ πρὸς οὐρανὸν καὶ γαῖαν ἐστήριξε φῶς σεμνοῦ πυρός, 1882-1883).

THE PARADIGM OF ACTAEON

The death of Pentheus at the hands of the maenads involves the metaphor of the inverted hunt, in which the hunter is mistaken for the beast of prey by the pack of hounds, who revert from the domesticated state to the wild and turn upon their master. It is a story told also about Actaeon, a cousin of Pentheus, and Euripides apparently considered Actaeon's fate as paradigmatic of Pentheus's death in the *Bacchae*, for he mentions Actaeon several times (230, 337, 1227) and specifies that the dismemberment of Pentheus occurred in exactly the same place on Cithaeron where the dogs had earlier torn Actaeon to pieces (οὗπερ πρὶν 'Ακτέωνα διέλαχον κύνες, 1291). Actaeon was the son of Autonoe

(230, 681) and Aristaeus, a son of Cyrene and Apollo who was associated with advances in horticulture, namely the tending of bees and the making of cheese and the hybridizing of cultivated olives from oleasters. Aristaeus also had a more sinister aspect, for he was responsible for Eurydice's abduction to Hades, and it is apparently this regressionary trait that surfaced also in the figure of his son. In the earliest accounts, Actaeon incurred his death by rivaling Zeus as suitor of Semele (Stesichorus, fr. 68; Acusilaos, fr. 33 Jacoby), and hence as a potential mortal sire for the Dionysian child. In terms of the *Bacchae*, we may surmise that it was someone like Actaeon who had the illicit affair with Semele that Pentheus and his aunts suspect. It is appropriate, therefore, that both Pentheus and he should meet the same end, since both represent regressionary primitivism with regard to the transmutation and evolution of Dionysus into Olympian times.

Traditionally, such regression is effected by Lyssa, a goddess of madness whose name means literally 'rabies'. Lyssa is a feminine formation of the word for 'wolf' (*lykos*), and the goddess represents the rabid madness that converts the domestic dog into its wild avatar, the wolf. A fifth-century vase from Attica in the collection of the Boston Museum of Fine Arts actually depicts Lyssa as a woman with a wolf's head as she maddens Actaeon's hounds against him, while Zeus and Artemis look on.[1] It may be that such a costume was traditional for Lyssa. Euripides used her as a character in his *Heracles* tragedy, where her lupine symbolism is an integral part of the plot. In that play, she maddens the hero into slaughtering his own wife and children, whom he had intended to rescue from the same fate at the hands of the 'wolf' Lykos, a primordial king of Thebes. Instead, he does what the 'wolf' intended, because Lyssa leads a pack of hounds against him (860, 898) and drives him into rabidity, infected with the primitive poisons of the monstruous beasts he had himself once hunted. The most recent of these conquests in the play is the netherworld's dog Cerberus and the poison of its rabid foam (Pliny, *N. H.* 27.22), aconite, which significantly for the pattern of the tragedy was called 'wolf-bane'.[2]

In the *Xantriae*, Aeschylus had also brought Lyssa on the stage as a character, inspiring the Theban maenads into madness against Pentheus (fr. 169), but in the *Bacchae*, Euripides seems to have intended Pentheus himself to be in some sense a Lyssa. Thus the prophet, as he prepares to dress Pentheus in female attire, prays to Dionysus to knock Pentheus out of his senses and insert a 'giddy

1. Simon, plate p. 132.
2. Carl A. P. Ruck, Duality and the Madness of Herakles, *Arethusa*, 9 (1) (1976) 53-75.

Lyssa' (ἐλαφρὰν λύσσαν, 851), explaining that otherwise Pentheus will not accept his new costume. While he is off-stage dressing as a maenad, the choral women imagine the joy of the mountain revel, comparing themselves to a fleeing fawn that escapes the hunter's pack of hounds, and they approve of the good sense that the god displays in hunting down his impious enemy (862 ff.). Their own joy in escaping the hunter is apparently the reciprocal complement to the fate warranted by the lawless, mad prey that the god hunts. After the ensuing episode, in which Pentheus is presented in his maenadic costume, they too identify this female attire as indicative of Pentheus's Lyssa-like appearance (ἐν γυναικομίμῳ στολᾷ λυσσώδη κατάσκοπον, 980-981), and they summon Lyssa's hounds to rouse the Theban women on the mountain in oestrual madness against this senseless, chthonic creature, while they imagine themselves rejoicing as they join in the hunt, led now by Justice herself and the god.

Since, as we have seen, Pentheus has the temperament of a poisonous herb and apparently, in his maenadic dress, is actually the rabid goddess of madness, his presence in the revel maddens his mother's pack of hounds (cf. 731) and they mistake him for the prey of the hunt. In view of the botanical ramifications of his identity, it is perhaps significant that the Theban women capture him as though he were a plant, uprooting the entire pine tree, which is itself a primordial version of Dionysus. There may be similar botanic implications in their use of the *thyrsos* as a weapon (733, 1099).

The lupine and serpentine connotations of Pentheus's identity mark him both as the enemy intruding upon the Golden Age and as the primitivism that cultivation must overcome, for the end of the Golden Age was issued in when serpents acquired their deadly poisons and the wolves began to plunder (Vergil, *Georgics* 1.129-130).

THE REGRESSION OF CADMEAN THEBES

The *Bacchae* concludes with a curious prophecy delivered by Dionysus. Cadmus and his wife Harmonia will be transformed into serpents and ride away in a carriage or chariot drawn by calves. Cadmus will become the leader of a barbarian host, presumably the Encheleis or 'Eel-people' of northern Epirus, amongst whom in historical times the earlier sovereignty of Cadmus was commemorated by the carrying of serpent ornaments as standards, in the same manner as the similar ornaments of the supposedly autochthonous Erechtheid lineage at Athens. With these people, Cadmus will eventually attack many cities, until finally he will be defeated in an assault upon Apollo's oracular sanctuary at Delphi. There at last, his barbaric horde will be routed and he and Harmonia alone will be rescued and transported to the Islands of the Blest by Ares, the god of war, who was Harmonia's father (1330 ff., 1352 ff.). In actual fact, such an oracle was current at the time of the Persian Wars, when Mardonius used it to justify his attack on Delphi, although it was well known that its true reference was to the Illyrians and the Encheleis (Herodotus 9.42 ff.).

In its context in the *Bacchae*, the prophecy is final proof of Dionysus's now vindicated Olympian lineage, for, as he says, he knows these things from no mortal father, but from Zeus (1340-1344, 1349). The corollary of that ascendancy is the destruction of his darker self in the victory he has just enacted over Pentheus. The fall of Pentheus and his pre-viticultural kingdom entails the demise of the entire civilization that Cadmus once had founded at Thebes, and the city, according to the prophecy, must now revert to its primitive state.

The fall of the house of Cadmus had been dramatized in the earthquake that shook the palace, and it was announced explicitly at the beginning of the messenger's account of the death of Pentheus. Cadmus, as the messenger says, was the one 'who sowed the earth-born harvest of the serpent snake in the land' (1025-1026). The failure of that primordial cultivation is lamented by Cadmus himself at the end of the play. He will be cast out of his house, 'he, Cadmus the Great, who sowed and reaped that superb harvest, the race of Thebans' (1314-1315). He and Teiresias had set out for the mountain revel at the beginning of the drama as two old men in hope of rejuvenation (187-188, 190), but now he returns from there unfulfilled, reproached by Agave for what she perceives as the ill temper of old age (1251 ff.), and bearing the mangled pieces of the young man (1218 ff.) who had inherited the culture he had once founded and who should have been his protection from the indignities of time (1303 ff.).

The founding of Thebes involved the mediation of indigenous and immigrant peoples, together with their dichotomous religious systems. Thus Cadmus, like another Apollo, whose directions he was following, destroyed the primordial serpent at Thebes and then planted its fangs, the so-called dragon's teeth, in the ground, from which grew the first crop of autochthonous creatures. To one, he gave his daughter Agave, thus mingling the blood lines and establishing the Indo-European traditions of patrilineality and patrilocality. Still another daughter brought an Olympian connection and the potential for dominance over the transmuted toxins of the earth. The success of Cadmus's foundation, as we have seen, was symbolized by his own patrilocal marriage to an Olympian female, Harmonia, whose name indicates the harmony between the realms, that was symbolized also by the attendance of the Olympians themselves at her marriage feast at Thebes. Since Harmonia was a half-sister to the primordial serpent (Sophocles, *Antigone* 126 *cum schol.*), she functions as an Olympian replacement for the autochthonous female originally associated with the serpent's spring.

A similar mediation can be seen in Apollo's victory over the serpent at Delphi. By destroying the serpent, Apollo established Olympian dominance over the sanctuary, that earlier had belonged to chthonic forces. It is ironic that Cadmus and Harmonia, as indication of their regression from Olympian harmony, will become 'dragon and dragonness' (1358) at the head of a host of serpentine 'Eel-people' and will finally themselves be routed in their attack upon this same Delphic sanctuary.

Their cow-drawn cart is similarly indicative of the reversion to the prefoundational condition, for Cadmus had been advised at the Delphic shrine to follow a cow into Boeotia, the land that would be named after it, and to found a city on the site where it lay down. He was descended from a line that twice had experienced a union with Zeus that involved taurine symbolism and migratory wanderings, first with Io, and again four generations later with Europa, the sister whom Cadmus was seeking when Apollo directed him into Boeotia. In the *Bacchae*, a taurine Dionysus has disrupted the city by sending its women rutting on the mountain, and again wandering cows will lead the Cadmean dynasty away from settled life.

At Thebes, the royal lineage will pass to the house of Oedipus, whose founder Labdacus was supposedly related to Cadmus via the latter's only son, Polydorus, a shadowy figure whose name as the 'one of many gifts' suggests chthonic associations with Hades and Plutus or 'wealth'. Labdacus is clearly a repetition of Cadmus, for Cadmus, as civilizer, was supposed to have introduced the Phoenician alphabet to Thebes, an event that also involves Labdacus, since another name for Cadmus's son was Pinakos, the 'writing tablet', and Labdacus seems to be named for *lambda*, the letter that follows the initial letter of Cadmus's name.[1] While Labdacus's son Laius is in his minority, the kingship will be exercised by the sinister ancestor and namesake of Heracles' opponent, the wolfish Lykos, like Pentheus, a son of one of the original Spartoi, Chthonius, a 'man of the earth'. His wife will be the maenadic Dirce, a woman associated with the Theban spring. Only after his death is Thebes again founded, this time by the

1. Kerenyi, *The Heroes of the Greeks* (Thames and Hudson, London 1959, translated from the German) 88. Since I follow Kerenyi's interpretation of the traditions about Cadmus, I have not cited original sources, which are documented in *Heroes of the Greeks*.

dissimilar brothers who were his nephews, Amphion and Zethus, the latter of whom married the Theban spring that gave the city its new name of Thebes.

Under Laius, the city will again suffer from the failure to mediate with the chthonic realm. He himself is supposed to have incurred a curse upon his house by the abduction of Chrysippus, an homoerotic affair that demonstrates his disregard for the fertile power of the earth, which in outrage will eventually manifest itself in the predations of the maenadic Sphinx, again on Cithaeron. His son Oedipus, at whose hands he will die, will have been inadvertently begotten in drunkenness upon a descendant of the serpentine Echion, and although he will at first rescue the city from the mountain madness, the sinister implications of his conception, against the advice of Apollo, and of his exposure to the mountain wilderness in his infancy, as well as his nurture by the wife of the cattle-tending Polybus, will eventually surface, uncovering his darker, pre-Olympian identity as the consort in the queen's matrilineal and matrilocal kingdom.[1] The city will return to fertility only when the pollution of this darker identity is recognized, in compensation for the previous, mistaken disregard of the Labdacids for chthonic primitivism. While the sons of Oedipus quarrel for control of the city in the great battle at the seven gates, a battle that pitched descendants of the autochthonous Spartoi against a host of foreign immigrants, the city will again be saved by an attempted mediation with the spirit of the slain primordial serpent, by offering a sacrifice of the last unwed descendant of the crop that Cadmus planted, so that the earth might take back a harvest for its harvest and mortal blood for its blood (Euripides, *Phoenician Women* 931 ff.). Even that pacification, however, will prove unstable, for the new regent, again the brother of the great queen, will demonstrate his lack of accord with the chthonic realm upon which his city rests, by burying the living and unburying the dead. And even in the next generation, the sons of the seven who came against Thebes will repeat their fathers' war.

This summary of the familiar mythical traditions about Thebes cannot, of course, do justice to the complexity of the subject, but is intended as an outline of what could be documented by a fuller analysis of the way Thebes figures in

1. Kerenyi, *Heroes* 88 ff. The Oedipean duality is indicated, as is common in the traditions about heroes, by the riddle of his own name. The pre-Olympian aspect of his identity has him gathered in the wilderness like a Dionysian child, a creature like a plant with a single foot. In Sophocles' *Oedipus*, he discovers his Dionysian primitivism vis-à-vis Apollo, whose Olympian nature is confirmed when Oedipus, like another Pentheus, becomes the polluted scapegoat.

tragic literature. As the city where Dionysus was born and initially rejected, Thebes was an important theme for Athenian tragedians. The story of Pentheus deserves to be viewed within the context of the entire body of Theban traditions, which seem to present the city as repeatedly unstable in its foundation because of a basic failure to maintain accord with the fertile sources of primitivism.

In the metamorphosis of Cadmus into a serpent, we can probably sense the regression of the supposed foreigner, the great civilizer and founder of an Olympian realm, to his own more primitive identity as an autochthonous chthonic figure, the form in which he was known in the mysteries of the Kabeiroi at Thebes and elsewhere. Thus Cadmus was said to be a son of a native, primal man, Ogygos, the child of Earth (Pausanias 9.5.1), in which case, the foreign realm from which he came was distant from Thebes only in the vertical plane, and the serpent whom he killed was his own primitive nature. In a similar way, the foreigner Medea was also aboriginal at Corinth. In the mysteries, Cadmus was apparently the father of a divine child, called Cadmilus or 'little Cadmus', another Hermes and, like him, represented by an ithyphallic herm. The foreign 'Eel-people' over whom Cadmus will rule suggest his own more primitive kingship over the eels of the lake in his native Boeotia, and the complex traditions about his journeys toward Thebes involve the story of his own taurine abduction of a bovine Harmonia, who was actually his sister, a Persephone-like figure who was mourned by the mother, in whose company Cadmus and his brothers were said to have wandered, searching for her at the ends of the earth.[1]

FROM POLLUTION TO FERTILITY

The *Bacchae*, as the work of an Athenian poet, presents a typically Athenian bias toward Thebes and Dionysian symbolism. Athens is a stable and eternal city, in the divine keeping of Athena, a primordial mother goddess, reborn as a virgin daughter of Zeus and successfully transmuted into the primarily masculine orientation of Olympian times.[2] Thus, for example, she wears male attire and was said to have helped the various sons of Zeus in conquering primitivism, including manifestations of her own primordial identity. Unlike Thebes, the traditions about Athens' autochthonous dynasties demonstrate that the city has successfully mediated the dichotomy of primitivism and culture.[3] In actual fact,

1. Kerenyi, *Heroes* 25-33.
2. Lyster.
3. John Peradotto, Oedipus and Erichthonius: Some Observations on Paradigmatic and Syntagmatic Order, *Arethusa*, 10 (1) (Spring 1977) 85-101.

the incorporation of rural Dionysian celebrations into the city's calendar of religious observances under the populist tyrant Peisistratus is living proof, enacted again each year, of Athens' acceptance of Dionysus. By the time of Euripides, the festivals of drama had become an important indication of the city's cultured life and a demonstration that the elsewhere dangerous god was a son of Zeus at Athens and a founder of civilization.

Typically, the regressive tendencies of Thebes cannot be solved there, but, in the Athenian view, can only be pacified through the intermediary of Athens, which, with its more stable foundation, will be able to provide the appropriate mediation to incorporate the rejected Theban primitivism into its own grand alliance of beneficent atavistic powers that sustain the civilized city. Thus, at the end of the *Heracles*, the former Olympian hero, polluted with the wolf-man's madness, is offered a tomb in Athens, to replace the altar to his father Zeus that at the beginning of the play had supposedly indicated his Olympian identity and his successful rout of the primitive forces threatening Thebes. In offering the tomb, Theseus, one of the mythical founders of Athens, is enacting the brighter version of his name as the 'placer', as opposed to his more sinister aspect as the one whose identity was indicated by the tokens 'placed' beneath the stone at Troezen, the city where he too was conceived, against the advice of Apollo, in irrational drunkenness. Ironically, Theseus in the *Heracles* had just been freed himself from the stone that had merged with his backside in Persephone's realm, and thus his entombment of the fallen Heracles is the counterpoise to his own ascendency, and the stone tomb in Athens supplants the stone of the now meaningless altar in Thebes.

As in the case of Heracles, there were also traditions about the reversion of Theseus to a darker persona. Thus it was sometimes claimed that he never returned from Persephone's realm, or that he died away from his native land in a controversy with a wolf-man named Lykomedes, while the kingship at Athens was regained for a time by the autochthonous dynasty. In a curious historical enactment of the basic mythical idea, here too the value of primitivism was recognized and reincorporated into Athenian traditions. What were supposed to be the bones of Theseus were recovered and returned to Athens for burial in 473 B.C., after his spirit had appeared to many in the recent battle against the Persians at Marathon (Plutarch, *Theseus* 35-36).

The burial of pollution at Athens is, in fact, the common theme of Theseus as the mythical Athenian king. In Sophocles' *Oedipus at Colonus*, another contaminated hero from Thebes is buried by Theseus at Athens. He enters into a covenant with Oedipus, whose rotting old body will be placed in Athenian land in the grove of the Eumenides, an alliance with the netherworld that will be an additional source of fertility and eternal stability amidst the vicissitudes of time, while the controversies at Thebes continue to rage in the warring of Oedipus's sons. Theseus also champions the cause of burying what Thebes refuses to place into its own ground in Euripides' *Suppliants*, where he espouses the supplication of the mothers of the Seven who fell in the war at the gates of Thebes, and retrieves their bodies for interment at Eleusis, thus again striking an alliance that will fortify his own city. His son Demophon, in Euripides' *Sons of Heracles*, will similarly strengthen Athens by providing burial even for Eurystheus, the archenemy and sinister double of Heracles who was defeated in a battle at Marathon. The theme can be noted even in Euripides' *Hippolytus*, where Theseus is reconciled with his own chthonic aspect in the person of his damned bastard son whom he mistakenly suspected of a Persephone-like abduction. Hippolytus too will be buried at Athens and incorporated into the city's religious foundations.

These burials at Athens demonstrate the same reconciliation with primitivism that we have already noted with regard to the conversion of the Erinyes into the beneficent Eumenides. These daughters of Night and sisters of Lyssa, who track down the prey they madden with wild delusions and contaminate with their excremental nature, could pollute the land with a 'lichenous' (λιχὴν, 785) plague of fungal-like parasitic sterility, until Athena in Aeschylus's *Eumenides*, caring for her city like a gardener (911), cajoles them into friendship by burying them in the earth, where their rotting poisons can function, not atavistically, but as a source of fertile growth for the Olympian institutions of the cultivated city.

The agrarian significance of such an incorporation of pestilential putrefaction as a benefit to the city was actually ritualized in Athens at the Skira and Thesmophoria festivals. Sacrificial pigs, animals akin to the netherworld deities, probably because of the characteristically obnoxious smell of their excrement, were tossed into subterranean caverns and allowed to rot, and, four months later, their putrefied remains were exhumed and spread upon the fields as fertilizer.[1]

Beyond the theme of actual burial at Athens, we can trace the similar theme of the reintegration of pollution into society in a number of other tragedies. In Sophocles' *Philoctetes*, the diseased and fit-prone hero is induced to abandon his exile and bring the contamination of his poisoned body and envenomed arrows to Troy, where his presence will allow his fellow Greeks at last to take the

1. H. W. Parke, *Festivals of the Athenians* (Cornell, Ithaca 1977) 159-160.

citadel. Reintegration seems also to have been essential to the theme of Sophocles' *Ajax*. Here too, the hero, who has regressed to a pre-Olympian identity, is finally reconciled with his enemies. Denied the inheritance of Achilles' armour, Ajax becomes a maddened cattle thief, and although he was supposedly named for the *aietos* or 'eagle' of Zeus, his darker persona will surface, the primordial Ajax, named for *Aia* or 'Earth' and the lamentation (*aiai*) of his tragic fate. Once he is dead, however, Odysseus, the new bearer of Achilles' armour and the particular enemy of Ajax, will side with the hero's surviving brother and convince the Atreidae to allow him burial.

In the context, therefore, of similar tragedies on the theme of primitivism and culture, the *Bacchae* is somewhat unique in not expressly enacting the reconciliation and reintegration. Although the chorus of Asiatic devotees joyously welcomes the deluded Agave as a fellow member of their revel band (1172), she will vow never to be a bacchant again as she goes into exile from her native Thebes (1384 ff.). A lacuna in the text of the *Bacchae* before the final prophecy of Dionysus obliterates a section of the play, that can, however be reconstructed from other sources.[1] The body of Pentheus was apparently reassembled onstage and prepared with lamentation for burial, but the truer reconciliation is probably the condemnation of the regressive Thebes and the vindication of the viticultural aspect of the god, who, as is implicit in the performance of the play at a Dionysian festival, has been integrated into the religion of another, more cultivated city.

TOWARD AN UNDERSTANDING OF TRAGEDY

Sometime in the early history of the drama festivals at Athens, it apparently became a stock criticism of a particular play that it had 'nothing to do with Dionysus'.[2] The phrase would seem to imply that a good tragedy was expected to concern itself with Dionysian themes, although the *Bacchae* is the only extant tragedy actually about Dionysus, and only a few of the lost plays appear to have been written on the actual subject of Semele, the bacchants, or the god's traditional enemies. The satyr plays and the comedies that were also part of the festivals could more easily maintain a Dionysian relevance, if for no other reason than their obvious phallic exuberance, but actually, given the great number of tragedies included at each performance, it is difficult to see how constant,

1. See Dodds, *Bacchae* 234-235. 2. Pickard-Cambridge 124-126.

simple repetition of the Dionysus myth would not have become unbearably tedious. The demand for Dionysian relevance in the tragedies must be understood as indicating something less literal than continuous reiteration of the god's myth. We have already seen that Dionysian themes can underlie the telling of apparently quite unrelated myths, and this argument could be expanded to encompass all the extant tragedies, if we were to consider themes other than the one germane to our discussion of the *Bacchae*. As conclusion, however, I should like to place the experience of ancient drama in its Dionysian context in order to demonstrate its relevance to the god as a religious celebration, since this too is an enactment of the transmutation of primitivism to culture.

Drama itself was a kind of madness. Actors are frequently portrayed in vase paintings and terra-cotta figurines contemplating the mask of the character they will impersonate on the stage. It is a commonly observed phenomenon that actors become quite literally obsessed by the personae of their roles, and ancient actors, in particular, by wearing the masks of the mythical figures they impersonated, can be expected to have experienced a kind of possession by the spirit of these dead heroes who returned, in the dramas, from the past. One of the early occasions for drama was, in fact, the performance of a hero's story at his tomb,[1] and in Athens, the earliest masking techniques of Thespis, the first tragic poet, suggest that the performers were intended to represent spirits of primordial times. Thespis disguised their faces with gypsum (Plutarch, *de Proverbiis Alexandrinorum* 30) or white lead (Suidas, *s. v.* Thespis), apparently to imitate the bloodless color of ghosts.[2] A similar disguise was associated with the primordial Titans who were said to have slaughtered and cooked the infant Dionysus (*Orphica Fragmenta* 209 Kern) in a regressive manner, contrary to the evolution of the culinary arts. Thespis apparently also used wine lees (*Anthologia Graeca*, Dioscorides, 7.411; Horace, *Ars Poetica* 275-277), the unfermented residue from the god's harvest as the grape. Perhaps even more significant was his use of wreaths of strawberry-tree (Suidas, *loc. cit.*), supposedly a primitive food of the Golden Age (Vergil, *Georgics* 147-149) and a fruit that today is used, as in the ancient manner, to fortify wine in some regions of Greece.[3] The aged Athenian lawgiver Solon was said to have disapproved of Thespis's performances of tragedy as a lie (Plutarch, *Solon* 29; Diogenes Laertius 1.59), perhaps because these early dramatic impersonations, unlike simply choral poetry, seemed to evoke the dead from the underworld.[4]

The enthusiasm of the actors who brought such figures to life in the service

1. Pickard-Cambridge 101-107. 2. Kerenyi, *Dionysos* 327. 3. *Ibid.* 4. *Ibid.*

of the god was, moreover, a contagious experience for the spectators as well. The people of the ancient audience, if they could read at all, were more accustomed to witnessing the performance of literature than to deciphering the written word in private.[1] In order to recapture the enthusiasm of the original audience, we must consider what manner of mentality would have been involved in witnessing drama, as opposed to reading it. The reader tends to stand apart from the communication and judge it rationally. This is less true when what is read is already familiar or to some extent even memorized, as was the more common case in classical times, for then the words serve merely to remind the memory of things already known and stored away as part of the cultural heritage of given truths. In performance, however, the words tend to capture the mind and imagination with a greater vividness. The judgmental processes recede to the dominance of emotional responses, especially when the performance, like classical drama, is musical and rhythmic, with imposing spectacle and dance. To an audience not accustomed to the detachment of reading and not yet desensitized, as in modern times, by too frequent an exposure to dramatic enactments, such emotionality would be even more pronounced. The whole audience might fall to weeping or be possessed by the contagion of laughter, enraptured by the impersonated spirits.

Wine itself seemed to have played a role in intensifying such a dominance of emotion over rationality in the ancient theater. We must imagine an audience in somewhat less than a perfectly rational state pharmacologically, for, as Philochorus, the fourth-century historian of Attica and its religious practices, records (fr. 171 Jacoby), the spectators prepared themselves by drinking throughout the days of dramatic performance, in addition to whatever drinking, presumably of a deeper nature, took place during the evenings of revelry. The wine drunk was called *trimma* (τρίμμα), like the one drunk at marriages, apparently so named from the fortifying additives that were 'ground' into it (Hesychius, *s. v. trimma*).[2] There were traditions also that claimed that the poets themselves were possessed by the spirit of the wine when they performed their dramas (Athenaeus 1.22, 10.429).

Such drinking in the theater should not be taken to imply a boisterous or ill-attentive audience, but one irrationally enraptured by the music and the dance and the age-old stories of what was supposed to be history, now again

1. Eric Havelock, *A Preface to Plato* (Harvard, Cambridge, MA, 1963).

2. The citation of Hesychius in Liddell, Scott/Jones omits the mention of the drinking of *trimma* in the theater.

come alive. Actually, we have an eloquent eye-witness description of the mesmerizing effect of dramatic poetry on both the actors and the audience in Plato's *Ion* dialogue. Plato had himself been a tragic poet before he turned to philosophy, and although he may exaggerate a little to make his argument against the irrationality of the poetic experience, his description must be accepted as authentic evidence about the general nature, at least, of what happened in the theater of the classical age.

The description purports to be Socrates' rebuttal to the claims of a renowned poetic expert, the rhapsodist Ion, who had made the conventional assertion that poetry is knowledge. It appears, however, that poets do not really understand their own poetry in any rational sense (533d ff.). All poets compose not by art or scientific skill, but because they become possessed and filled with divinity. Music and rhythm lead them into a condition where they are no longer in control of their own wits, but are actually possessed by the subject or figure they are impersonating. They are, in fact, like people entranced or bewitched. The god has removed their minds and substituted his own, using them as his servants, the vehicles for a communication that simply seems to pass through them, although it is not their own. They are like prophets and oracles, who speak for the god, but do not comprehend or at times even remember what words they spoke when the possessing spirit came upon them.

This enchantment, moreover, is a contagion that spreads to the audience as well. The god, according to Plato, is like a magnet drawing the poet or performer into bondage with its attractive force, and through his inspired servants, the binding attraction passes on to the spectators, uniting them all like so many iron rings drawn ineluctably into a continuous chain.

Both poet and audience, in fact, are drunk, but on a potion superior even to that of wine, for the god, in this celebration of his evolution to culture, transports and reunites his people with primordial times of the Golden Age. The drama itself is a drink that the poets have fetched from the magical springs that flow in the gardens of the Muses, a potion composed of the commingled nectars of flowers that are tended not by human agents, but simply found in a metaphysical wilderness by the ecstatic poets, as they go, like bees, from each to each. It is this special drink that the poets offer, and through it, the whole world seems metamorphosed, with rivers, as on Cithaeron, that flow with milk and honey. In the throes of this intoxication, the whole theater will fall to weeping along with the actor although they are celebrating a joyous festival, or their hair will stand on end for fear although they sit amidst their closest friends.

In a deeper sense, it is not the reanimated dead who have so captivated and enthralled the actors and their audience, but rather the culture's heritage of myth, the ancient patterns of story and metaphor that have accompanied the people in the long course of their history from primordial times. The meanings of these stories are elusive, for they have been told over centuries and have had a multiplicity of referents and they seem always to suggest subtleties receding beyond the frontiers of conscious knowledge. The ancient poets were trained in the skill of telling these stories, molding them in accordance with criteria of balance and harmony, but, as Socrates testifies in the *Apology* (22b ff.), not themselves really capable of explaining what they intended as meaning. Traditionally, these inspired transmitters of myth ascribed the source outside their own conscious control to the Muses, who were the daughters of Memory, the repository of the cultural heritage. In performance, these poets and their actors led the audience back into the world of myth, imparting to it their own sense of its deep, although elusive, worth and relevance for the present.

This confrontation with myth not only brought the people back to its historical past, but, as ontogenesis as well, it reunited the individual with the primordial and darker versions of the self that underlay the persona of civilized life, the infant in the adult and the wild in the cultured. What Aristotle was to call the tragic flaw had not only such a reference to the personal psyche, however, but to the whole of society as well, which was reconfirmed in its civilized state by experiencing this journey back to primitive origins.

Such a journey is basically Dionysian and does not require the story specifically of Dionysus to be told. From the viewpoint of the tragic poets, there were particular ways of telling a story that pertained to their god and his area of symbolism, different, for example, from the ways of the epinician poets. The latter celebrated the masculine virtues of Olympian heroes and of the victorious athletes who surpassed for a time the limits of their own mortality, reasserting their families' aristocratic claim to divine lineage. But the tragic poets told instead of the hero's fall from Olympian grace into the dominance of women and the foredestined tomb. When freed from the personalism of the Aristotlean bias, the mythopoeia of the tragic poets can be shown to represent a consistent pattern or design, in which the hero's fall repeatedly involves Dionysian symbolism, the regression to a more primordial identity, and the restitution of fertility to the civilized world, or some favored part of it, by the incorporation of the polluted, non-Olympian persona. In this manner, the inspired enthrallment of the theater experience was itself an analogue to the stories enacted in the dramas that celebrated the god who himself submitted to death in order to be reborn with his gift of wine.

CHAPTER EIGHT

THE OFFERINGS FROM THE HYPERBOREANS

INTRODUCTION

The Hyperboreans were a mythical people, living beyond the frontier of the world known to the classical Greeks, in what was reputed to be the original homeland of the god Apollo. Each year, however, these supposedly imaginary people joined the real cities of Greece in sending actual offerings to the god at his sanctuary on the sacred island of Delos. The other cities all sent envoys with sheaves of grain, the so-called first fruits of the year's crop, harvested before they had completely ripened, but the sheaf of wheat from the Hyperboreans was special for it was supposed to conceal some other plant, a secret offering bound within it.[1] Whoever actually sent this special gift from the lands of myth, the plant itself, we may assume, would have to have been something that was considered particularly appropriate to the supposed Hyperboreans,[2] as well as

1. Herodotus (4.33) mentioned 'sacred things bound in wheat-straw' and Pausanias (1.31.2) called them 'first fruits hidden in wheat-straw,' adding that their identity 'was known by no one.' Callimachus, however, in his *Hymn to Delos* (4.275 ff.), seems to identify these Hyperborean offerings as nothing more than 'a stalk and sacred sheaves of grain' (thus, M. Cary, *Oxford Classical Dictionary*, Oxford 1970, s. v. Hyperboreans), but a closer examination of the context reconciles his account with the other two. Callimachus is describing the general convergence of first fruits upon Delos, sent from all the cities of the Greek world, amongst which the land of the Hyperboreans is mentioned as the most distant. He then goes on to give the aetiological myth that explained the special manner in which the Hyperborean offerings were conveyed to Delos, not in person by the Hyperborean emissaries, as in the case of the other cities, but indirectly through a series of intermediaries. In this context, there was no reason to distinguish the special contents of the Hyperborean offerings from the general tribute of first fruits. Callimachus's point is simply to illustrate the glory of Delos in receiving tribute from even the most distant of the Greek lands. If the 'sacred things' or 'first fruits' were still a secret in the second century A.D., when Pausanias gathered his information, it is unlikely that Callimachus, three centuries earlier, would have known that the whole tradition was merely a pious hoax, nor would such a revelation suit the context of a hymn, in the Homeric manner, in praise of Delos. As an antiquarian poet, it is just such traditions that he would have wanted to perpetuate.

Nor is it clear that the Hyperborean offering was actually a sheaf of grain, for 'wheat-straw,' 'stubble,' or 'stalk' (*kalame*) is not the same thing as 'sheaf' (*dragma*, literally, a 'handful' or 'as many stalks or *kalamai* as the reaper can grasp in his left hand'). Since the Hyperborean offering, as we shall see, had a longer distance to travel, it is unlikely that it could have been cut at the same time as the other offerings of first fruits. That it was a 'first fruit' is documented by Pausanias, but the 'straw' may have been intended merely to hide it or preserve it over the journey.

2. Tithes and first fruits were often of a kind particularly identified with the traditions of the donor and could even on occasion be represented by a model, as, for example, a head of

to the pre-Hellenic identity of their original god and to the meaning of such ritual presentations of first fruits.

THE ROUTE FOR THE OFFERINGS

The Hyperborean offering was transmitted from its origin indirectly along its way to Delos through a succession of intervening peoples. Somewhere along this route, the actual sheaf with its secret contents must have materialized out of the land of myth.

The route for the transmission is recorded in three ancient authors,[1] who are in essential agreement that the offerings traveled a strangely indirect, zig-zag course, up the Danube, then south along the shore of the Adriatic, and eastward through Dodona and across the Thessalian plain, before finally going south through Euboea and the adjacent islands to Delos. This was obviously not the easiest nor most direct route from Scythia, through which the offerings had initially passed on their way from the Hyperboreans. They could more simply have been sent through the Hellespont and along the northern shore of the Aegean. The careful preservation of this Danube and Adriatic route must have had symbolic significance, and it may retrace the historical route of a tribal migration of Indo-Europeans into the Greek lands from central Asia.

At the other end of the journey, beyond the Scythians, we hear of only one further people before we enter the lands of myth. These are the Issedonians (Pausanias 1.31.2), a nomadic Indo-European tribe living along the forested south-western slopes of the Altai Mountains, which form the western fringe of the central Asiatic massif.[2]

Beyond them were the Hyperboreans, who either transmitted the offerings through the intermediary of the Arimaspeans (Pausanias, loc. cit.) or perhaps

celery from Selinus or a head of the precious drug plant silphium from the people of its native Libya. In the same manner, we hear of a golden radish, a silver beet, and a turnip of lead, apparently from private donors, as well as a silver duck from a poulterer, and so on. See William H. D. Rouse, *Greek Votive Offerings* (University Press, Cambridge, U. K. 1902, reprinted by Arno Press, New York 1975) 60-94. We can expect that the secret offering was considered to be the special Hyperborean plant.

1. For the ancient testimony, see p 225 note 1. The three documents cover the same route, but mention different places along the way. The one divergence is the insertion of an Athenian role in the final delivery of the offerings, according to Pausanias's account. This apparently reflects Athenian dominance over the sacred island, dating from sometime after the writing of Herodotus, and the innovation may have coincided with the Athenian reorganization of the Delian festival around the year 418 B.C., when Athens dedicated the new temple to Apollo.

2. J. D. P. Bolton *Aristeas of Proconnesus* (Oxford 1962) 104-118.

were themselves identical with these Arimaspeans (Callimachus, *Hymn* 4.291 *cum scholia*; Antimachus, frg. 118). The name of these Arimaspeans is supposed to be descriptive of them in the Scythian language. They were a people who had only a single eye (Herodotus 4.27). They lived near the Gorgons (Aeschylus, *Prometheus* 790 ff.; Pindar, *Pythia* 10.45)[1] amongst monstrous griffins, whose gold they were said to steal.

HYPERBOREANS

These Hyperboreans, as the Greeks understood their name (Herodotus 4.36; Pindar, *Olympia* 3.31; Callimachus, *Hymn* 4.281; etc.),[2] lived in a paradise 'beyond the North Wind,' who was personified as Boreas. Although north of the Greek lands, the Hyperboreans appear to have been imagined as living also considerably toward the east, for Boreas, in early Greek cartography, did not stand for the cardinal point until later advances in astronomy, and Boreas could shift around from place to place to indicate the direction from which the north wind would appear to blow at different locations. In the region of the Hyperboreans, beyond the Issedonians on the slopes of the Altai Mountains, the bitter prevailing winds sweep westward down through the Dzungian Gate. On the other side of the mountain pass, the Hyperboreans lived. Boreas himself was supposed to have had his home in a cave, which can perhaps be still identified with an actual Cave of the Winds that is located there within the mountain pass in Asiatic lore.[3]

The journey to the mythical land of the Hyperboreans was to be accom-

1. The placement of the Gorgons in the east (instead of the more customary west) seems to have derived from the *Arimaspea* of Aristeas. See Bolton 61 ff. It is probable, however, that the Gorgons were traditionally placed near each of the Greek versions of paradise or the otherworld. Thus they are found also to the south amongst the Ethiopeans, as well as with the Hesperides in the west. See Joseph Fontenrose, *Python: A Study of Delphic Myth and its Origins* (University of California Press, Berkeley and Los Angeles 1959) 288.

2. The ancient etymology has been questioned in the modern era. Ahrens suggested that the name was actually derived from a supposed variant, Hyperphoroi, and thus the Hyperboreans were simply the same as the 'Perpherees,' the name that Herodotus records for the emissaries or 'conveyers' who delivered the offerings to Delos. Schroeder, on the other hand, assumed that 'Boris' was a variant of the word for 'mountain' (*oros*) and interpreted the Hyperboreans as the people who lived 'beyond the mountain.' See Lewis Richard Farnell, *The Cults of the Greek States* (Oxford 1896-1909) 4.102 ff. Further references are found in Pierre Chantraine, *Dictionnaire Etymologique de la Langue Grecque* (Klincksieck, Paris 1968) 1157-1158. Farnell enthusiastically endorsed Ahren's interpretation, but there is probably nothing wrong with the etymology current in antiquity. It is accepted as correct by E. R. Dodds, *The Greeks and the Irrational* (Berkeley 1951) 162, and Bolton 195.

3. Bolton 94 ff.

plished only through inspiration and mystical transport, as would be expected, for there is no other way to find the long pathway to another world. There was a poem, entitled the *Arimaspea*, about such a journey to the Hyperboreans. It was ascribed to a certain Aristeas of Proconnesus, an island in the sea of Marmara. Since Aristeas is supposed to have reappeared in Italy amongst the Metapontines in the fifth century, some two and a half centuries after his death (Herodotus 4.15), he is probably not so much a real person as the traditional persona that was assumed by a poet in reciting that type of poem. Such poems, like the songs of Hesiod, were originally oral in composition and were perpetuated by a religious society of similarly inspired poets, who could all speak in the biographical persona of their supposed founder.[1] Just as Hesiod appears to have been a Boeotian farmer with an evil and greedy brother, the Aristean persona is characterised by his experiences of shamanic rapture. He was said to have journeyed to the Hyperboreans while 'possessed by Apollo' (*Phoibolamptos*, Herodotus 4.13),[2] an experience that was thought to have happened to him first in a fuller's shop in Proconnesus, but which was repeated, according to some sources (Apollonius, *Mirabilia* 2), over a long period of time. During these seizures, he had the appearance of being dead, while his soul would leave his body (Suidas, s. v. Aristeas; Maximus of Tyre 10.2 ff.) in the form of a raven (Pliny, *Natural History* 7.174), a bird sacred to Apollo and associated, in particular, with the god as his spiritually possessed 'bride' or mate and devotee.[3] As this animal familiar of the god, Aristeas would travel far and wide. He was also

1. Gregory Nagy, *Hesiod* (T. J. Luce 1982).

2. K. Meuli (1935) Scythica, *Hermes* 70, 121-176. Bolton, 125 ff., disputes what has become the common acceptance of Aristeas as a shaman. He argues that Aristeas was simply someone who was somewhat of a religious fanatic about Apollo and that because of his love for the god, he set out on an actual trip to what he believed to be the topographical homeland of the god, going only so far as the Issedones and hearing from them of a civilized race beyond the central Asiatic massif, who in reality were probably the Chinese. Although Herodotus does claim that Aristeas did not go so far as the Hyperboreans – a strange shortfall for a shaman's journey, as Bolton points out – we should note that not all the sources, who presumably also had access to the *Arimaspea*, agree that he failed to reach the goal of his travels. Bolton further argues that the reappearance of Aristeas amongst the Metapontines was a resuscitation of his memory by the Pythagoreans as a justification for their own vegetarianism, a trait that they shared, as we shall see, with the Hyperboreans.
The diverse traditions about Aristeas, however, are probably not to be reconciled with reality, but indicate, as I have suggested, the persona of an oral tradition of poetry about the journey to the Hyperboreans, nor should we assume that the so-called *Arimaspea* was a fixed text without variants.
For a refutation of Bolton's view, see Ken Dowden (1980) Deux notes sur les Scythes et les Arimaspes, *Revue des Etudes Grecques* 93, 486-492.

3. C. Kerenyi, *Asklepios: Archetypal Image of the Physician's Existence* (Pantheon, New York 1957, translated from the German of 1947) 87-100.

thought to have the gift of prognostication and was closely identified with Apollo in certain of his cults.

It was not only Aristeas, however, who experienced such Hyperborean rapture. The shamanic nature of the journey was a traditional theme. Abaris, who, like Aristeas, was the assumed author of another collection of verses, was himself supposed to have been a Hyperborean and was said to have traveled about the earth on an arrow from Apollo's temple amongst those imaginary people (Herodotus 4.36; Suidas, s. v. Abaris).[1] Pindar thought that Abaris was a contemporary of Croesus (frg. 283 Bowra), although, like Aristeas, he too seems to have reappeared at a later date, both in Athens (Suidas, s. v. Abaris) and amongst the Spartans, whom he directed in the performance of sacrifices to avert plagues (Apollonius, *Mirabilia* 4), a ritual that, as we shall see, had definite Hyperborean connotations.

Another of these Hyperborean travellers was Olen, the reputed composer of certain very ancient hymns that were sung at Delos on the subject of the first Hyperborean offerings and a similar purificatory ritual (Herodotus 4.35; Callimachus, *Hymn* 4.304-305). He was claimed as the founder and first prophet of the oracle of Apollo at Delphi (Pausanias 10.5.7), and hence, he too, like Aristeas and Abaris, was presumably the traditional persona of a shamanic poet possessed by the god. He was either a Lycian who came from the Hyperboreans (Pausanias 5.7.8) or was actually himself a member of the Hyperborean race (Pausanias 1.18.5, 8.21.3; Hesychius, s. v. Olen).[2]

It was the wind Boreas himself who took such ecstatic poets to the Hyperborean world that lay just beyond the wintry passage through his cave in the Dzungian Gate. The wind is traditionally an abductor to the otherworld, for the metaphor of 'inspiration,' which in Latin literally implies 'blowing upon' (*inspirare*), existed also in Greek as *empnein*. Thus, for example, the Muses, according to Hesiod, 'breathed song into' him at the moment of his inspiration upon Mount Helicon (*Theogony* 31). So too, 'breath' was soul or *psyche*, just as in Latin it was *spiritus*.[3]

1. Herodotus differs from the later sources in saying that Abaris traveled carrying the arrow, unless the text is to be emended to reconcile it to the other traditions. See Reginald Walter Macan, *Herodotus* (MacMillan, New York 1895, Arno Press reprint 1973) note on 4.36.3.
The idea of traveling on a sacred arrow may imply shamanic rapture, for the word in Greek for 'arrow' (*ios*) is homonymous with 'toxin,' and the arrow traditionally was drugged or poisoned and conveyed the metaphor of intoxication.

2. On the confusion of Lycia with the land of the Hyperboreans, see my discussion below under Lycians.

3. Bruno Snell, *The Discovery of the Mind* (Harvard University Press, Cambridge, MA 1953, translated from the German of 1948, 2nd edn.) 8 ff.

The myth of Oreithyia suggests, as we might expect, that the inspired journey to the Hyperborean paradise beyond the North Wind had connotations of shamanic herbalism, for it was the 'breath' or *pneuma* of Boreas (Plato, *Phaedrus* 229c) that carried her to the otherworld while she was playing with her maiden companion, named Pharmakeia or the 'use of drugs'. The spirit thus brought Oreithyia to what was called the 'ancient garden' of Apollo amongst the Hyperboreans (Sophocles, frg. 956 Pearson). It was in that garden that the Hyperboreans would have harvested their special offering to the Delian god. What magical plants grew there in paradise?

THE GARDEN OF APOLLO

One of those plants was the olive (Pindar, *Olympia* 3.13 ff.). Heracles was supposed to have seen it growing in the land of the Hyperboreans when he went there in pursuit of the so-called golden-antlered hind of Apollo's sister Artemis, an animal that must originally have been the reindeer, for only in that species does the female deer bear horns.[1] Up until then, it was said, the olive was unknown in our world. Heracles was supposed to have transplanted it to the sanctuary that he founded in honor of his divine father Zeus at Olympia, which previously had been completely treeless. Henceforth, the Hyperborean olives provided the wreathes that crowned the victorious athletes who competed in the games at Olympia.

In Delian traditions also, the olive had a sacred association with the Hyperboreans. The grave of the maidens who were the first Hyperborean ambassadors to Delos with the secret offerings was marked by an olive tree that grew upon it, in the area of the sanctuary that was set aside for the goddess Artemis (Herodotus 4.34). It was believed to be one of the oldest trees in existence (Pausanias 8.23.5), and was the object of a bizarre ritual, that dated back to the visit of Theseus upon his return trip toward Athens, after slaying the Cretan Minotaur (Hesychius, s. v. *Deliakos bomos*). Apparently, it was the custom to dance around the altar with whips, while boys, with their hands bound behind their backs placed themselves in symbolic contact with the divinity resident within the tree by biting its trunk (Callimachus, *Hymn* 4.316-324).

From these traditions, it would appear that the Hyperborean plant had connotations of the grave and ritual sacrifice, that it was, moreover, an entheogen

1. W. Ridgeway (1894) The Legend of Herakles and the Hind with the Golden Horns (Pindar, Ol. III 31), *Proceedings of the Cambridge Philological Society* 37-39, 14-15.

capable of effecting the ecstatic journey to the otherworld, and that it was symbolic of the advent of the Olympian strain of religion that came to the Greek lands with the arrival of the Indo-Europeans. It was this triumph of Olympianism over the previous indigenous religions that was commemorated by the tradition that Olympia was purified and refounded by Heracles in honor of Zeus, and the athletic games that were celebrated there were thought to prove the victor's continuance in that divine heritage. Theseus's visit to Delos similarly symbolized the triumph over the primitive chthonic implications of the Cretan labyrinth.

The olive itself, however, can only be a symbolic substitute for the original Hyperborean plant, as it was before being transplanted to this world, for the olive is not native to the northern latitude of the Hyperborean homeland.[1] Before its transplantation, the Hyperborean plant, with the full magical character of the original entheogen, was known metaphorically as the tree upon which grew the golden apples. Although the route for the Delian offerings preserved the remembrance of an Asiatic homeland for the Hyperboreans, that land lay beyond this world, and the various entrances to the otherworld all led to the same place. Thus the Hyperboreans could also be found in the garden of the Hesperides, in the far west beyond Gibraltar, at the frontier of life and death, where the sun went down (Alcman, frg. 10 Page; Apollodorus 2 5.11), and the same Heracles who discovered the olive was said to have brought the apples back as well, from the journey that had taken him north into Hyperborean territory in quest of the magical reindeer.

There was, however, another Hyperborean plant that, like the olive, could be found in this world. This was the *daphne* (*Laurus nobilis*), a laurel or bay. Although the plant itself contains no psychoactive drug,[2] the Greeks considered it a symbolic entheogen. The eating of its leaves was thought to induce the mantic possession of Apollo's Delphic priestess, who, like Aristeas, became *Phoibolamptos* (Lycophron, *Alexandra* 6, 1640). Olen, with the two Hyperboreans, Pagasus and Agyieus, was supposed to have constructed the first temple of Apollo at Delphi out of branches of *daphne* that he brought with him from the valley

1. For Greece, the olive does not grow north of the plains of Thessaly. Pindar (*Olympia* 3. 13 ff.) claims that Heracles found it growing at the head-waters of the Danube, a region that was considered to lie within the territory of the Hyperboreans.

2. Dr. Albert Hofmann, in personal correspondence, assures me that, despite the common knowledge that the Delphic priestess chewed the leaves of *Laurus nobilis*, the plant contains no chemically active principles that could induce her prophetic ability, nor is he aware of any other laurel with such properties.

of Tempe, the narrow passage north into the Thessalian plain (Pausanias 5.7.8; 10, 5, 7). That origin for the plant was commemorated by continuing to gather from there the leaves that were used, like those of the olive at Olympia, to weave the crowns for the athletes and musicians who were victorious in the Pythian contests (Aelian, *Varia Historia* 3.1; Argument 3 to Pindar's *Pythia*).

It was said that Apollo himself had sought refuge in Tempe with a suppliant branch of *daphne* after having slain the serpent monster Python and that he had been purified there before his return to Delphi. The *daphne* leaves for the victor's crowns were gathered in Tempe in a ritual that recalled the god's polluted sojourn there. Every ninth year, the Septerion (or Stepterion) Festival was celebrated at Delphi, coinciding originally with the performance of the Pythian contests, which were said to commemorate Apollo's victory over the Python. In the Delphic sanctuary, opposite the Portico of the Athenians, there was a level area called the threshing floor. Here a temporary structure representing a royal habitation was set up, with a table beside it. A band of youths, escorting a boy, who apparently was thought to impersonate the god, silently attacked this hut and set it afire with torches, overturning the table. They then fled immediately all the way to Tempe, where they were purified of their crime which was no less, as it was imagined, than the ritual slaughter of some kingly person, an impersonation, that is to say, of Apollo's own murder of the Python. The youths then gathered the boughs of *daphne* and carried them triumphantly back to Delphi, accompanied by the music of flutes and pipes (Plutarch, *Moralia* 293c, 418ab, 1136a; Aelian, *Varia Historia* 3.1; Pausanias 2.7.7).

Tempe was apparently considered a nearer version of the Hyperborean world, an analogue to the northern land, like the entrance to the otherworld beyond Gibraltar, and the boughs of *daphne* are a Delphic version of the Delian ritual of the secret offerings. Thus the slaughter of the Python, followed by the expiatory sojourn in Tempe, is comparable to the tradition that Apollo was banished to the Hyperboreans for a period of servitude and absolution after his murder of the one-eyed Cyclopes (Apollonius Rhodius 4.612-616). This same murder of the Cyclopes was also given as a reason for Apollo's sojourn in the service of Admetus, whose kingdom lay in the nearer Hyperborean otherworld in the region of Tempe (Euripides, *Alcestis* 1-7). The Cyclopes and the Python were both more primitive identities of Apollo himself, and thus the murders quite naturally required his own descent for a stay in the underworld.

Both the *daphne* and the olive were trees that marked the transition to the otherworld and had connotations of a death that occurred at puberty. The maiden Daphne, for example, died in the region of Tempe as she attempted to escape the courtship of Apollo and was transformed into the plant that bears her name (Ovid, *Metamorphoses* 1.452 ff.). Similarly, Hippolytus, the virgin youth who was devoted to Artemis, was said to have died when the reins of his maddened horses became entangled in the crooked branches of an olive (Pausanias 2.32.10).

The basic identity of Tempe as a Hyperborean land can also be sensed in the traditions involving both places with Apollo and wolves. Apollo himself bore the epithet Lykegenes, meaning 'born from the she-wolf',[1] and it was said that his mother Leto had been escorted from the Hyperboreans by wolves, herself as a she-wolf, at the time of her labor (Aristotle 580 a 17), and that after the death of Python, it was a wolf that first brought Apollo the *daphne* from Tempe (Servius, on Vergil's *Aeneid* 4.377).

The wolf was a metaphoric version of the god in his polluted state, and thus Apollo was also called Lykoktonos, as the 'one who slew the wolf' (Sophocles, *Electra* 6). The stories of Apollo's murdered victims really mask the god's sacrifice of his own primitive precedents in order to supplant them with his evolving Hellenic persona as a deity of more civilized times.[2] In this manner, the primitive Apollo could himself be represented as a wolf or, like Python, as a serpent (Bode, *Scriptores Rerum Mythologicorum* = Farnell 4.359 R 7n). It was as a wolf that he abducted the maiden Cyrene, like Daphne, from the region of Tempe (Servius, on Vergil's *Aeneid* 4.377), and the wolf was his special animal and a fitting sacrificial victim in his worship (Pausanias 10.14.7, scholia to Sophocles' *Electra* 6).

LYCIANS

Amongst the god's primordial victims was a race of evil wizards called the Telchines. Originally associated primarily with the island of Rhodes, they also inhabited Argos and Crete and migrated to Lycia under the leadership of Lykos or 'wolf' and founded a temple of Apollo Lykios by the river Xanthus in south-

1. Thus, Farnell 4.114. Even in antiquity, there was an attempt to derive Lykegenes from a supposed *lyke*, meaning 'light,' and thus Apollo was associated with solar symbolism, but this is a result of the attempt to obliterate Apollo's pre-Indo-European identity. The same pattern can be seen in the explanation of his epithet of Phoibos as meaning the 'shining one,' whereas its original significance apparently designated him as the consort, named with the name, in matrilineal fashion, of his Great Goddess, Phoibe, who was associated, not with the masculine sun, but with its feminine counterpart, the moon. See Kerenyi, *Asklepios* 90 ff. Phoibos is thus a primordial name and identity retained as an epithet of the Hellenic god, in the same manner as the epithet of Bacchus (Bakkhos) for the Hellenic Dionysus.

2. Fontenrose 470 ff.

western Asia Minor (Diodorus Siculus 5.56). Others claimed that it was actually wolves themselves who met Apollo's mother Leto when she was in labor and that it was they who brought her to the same site by the river, where she was delivered of the divine twins (Antoninus Liberalis 35). These wolves were apparently nothing other than the Telchines themselves, for one version of their origin had them metamorphosed out of Actaeon's hounds (Bergk, *Poetae Lyrici Graeci*, Leipzig 1882, 3.232). Traditionally, these hounds represented the recidivism of the domestic dog into its wild avatar, the wolf, a transformation that was effected through the agency of rabies, which was called the 'wolf-madness' or Lyssa. The Telchines, therefore, were the 'mad' or inspired ministers of the primitive Apollo. The classical god, who was supposedly born on Delos, was ritually insulated from his own recidivous tendency by prohibiting all dogs from landing or living upon the island (Strabo 2.8.6). The homeland of the god's lupine predecessor, who was born instead in Asia Minor, was named for the Telchines' deity. It was called Lycia, from the epithet of their god, Apollo Lykios, for Lycia is a Greek word and not the country's ethnic name in the native language of its inhabitants. For the Greeks, Lycia was known as the 'wolf-land.'

This wolf-land of Lycia, it would appear, was another version of the Hyperborean world, for it too was claimed as the paradisiacal garden where Apollo spent his annual sojourn (Vergil, *Aeneid* 4.143-144; Suidas *omega* 71). Thus, the Olen who brought the first *daphne* to Delphi came, as we have seen, with two Hyperborean companions, but was himself a Lycian (Pausanias 5.7.8). Apollo's name in fact, appears to be derived from that of a Hittite deity of entrances, and hence of weather and the seasons.[1] Moreover, the cave of the Python at Delphi, which was the original site of the oracle on Parnassus, is a Hellenic importation of a religious cult from Cilicia, on the southern coast of Asia Minor, eastward beyond Lycia.[2]

This Corycian Cave, as it was called at Delphi, seems in fact, to have had the same name in Cilicia, as well as at its various other Anatolian locations. These caves were all considered to be entrances to the otherworld. The Delphic Corycian Cave was administered by a tribe that lived in the nearby town of Lykoreia, high on the Parnassian plateau, before they later moved further down the mountain to occupy the site of the classical Delphic sanctuary, sometime before the year 800 B.C. (Strabo 9.3.3). Lykoreia is etymologically the 'mountain

1. B. Hrozný (1936) Les Quatre autels 'Hittites' hieroglyphiques d'Emir Ghazi et d'Eski Kisla, et les divinités Apulunas (?) et Rutas, *Archiv Orientální* 8, 171-199. Emmanuel Laroche, *Recherches sur les noms des dieux Hittites* (Maisonneuve, Librairie Orientale et Americaine, Paris 1947).

2. Fontenrose 406-403.

city of the wolves,' and its original location was supposedly chosen by wolves, who led the Lykoreians there to save them from the waters of the great flood (Pausanias 10.6.2 ff.). Its founder was a certain Lykoros, the 'wolf-warder,' or, by some accounts, simply Lykos himself. Here too, we can discern the wolf as a primitive version of the god and hence the primordial enemy of the classical deity who evolved from him, for it was a Lykos who was said to have desecrated the god's temple by attempting to steal the sacred tripod upon which the oracle sat. For this reason, Lykos was stoned to death (Hippocratic Corpus 9.412 Littré; Pausanias 10.14.7; Aelian, *De Natura Animalium* 10.26).

The cave on Parnassus was apparently another passageway to the god's primordial realm amongst the Hyperboreans. The oracle there was spoken by three winged sisters who were said to become inspired by eating honeycomb (Homeric hymn 4.533-567). They were called 'bees,' a title that persisted into the classical era for the priestess of the oracle, even after the transposition of the rite to the Delphic sanctuary. This cave of the bee-maidens was said to have been the second Delphic temple, replacing the first of *daphne*, and it was reputed to have been constructed out of honeycomb and feathers by bees (Pausanias 10.5.9 ff.). Like the *daphne* temple, it too would appear to be a metaphoric substitute for the golden fruit of the otherworld, for Apollo, on usurping the site from the Python and claiming it for his own Hellenic persona, was supposed to have dispatched the honeycomb temple to the land of the Hyperboreans (Pausanias, loc. cit.; cf. Strabo 9.3.9). Whereas the classical Apollo transmitted oracles from his Olympian father, this Corycian version of the god sent up dream phantoms from the dead in the service of the Great Mother, who was Earth (Euripides, *Iphigenia in Tauris* 1259-1269; Aeschylus, *Eumenides* 1-8).

Since the Corycian Cave could be viewed as an entrance to the Hyperborean world that lay beyond its depths, the Delphians themselves were called Hyperboreans (Mnaseas, frg. 24 Müller). The cave was the way to the golden fruit. Hence, the cave itself was said to have had its chambers lined with gold, and its maiden priestesses were clothed in golden raiment (Philoxenos, frg. 14 Bergk).

It is not surprising, therefore, that the Telchines, who served the primitive god in his Lycian temple, were notorious metalsmiths, working the precious ores extracted from the chthonic depths. Their name was etymologically derived from the words for 'melting' (*texis*) and 'enchantment' (*thelxis*) (Hesychius, s. v. Telchines),[1] and they were apparently the Lycian version of the Cyclopes,

1. See Herter, in Pauly-Wissova, *Real-encyclopädie der classischen Altertumswissenschaft*, s. v. Telchinen.

who were similarly subterranean smiths, as well as of the Hyperborean griffins, who dug the gold that the one-eyed Arimaspeans stole from them (Herodotus 3.116). Like the bee-maidens, the Telchines were ecstatic creatures (Nonnus, *Dionysiaca* 14.42) with a reputation for sorcery and drugs (Callimachus, frg. 6.64, Diodorus Siculus 5.55; Hesychius, s. v. Telchines). They were also herbalists, for their so-called metallurgic arts involved the making of special potions with the roots they dug from the earth (Eustathius p. 771, 60 ff.), and the single eye that characterized the Cyclopes and the Arimaspeans was known for them as the power of their evil eye (Ovid, *Metamorphoses* 7.366). The classical god in killing these ancient ministers of his religion, redeemed mankind from their supposed wickedness, for, like the bee-maidens, their shamanism was chthonic. They stood accused of having sprinkled the islands of Rhodes and Cos with the waters of the underworld, thereby annihilating all life (Strabo 6.4.5).

APOLLO

Apollo, it would appear, had two homelands, one amongst the Hyperboreans on the slopes of the Altai Mountains, and the other amongst the Lycians who tended the Corycian caves of Anatolia. This is not surprising, for in his classical form, Apollo, like the other Olympians, was actually an assimilation and reconciliation of deities from two basically different religious traditions.[1] One was that of the Indo-Europeans, in which male deities dominated over females and were associated with the heavens and spiritual immortality. The other was the Anatolian tradition, where there was a Great Mother goddess, associated with the earth, agriculture, the tomb, and an eternity of corporeal resurrections and deaths. In Lycia, Apollo would have been originally the lesser consort of a superior goddess, amongst a people who still in classical times alone of all men known to the Greeks reckoned lineage by matrilineal descent (Herodotus 1.173). The myth of his birth as a son of Zeus is more exactly, like that of the other children of Zeus, the story of his assimilative rebirth into his new identity as one of the Olympians, along with his former Goddess, who has been transformed into his twin sister, Artemis.

The basis for the assimilation of the 'northern' and Anatolian Apollos seems to have been that both gods were involved with oracular activity, in which they functioned as intermediaries with another world, a role that probably developed

1. For a summary of the two points of view about Apollo's origin, see H. J. Rose, *A Handbook of Greek Mythology* (Dutton, New York 1959) 135, 138.

from their supposed control over seasonal change and hence over the entrances to life and death. The shamanism of the Hyperborean Apollo, however, would have differed from that of the Lycian with regard to its orientation. To judge from Orphism, which was a classical evolution of northern Apolline traditions, the shamanism of the Indo-European Apollo was directed toward the celestial realm and strove to liberate the spirit from the body, whereas the Lycian god, through death and rebirth in the embrace of the Earth, showed the way to the body's renewal in its passage through the tomb.

It would, however, be an oversimplification to assume that the assimilation of the two religious traditions occurred solely in the Hellenic context. The Anatolian peoples may well have been influenced by their eastern and northern Indo-European neighbors before their Lycian deity confronted the Hyperborean after the migration of the Indo-Europeans into the Greek lands. So too, the myths cannot be separated clearly at all times into two distinct traditions.

The typical mythical pattern for this assimilation presents the gods of a newer Olympian generation asserting their dominance over their own avatars. Since the Indo-European immigrants were to dominate politically and impose their language, which was to become Greek, upon the indigenous peoples, the gods of this new order are characterized by the Indo-European cultural ideals of male dominance and celestial orientation, but versions of their avatars persisted into the classical period, particularly in agrarian and funereal rites, and, in various ways, the Olympians, like the people who worshipped them, had to strike an accord both with their own particular precedents and with a whole class of deposed chthonic deities, who were the children of an earlier race.

In this manner, although Apollo's predecessors were supplanted and often discredited as his evil antithesis, it was nevertheless felt necessary to appease their angered spirit by some semblance of accord and reconciliation. Thus at Delphi, the Python, who was the original deity of the Corycian Cave, continued to be honored in biennial nocturnal rites that were an atavistic regression to the times of the Hyperborean bee-maidens and their Lycian god. During these rites, the whole sanctuary fell under the dominance of Dionysus, who often functioned as the chthonic opposite of his celestial brother, while Apollo himself withdrew to his primordial home amongst his chosen people in the otherworld.

SACRIFICE

Such acts of expiated slaughter, by which the god supplanted his predecessors, are paradigmatic of the accord with the past and its primitivism that was repeatedly renewed through the ritual of sacrifice. The victim for the offering had a role of special honor, for typically it was an animal that was felt to have some particular kinship with the deity, often being associated with the god's sinister persona.[1]

Although some sacrificial ceremonies required that the victim be given over totally to the deity or spirits, either through holocaust or by being simply left to rot, the sacrifice was usually a communion meal that the worshipers shared with the gods. Even in the former case, the sacrifice was meant as food that was offered to the deity whose appeasement was sought. In feeding the deity, the worshipers nourished and bound it to the persona elicited though their invocation and ritual, seeking to avert its regression to less beneficent manifestations. The sacrifice itself was a cultivated and civilized art, usually involving the act of cooking, although certain ceremonies in honor of primitive personae required the eating of the flesh raw. Ordinarily, however, the manner in which the victim was butchered and prepared for consumption was intended symbolically to reassert and strengthen the progress of evolution, for the ceremony recapitulated the supposed ontogeny of the animal itself, as well as the imagined history of the culinary arts since primitive times.[2]

In addition to ritualizing the manner in which mankind of necessity partakes of death in order to nourish life, the ceremony of sacrifice signified man's essential role in the reconciliation between the primitive and civilized deities and between the chthonic and Olympian realms. The chthonic gods, who presided over the tomb, were accustomed to eating the corruptible matter of life, but the Olympians ordinarily avoided pollution with the blood and flesh of mortality

1. Thus, a dog could be sacrificed to the nether goddess Hecate, a horse to Poseidon or the Winds, a goat to Dionysus, a sow to Persephone and Demeter, etc. The animal was thought to represent the form in which the deity formerly appeared and the victim was thus chosen to intensify the resemblance, as, for example, a red dog to the Latin Robigus, who was the spirit of the reddish fungus or ergot that attacks grain. So too were virgin animals appropriate to the virgin goddesses Artemis and Athena, and black ones for the chthonic gods, but white for the celestial. The bull was a typical sacrifice to Zeus, and we can sense the god's sinister persona in the myth of his abduction of Europa, whom he possessed in the form of a bull that breathed the fragrance of the magical herb it had grazed upon.

2. Marcel Detienne, *Dionysos Slain* (Johns Hopkins University Press, Baltimore 1979, translated from the French of 1977) 68 ff.

and were nourished instead upon their own special food and drink, their ambrosia and nectar,[1] which had the power to confer immortality even upon mortals (Pindar, *Olympia* 1.61-64) and were the reason that the Olympians were a race apart, with serum-like ichor instead of blood in their veins (Homer, *Iliad* 5.339-342). Because of this basic difference, the pure Olympians at first had little use for humans, who were created out of clay (Pausanias 10.4.4) and were closer by nature to the chthonic gods, who shared with them the traumas of birth and death. Through the communion meal of sacrifice, even the Olympians, however, were incorporated into the universal interdependency of life and death in the sources of nourishment.

Before Zeus's great reconciliation with humans and the creatures of Earth, he had originally intended to destroy mankind and he and his new hierarchy of gods were cruel and tyrannical. Pursuant of his plan, he took fire away from the volcanic forge of the subterranean smiths and hid it from humans (Hesiod, *Theogony* 561 ff.; Aeschylus, *Prometheus* 7). This fire was the magical plant of chthonic shamanism, and without it, mankind was no better than the beasts of the wilderness, eating their foods raw and lacking in all the civilizing arts (Aeschylus, *Prometheus* 436 ff.). Before Zeus could complete their destruction, however, Prometheus championed the cause of men, who were beings of his own creation, and retrieved fire for them back from the heavens so that they would not remain utterly at the disposal of the tyrannical god. Although himself born of Earth, Prometheus had at first sided with Zeus in the battle that subdued the chthonic creatures, but since Zeus would not rule with justice, it was the role of Prometheus to endure shamanic torment until he could manage to reconcile the two opposing realms and demonstrate the interdependency of both upon the intermediary lot of mankind.

In this reconciliation, chthonic fire became identified with the fire from heaven, for the chthonic smiths are also the Cyclopes who make the celestial thunderbolts of the supreme Father (Hesiod, *Theogony* 149), and thus, the magical plants of the two traditions of shamanism merge. In effecting this reconciliation, Prometheus showed Zeus the way toward justice and the evolution of a better world. In return for his own freedom, Prometheus showed Zeus that the new

1. *Ambrosia* is etymologically a negative formation of *brotos* or 'mortal,' and hence a designation of the nourishment of immortals. *Nektar*, which often indicates the gods' drink, may be derived similarly from *nekus* or 'corpse,' plus a second element indicating 'against.' The word has also been interpreted as composed of an initial negative (*ne-*), plus *ktar*, which may be related to *kteres*, a synonym for *nekroi* or 'corpses' (thus, Hesychius). There is, however, no generally accepted etymology for *nektar*. See Chantraine.

order of Olympians would be eternal only if the supreme god avoided his own demise by passing on to a human the allotment of mortality that would have been his.[1]

In this manner, it became a human who was to bear the darker persona of the supreme Olympian, and it fell to the lot of mankind continually to reinstate the terms of the accord upon which the new order of the world depended. To the most sinister aspects of the chthonic deities, the sacrifice was typically performed at night in a pit in the ground, and the victim was often not considered an edible species and was simply left to rot. The Olympians, in contrast, were characteristically worshiped in the light of the sun, and, according to the procedure established by Prometheus, the inedible parts were burnt upon an altar for the gods, while humankind cooked and consumed the rest (Hesiod, *Theogony* 535 ff.).[2] In such sacrificial rituals, the magical power of fire transmuted the gods' portion into fragrant smoke, that would ascend to the heavens, where the Olympians, or the brighter aspects of the evolving chthonic gods, fed upon the destruction of their own primitive avatars. Thus they were strengthened in their separate estates, with humans as intermediaries to reinforce the advance of the Olympian age.

THARGELIA

The offerings of first fruits were presented to Apollo toward the beginning of June, on the seventh of the month Thargelion, which was so named after these *thargela*, the still unripe samples of the coming harvest. It is at this time that we may infer that the Hyperborean offering must have also arrived at Delos, amidst the offerings of sheaves from the other Greek cities. Because of the greater distance that it had traveled, however, it is improbable that the secret offering could have been cut at its supposed Hyperborean origin that spring. The sheaf may have been added later along the route, but the special Hyperborean plant

1. Thus, the nymph Thetis, by whom Zeus would have begot his own successor, was given in marriage to Peleus, and Zeus avoided that chthonic union, for Thetis is another of the abducted Persephone-like females, and Peleus is named for 'clay' or 'mud' (*pelos*). Achilles, who is born of the union, therefore, is the bearer of Zeus's mortal potential, a mortal son of an immortal father.

2. The verb for sacrifice when directed to a celestial god was typically *thuo* (or *thyo*) and meant basically 'to make smoke.' A different verb was used for chthonic sacrifice, *enagizo*, which implies involvement with 'pollution' and 'curse' by association with the dead. These distinctions in nomenclature and ritual for celestial and chthonic deities were not universally observed, but that is probably because it was possible to invoke the celestial aspect of a chthonic deity, like the paired Demeter and Persephone, or the more sinister persona of an Olympian.

would have to have been available earlier in the year. The arrival of all these *thargela* was the occasion for the great gathering of Ionian Greeks on Delos to celebrate their Apollo as an Olympian god with music and dance, these highest manifestations of the Hellenic culture inspired by him (Callimachus, *Hymn* 4. 300 ff.; Homeric hymn 3.146 ff.).[1]

During the entire period of this festival, the Greek cities were considered to be in a state of ritual purity, as befitted the god they were honoring at this Thargelia Festival. To maintain this purity, they had to avoid all contamination with blood pollution, for that would have involved them with the chthonic realm and endangered the persona of the deity they intended to invoke and nourish. Thus it was, for example, that Socrates remained so long in prison before his execution, for the Athenian ambassadors with the first fruits had already set sail for the sacred island just the day before the trial and condemnation, and during the state of purity, no public execution or blood offering could be made (Plato, *Phaedo* 58a ff.).

On the day before the Thargelia, however, as it appears to have been celebrated in the various Greek cities, the ultimate sacrifice to a chthonic deity had been made, a piacular victim 'upon whose flesh no one could feast' (Aeschylus, *Agamennon* 151). This was the offering of a human sacrifice, or, at least, the tradition of such an unspeakable offering. It is not clear from our evidence whether in the classical period this sacrifice was still enacted regularly, although both myth and archaeological finds testify to its occurrence in Minoan and later times. The human sacrificial offering may have been reserved by the classical Greeks for times of extraordinary peril, such as pestilence or war, when the more sinister aspect of the healing Apollo would need special appeasement. It is also possible that by the classical period the actual immolation had become a symbolic or token imitation. Despite our modern repugnance,[2] however, the ritual

1. It is unlikely that the great assembling of peoples at Delos (Homeric hymn 3.147 ff.) was separate from the Thargelia, for that would have required the mounting of two annual ambassades to the sacred island. See Farnell 4.289 ff.

2. S. Eitrem and J. Fontenrose in the *Oxford Classical Dictionary* (s. v. Sacrifice) discount the evidence as untrustworthy, probably arising from strangers' misunderstandings of hearsay reports of rites, and they cite the piacular killing of a criminal at Marseilles and the occasional slaughter of captives of war as hardly evidence for human sacrifice amongst the Greeks and Romans. It is true that a spurious work attributed to Plato (*Minos* 315 ff.) unequivocally states that human sacrifice was not the custom amongst Greeks, although it was amongst other peoples, but it is now clear that human sacrifice was once enacted amongst the Greeks also and that they maintained a remembrance of it in their mythical traditions and continued to enact various transmutations of the rite in classical times, although actual im-

was known even in classical Athens and perhaps practiced there (Aristophanes, *Knights* 1405; Lysias 6.53).

The victim was called the *pharmakós*, a scapegoat or atonement, but a word that in Greek is derived from the same root as 'drug' or *phármakon*.[1] A mythical tradition preserved an awareness of the obvious relationship between the two words, for a figure, personified as Pharmakos, was remembered as an ancient enemy of Apollo, another of the god's supplanted predecessors. Pharmakos was said to have incited the god's wrath by stealing his sacred drinking cups, for which reason the deity had him stoned to death (Istros, frg. 33 Jacoby; Suidas, s. v. Pharmakos). The myth is clearly aetiological for the *pharmakos* ritual, but it suggests an original controversy about the two traditions of shamanism and the magical plant.

Our earliest source for the manner of performance of this ritual at Athens is the third-century B.C. historian Istros (or Ister, as he is sometimes called), an Alexandrine pupil of Callimachus who collected information about cults and festivals in Athens during the early, mythological period. According to him two men were chosen as victims, one on behalf of the men, and the other on behalf of the women of the city (loc. cit.). We do not get further details until the third century A.D., but the similarity of the wording of the quoted material suggests that the original source was again Istros. The victim for the males, we are told, was draped with black figs, the other with white, and the two were called *subakkhoi*, a word whose etymology is unknown, probably assimilated from a pre-Hellenic language (Helladios, in Photius, *Bibliotheca* 534 Bekker). Apparently, moreover, the use of a male victim on behalf of the female populace was not always the custom, for we also hear of a pair of victims, a man and a woman (Hesychius, s. v. *pharmakoi*).

The occasion for the first offering of such *pharmakoi* was supposed to have dated back to Minoan times, when the Athenians were compelled by a plague to send seven males and seven females to die in the labyrinth at Knossos. Every year thereafter, the Athenians had sent the same tribute of human victims until they were finally released from this bloody obligation of appeasement

molation may, in most cases, have been avoided, or the victim chosen as being, for some reason, justifiably expendable.
The repugnance of modern scholarship to human sacrifice amongst the Greeks can be sensed from Wilamowitz-Möllendorff's attempt to emend Harpocration's testimony to read two 'rams' (*arnas*) for the two 'men' (*andras*) indicated as the sacrificial victims. See Paul Stengel (1887) 'Thusiai Aspondoi,' *Hermes* 22, 647.

1. Although the etymology of *pharmakon* is not clearly established, its relationship to *pharmakos* seems assured. See H. Frisk, *Griechisches etymologisches Wörterbuch* (Winter, Heidelberg 1954-1970).

when Theseus sailed as a victim to Crete and managed to slay the Minotaur. This tradition, like that of Pharmakos, similarly implies the transition from primordial to more civilized times, and Apollo, in his Delian purity as an Olympian again figures in a redemptive role, for Theseus, on his way back to Athens, transmuted the sinister and chthonic implications of the labyrinth into higher culture on the island of Delos as the intricate windings of a line-dance by the troop of victims he had rescued from the Minotaur. This was the aetiology of the first Thargelia, and the tradition was commemorated, as it was believed, by employing the very ship of Theseus, which had been preserved and perpetually restored as a precious antique, to convey the Athenian contingent to the Delian Thargelia with the city's first fruits in classical times (Plato, *Phaedo* 58a ff.).

Although the *pharmakoi* were human offerings, the manner of their immolation suggests that they were symbolic, in a broader sense, of the whole regenerative agrarian cycle. The victims, holding cheese and breads, were beaten seven times on their genitals with branches of the wild fig, squills, and other wild plants (Hipponax, frg. 7, 11 Diehl, quoted with amplification by Tzetzes, *Chiliades* 5.726; scholia to Aristophanes' *Knights* 1133). This symbolic seven fold flagellation is reminiscent of the whipping of adolescents at the Delian olive and identifies the victim's sexuality and its relationship to primitivism and the otherworld as the particular aspect of them that was offered in piacular sacrifice. The victims themselves were apparently selected for the same symbolism, for they were social and physical miscreants, chosen because of their extraordinary ugliness or low birth.

In preparation for their ordeal, they were glorified (Hipponax, frg. 13 Diehl, quoted with amplification by the scholiast to Lycophron's *Alexandra* 436), as befitted their sanctified role as the god's avatar. They were fed at public expense (Suidas, s. v. *pharmakous*) and purified by a vegetarian diet of bloodless foods, the cheese and breads that they were made to hold for the flagellation, as well as the wild fruits of the branches that were used as whips (Hipponax, frg. 9 Diehl). This appears to have been the custom also in the Greek colony of Marseilles, where the same ritual was still known in the fourth century A.D. (Servius, on Vergil's *Aeneid* 3.57). There, we are told, the victims were sumptuously maintained on such foods and luxuriously dressed.

Then, like the mythical Pharmakos, they were stoned to death, a form of execution that avoided incurring individual blood guilt. Their bodies were burnt with the wood of wild fruit trees, and their ashes were scattered to the winds, which took their spirits to the otherworld and spread their mortal remains upon the earth to enrich and fertilize it for the new growth of cultivated plants that they, as impersonations of the wild and primitive, liberated through their deaths (Tzetzes, *Chiliades* 5.736; scholia to Aristophanes' *Knights* 1133).

The Hyperborean offerings to the Delian Thargelia appear to be a transmutation or substitution for such *pharmakos* victims. It is for this reason, no doubt, that the Hyperborean maidens who were the first ambassadors to arrive in person with the secret offerings never returned to their far-off land, but were buried on Delos within the area of the sanctuary that was sacred to Artemis (Herodotus 4.34), a signal honor that was accorded them, despite the general prohibition against all contamination with funerary custom that prevailed otherwise at the sanctuary. The myth of their simple death glosses over the tradition of what was originally their sacrifice on the sacred island and thus protects the classical god from the sinister connotations of his more primitive persona as a chthonic deity.

According to Herodotus, however, these two maidens, with their male escorts, were actually not the first visitors from the Hyperboreans. They were said to have been preceded by two other girls, a doublet variant of the other myth.[1] They came from the Hyperboreans by the same route and at the same time as the pregnant Leto and brought with them thank-offerings for her easy delivery of the twins, the rebirth that gave them their classical personae. They too apparently died, or were sacrificed, on Delos and were buried and honored within the sanctuary. These Hyperboreans, according to another variant, were none other than the goddess of travail herself, who came to aid Leto in her labor, and the two traditions of primitive Apolline worship are transparent in the confusion about whether this goddess of travail actually came from the 'northern' Hyperboreans or, as some claimed, from Minoan Crete and the labyrinth that had claimed the Athenian victims up until the time of Theseus's triumphant visit to the sacred island after the death of the Minotaur (Pausanias 1.18.5).

The two commemorative graves of these two groups of Hyperborean visitors to Delos were ritually honored in classical times by rites of passage, for the maiden Hyperboreans were themselves symbolically the first fruits of pubes-

1. The names of all the girls are recorded, but there are variations concerning who was in which group, probably indicating that the two separate groups are doublet variants of the same tradition. The first visitors were Arge and Opis. The second ambassadors were either a group of three, named Oupis (a variant of Opis), Loxo and Hekaerge, or a group of two, like the first visitors, but named Hyperoche and Laodice. The names appear to be bynames or epithets of Artemis.

cence, originally offered to the chthonic persona of the god. Thus it was the custom for Delian maidens in classical times to make a substitute offering at pubescence, a lock of hair, wrapped about a spindle and placed upon the grave of the Hyperborean maidens when they themselves prepared for marriage. Similarly, pubescent males on the island would make a 'first fruit offering' of their facial hair, wrapping it about the shoot of some young plant (Callimachus, *Hymn* 4.296 ff.).

The other of these two graves on Delos, that of the Hyperboreans who aided Leto's delivery, was also honored ritually. Delian women, who, like the goddess, had given birth and passed beyond the threshold of maidenhood into matrimony, would collect the ashes from the sacrificial animals burnt upon the classical god's altar and scatter them upon the tomb of these Hyperboreans who had died so that the god could be born.

Apollo and Artemis, moreover, are frequently associated with rituals of human sacrifice in a Hyperborean context. The most interesting of these victims is Orion, who was associated with a pre-classical intoxicant, a predecessor of the Dionysian wine. Orion was the son-in-law of Oinopion, a primitive 'wine king',[1] who made him drunk and blinded him. Orion himself was said to have been born out of an oxhide upon which the gods Zeus, Poseidon, and Hermes had urinated, and his name was etymologically derived from this act of urination, *ourein* (Ovid, *Fasti* 5.495 ff.; Nonnos, *Dionysiaca* 13.96 ff.; Servius, on Vergil's *Aeneid* 1.535). He seems to have regained his sight through the aid of one of Hephaestus's Cyclopes and to have died at Artemis's hands when he tried to violate one of the maiden Hyperborean visitors to Delos at the time that the classical twins were born (Apollodorus 1.25-27).

Like all victims, the *pharmakos* ideally had to accept its fate. The Hyperboreans, themselves, were supposed to have enjoyed a blessed, long life, during which they too abstained from eating meat, living instead upon the fruits of trees (Hellanikos, frg. 96 Jacoby). At the end of their lives, they voluntarily offered themselves to death by jumping off a cliff (Pliny, *Natural History* 4.89; Mela 3.37). Such a leap off a cliff to one's voluntary death is well attested in Apolline ritual and mythical traditions.[2] Symbolically, it enacts the descent to the netherworld in the wind's embrace,[3] and Apollo himself was called Katai-

1. On the connotations of these mythical kings with names constructed upon the word for 'wine' (*oinos*), see C. Kerenyi, *The Heroes of the Greeks* (Thames and Hudson, London 1959) 113.

2. Farnell 4.274 ff.

3. Thus Oreithyia (see p. 222) was blown to her death off a mountaintop, in the rationalized version of the myth of her abduction by Boreas to the Hyperborean garden of Apollo.

basios, as the god of the descent, although the epithet could also be interpreted in a less sinister manner as the god who oversaw the return to one's country and homeland (scholia to Euripides' *Phoenician Women* 1408).

The most famous Apolline leap was the one from the Leucadian rock, the sheer limestone cliffs on the west coast of the island of Leukas in the Ionian Sea, off the coast of Acarnania. By one account, the priests of the god threw either themselves or some sacrificial victims off the rock into the sea (Photius, s. v. *Leukates*).[1] This so-called 'White Rock' was a particular topographical localization of another cliff, found only in the lands of myth, at the edge of the world and reputed to be an entrance to the country of dreams, sleep, and death, the gateway where the sun went down or rose again from its repeated passage through the abyss of night (Homer, *Odyssey* 24.9 ff.).[2] Typically, it was a wind that snatched its victims from that rock, and the mythical leap was located elsewhere as well, wherever the boundary between consciousness and unconsciousness was felt to lie. At Cape Leukas, however, the traditional concept was defined by the purificatory ritual of an annual sacrificial leap in honor of Apollo. The leap from the Leucadian cliffs was reputed to be a cure for intoxication and madness (Anacreon, frg. 31 Page) and even the poetess Sappho was supposed to have plunged there into the sea for love of Phaon (Menander, frg. 258 Koch), who is a doublet of Phaethon and hence a mortal son of his divine father, the sun-god Helius. In the case of Euripides' Silenos, who was the leader of the satyrs or primitive Dionysian spirits, this madness was a joyous affliction caused by drinking a potent drugged wine that came originally from a northern priest of Apollo (Euripides, *Cyclops* 412; Homer, *Odyssey* 9.196 ff.),[3] so that, as he says, he would gladly leave his life amongst the race of Cyclopes and leap from the Leucadian rock (Euripides, *Cyclops* 264 ff.). Since Aphrodite herself was supposed to have been the first to find this famous leap as a cure for her love of Adonis (Ptolemaios Chennos, in Photius's *Bibliotheca* 152f Bekker), it is clear that the tradition of the Leucadian rock implies not only the magical herb and the shaman's rapture to the otherworld, but also the transition from primitivism to the Olympian age, for the love-goddess Aphrodite was one of the forms in which the Earth Mother was assimilated as an Olympian, and Adonis, whose name appears

1. Farnell 4.431 emends 'them' (*autous*) to 'themselves' (*hautous*), an easy emendation (requiring only a change of breathing from smooth to rough or aspirate) that supplies an otherwise absent appropriate object for the verb in this context.

2. Gregory Nagy (1973) Phaethon, Sappho's Phaon, and the White Rock of Leukas, *Harvard Studies in Classical Philology* 77, 137-189.

3. The wine was called Maronites, after Maron, a priest of Apollo, and its extraordinary potency required twenty-fold dilution with water.

to be related to Semitic Adon or 'lord', was her dying consort, whose fate was symbolized in classical times in the withering pots of seedlings, the so-called Gardens of Adonis, that were mourned as a commemorative ritual by Greek women.[1]

In actual custom, each year at Leukas, it was an ancestral rite to throw some convicted criminal off the cliffs as a purificatory sacrifice to Apollo. The substitution of a criminal for the *pharmakos* victim in classical times was an appropriate transmutation of the original symbolism, for the adjudged criminality of the victim certified him as an antisocial and recidivous force within the civilized group. The god, however, was supposed to have been lenient to the sacrificial offering, who was said to sprout feathers during the descent and to be uplifted by birds, so that he would land safely in the shallow waters at the base of the cliffs (Strabo 4.5.2). We are reminded of the god's similar kindness to one of his own avatars, Kyknos, like the wolf and the Python, a primordial enemy, who used to slay pilgrims on their way to the Delphic sanctuary. Apollo turned him into the 'swan,' after which he was named, the god's own prophetic bird (Palaiphatos, *De Incredibilia* 12; Antoninus Liberalis, *Transformationes* 12.12). As part of the Leucadian rite, moreover, an ox was slaughtered and, like the human victim, not feasted upon, but left to rot and attract flies, which, after drinking the blood, were said to disappear (Aelian *De Natura Animalium* 11.8).

The White Rock, as a mythical idea, is probably just one of several attempts to locate in reality the 'White Island' of Leuke. Other topographical placements found it somewhere in the Black Sea (Pindar, *Nemea* 4.49; Euripides, *Andromache* 1262), and thus it was sometimes identified with an island lying before the estuary of the Danube, a place that became confused with the so-called Islands of the Blessed, where the gods of an earlier age presided over the souls of the departed. It was there that Kronos, the father and deposed predecessor of Zeus, was king, and like the other versions of the Hyperborean land, it was a magical garden where golden flowers grew upon resplendant trees and in the offshore shoals (Pindar, *Olympia* 2.68 ff.). The western gateway of the Hesperidean garden and the analogous Leucadian Rock thus had its antipodal counterpart in the blessed island glowing white in the light of the rising sun. It was to this eastern entrance that Orion was transported upon his death after his attempted violation of the Hyperborean maidens (Homer, *Odyssey* 5.121-124). The sacred island of Delos itself was so-called because of the way its barren coasts shone from a distance amidst the Cyclades in the light of the sun.

1. For the Adonis Festival and its botanic symbolism, see Marcel Detienne, *The Gardens of Adonis* (Humanities Press, New Jersey 1977, translated from the French edition of 1972).

SOMA

In Vedic traditions, the White Island can also be found. There it is called Súetadvīpa, and the paradise beyond the wind appears as Uttarakurus.[1] This is what would be expected, for the Indo-European tradition of shamanism can be traced in the other lands to which these peoples migrated. The ambrosia and nectar upon which the Olympians feasted is a Hellenic version of what in the Aryan or Indo-Iranian context was called Soma or haoma.[2] This is the original identity, or at least Sanskrit name, of the magical plant that grew in the gardens of paradise and marked the gateway to the 'northern' otherworld. It is this that is the object of the hero's quest, not only in Hellenic traditions, but also in the lore of their Anatolian neighbours, and Soma is an aspect of the atavistic personae of the classical gods. The concept of this magical food reached Greece not only, as in the Hyperborean traditions, along with the tribal migrations from central Asia, but also indirectly through dissemination and assimilation amongst the different peoples and cultures of Anatolia, where it was equated to their own versions of the shaman's plant.

Although the intoxicating properties of Soma were recalled in the oral poetry of the Indo-Iranians, numerous symbolic substitutes, which were not entheogenic, were commonly employed in the ritual that centered upon the preparation and drinking of the ceremonial potion. The reason for these substitutions seems to have been that the original plant, which was to be found in the homeland of the Indo-Europeans before their various migrations and whose attributes were preserved and perpetuated in the formulaic phrases of their oral poetic traditions, was no longer easily available in their new environments and had, with the course of time, lived on chiefly in the memory of the Brahmans and priests.

So too, the magical plant of the Hyperboreans became identified in Hellenic traditions with various substances that were, in one way or another, appropriate to the religious and symbolic context, but which did not share the original's physical properties for inducing mantic inspiration. Such was the case, as we have seen, with the *daphne* at Delphi and the olive at Olympia and Delos. Both are clearly not the plant actually recalled in the traditions of the Hyperborean

1. Ken Dowden (1979) Apollon et l'esprit dans la machine: Origines, *Revue des études Grecques*, 92, 293-318.

2. Fontenrose, 430, 549, comes to this conclusion on the basis of an extensive examination of the myth of the god or hero's combat with the primordial serpent monster in Mediterranean and Near-eastern cultures.

entheogen, which more poetically could also be metamorphosed into the golden fruit or flowers, subterranean honey, the Gorgon's head, or the creatures with a single eye.

It became, above all, the god's victim, to be appeased and offered in sacrifice, for the plant belonged to the wilderness that had preceded the growth and evolution of the superior Olympian age of assimilated and reconciled divinites who presided over the perfection of Hellenic culture. Thus it became also the *pharmakos* offering, either the actual giving of human lives or, as became increasingly appropriate to the god's own civilized persona, the token offering of the same. In this way, criminals were used for the annual leap at Leukas, or, as in Thessaly, the people promised each year to sacrifice 100 men, a full hecatomb, to Apollo Kataibasios and each year postponed the offering until the next (scholia to Euripides *Phoenissae* 1408). At Delphi, as we have seen, the Python was murdered again in sham. On Delos, the Hyperborean visitors were replaced by the symbolic flagellation at the sacred olive and, as elsewhere, by rites of passage at puberty, for the youthful and virgin persona has to die at adolescence to liberate the fertile adult, just as the god himself and his sister had grown to maturity only in the Hellenic age. As with their human devotees, so also in the agrarian cycle could the same token offering be made in the form of the botanic first fruits, given as piacular victims to assuage the honor of the primitive spirits who are again and again deposed in the arts of cultivation but whose chthonic beneficence is required if the crop is to grow to fruition.

DAPHNEPHORIA

The olive and the *daphne* were coupled in the Apolline ritual of the Daphnephoria or the 'bearing of the *daphne*.' Like the ritual of the *pharmakos*, it appears to have been an annual purificatory ceremony. It was performed in Boeotia each year (Pausanias 9.10.4), with a more elaborate performance of the ceremony every ninth year, like the Delphic Septeria (Proclus, *Chrestomathia* C. 26 = Photius, *Bibliotheca* p. 321 Bekker). In this ceremony, a log of olive wood was wreathed with *daphne* and various flowers. At its top was attached a bronze sphere, from which were suspended smaller balls, arranged around 365 purple garlands that encircled the middle of the log. The bottom of the log was clothed in a saffron *krokotos*, which was an effeminate robe commonly worn by Dionysus or by his devotees at his festivals. The *krokos* blossom, from which the saffron dye was prepared, itself had associations with the *pharmakos* offering to the pre-

Olympian Apollo,[1] and the entire Daphnephoria effigy seems to have been intended as a token representation of the primordial god or his scapegoat.

Consistant, however, with his newer, assimilated identity, as indicated by the botanic transmutations of the *daphne* and the olive, the bronze spheres did not represent the golden fruit of the Hyperborean tree, but were interpreted instead as symbolic of the celestial universe, the sun, moon and stars, with the garlands as an enumeration of the days of their annual course.

In place of the royal victim, who seems to have been the original sacrifice,[2] a handsome boy of noble ancestry, touching the effigy, was led in procession by his nearest male relative, who himself carried the decorated log. The boy followed like the god, wearing a golden crown and resplendant clothing that reached to his feet. Behind him came the rest of the procession, composed of maidens, holding suppliant branches and singing hymns. In this manner, they brought the sacred *daphne* to the god's temples.

THE SECRET OFFERING

Although, as we have seen, there were several plants associated symbolically with Apollo, the secret offering enclosed in the sheaf of wheat from the Hyperboreans was probably none of these commonly known, yet it would have had to display certain characteristics to suit the meaning of the Thargelia and the *pharmakos* offerings. Since two strains of shamanism were assimilated in the evolution of the classical god, a plant not known to the Indo-Europeans before they found it amongst the earlier Mediterranean peoples would not be a likely possibility, for although the Hyperboreans, as a metaphor, could be encountered wherever there was an entrance to the otherworld, the careful preservation of the route for the supposed transmission of the secret offering to Delos would indicate a pre-Hellenic plant originating on the forested slopes of the Altai Mountains, the 'northern' homeland of the Hyperboreans. For this reason, the olive is an unlikely candidate.

The token offerings of first fruits, moreover, were meant to liberate the coming harvest from the contamination of its own primitivism, and thus the secret offering should be characterized as the god's pre-classical avatar. The

1. In Euripides' *Ion*, the queen of Athens, in pre-Olympian times, conceives a child by the god in decidedly chthonic circumstances while gathering *krokos* blossoms.

2. Farnell 4.274 ff.

daphne, therefore, like the olive, would have the wrong symbolism, for they both signify the god's completed transmutation to Olympian status.

The most striking characteristic of the Hyperborean original, of course, is its properties as an entheogen. It should be a wild, northern plant, associated with Indo-European traditions, and since it was sent as a secret offering, we should expect that knowledge of its identity was restricted.

R. Gordon Wasson, working with the Sanskrit tradition of the *Ṛg Veda*, has postulated that the original identity of Soma in the homeland of the Indo-Europeans before their migrations into the Indus valley and the plateau of present-day Iran was a particular species of mushroom, *Amanita muscaria*, sometimes called the 'fly-agaric' in English. As would be expected, the Hellenic branch of these same peoples brought with them into the Greek lands a remembrance of a special symbolism for the fungi in religious contexts. Wasson and his colleagues have detected it in the religion of the Eleusinian Mysteries, as well as in the rituals of viticulture and its god Dionysus. We should expect, as well, to find this same fungal symbolism in the traditions of the secret Hyperborean offering, especially since that carefully perpetuated ritual, more than any other, preserved a mythical idea of the original Indo-European homeland and its native entheogen.

A mushroom, first of all, would have the perfect symbolism for its piacular role as a *pharmakos* offering. It was a wild plant, uncultivatable and belonging to the pre-agrarian, primordial world of hunter-gatherers. In the form of ergot, a fungus with fruiting bodies of the characteristic mushroom shape that is parasitic on various wild and cultivated grasses and grains, the mushroom actually blighted and poisoned the ripening harvest and was thought to pose a threat of regression for the whole evolutionary process that had yielded the edible foods and the progress of higher culture and civilization. Ergot was apparently felt to represent some aspect of Apollo's supplanted avatar, for he bore the epithet Erysibios (Strabo 13.1.64), literally the metaphor of the fungus as the reddening corruption or 'rust' (*erysibe*) upon the grain.[1]

1. It was an epithet that he shared with Demeter, who could be called Erysibe (*Etymologicum Gudianum* 210.25). She was the Mother Goddess in her Hellenic manifestation, assimilated to Olympian traditions as a sister of Zeus and the overseer of the cultivated grains. The same epithet also appears for Apollo in dialectal forms as Erethimios (*Sylloge Inscriptionum Graecarum* 724) and Erythibios (Strabo 13.1.64). If Erithios, a Cypriote epithet of the god, is also a dialectal variant (and not to be related instead to *erithos* or 'hired-servant'), there is an intriguing tradition that it was this Apollo Erithios who counseled Aphrodite to take the first sacrificial leap off the Leucadian Rock in order to assuage her yearning for Adonis (Ptolemaios Chennos, in Photios, *Bibliotheca* 152f Bekker).

This rust appears as the ingredient of a magical potion derived from a sacred tree with connotations of a fertility sacrifice and rite of pubescent passage in the mythical traditions about the seer Melampous, or 'blackfoot,' as his name implies. Melampous was the first prophet of Dionysian religion in Greece and was supposed to have learned divination from none other than Apollo himself. On the mainland near the Malaic Gulf, there was said to have been a king whose son was impotent. Melampous discerned that the boy's problem had been caused by the fact that he had witnessed a traumatic incident. He had seen his father gelding rams, and when the knife by chance had fallen close to him, he fled in terror, as well he might, for as the king's son, he was a likely candidate for the role of victim himself. The furious father, in his frustration, had thrust the knife into a sacred tree, where it had 'rusted,' the same metaphor in Greek, as in English, for the reddening corruption that also destroys iron through oxidation. Melampous was said to have cured the youth's impotency by administering a potion composed of the rust scraped from the blade (Apollodorus 1.9.12; scholia to Homer's *Odyssey* 281).

Ergot, moreover, is an entheogen, containing water-soluble alkaloids that are closely related to LSD. The Indo-European migrants would have first encountered the entheogenic ergot amongst the grain-growing peoples through whom they passed, and thus in the Greek branch as well as the Indian, one of the first surrogates for Soma would appear to have been fungal. It was used as a Hellenic substitute for Soma in the potion that was drunk by the initiates at the Greater Eleusinian Mystery in order to induce the communal shamanic experience of a descent and return from the otherworld. Its entheogenic properties, furthermore, were apparently responsible, according to mythical tradition, for the Apolline art of divination. Apollo himself was supposed to have been taught clairvoyance by a certain Glaucus (Nicander, frg. 2 Schneider), who seems to have acquired the ability when he discovered the magical properties of a wild grass, *Paspalum distichum*, a plant commonly infested with a species of ergot that, unlike the others, contains pure, uncontaminated entheogenic alkaloids.[1] It was supposed to grow on the Islands of the Blest, that Hyperborean paradise, where the deposed Kronos was said to have planted it, and it was responsible for the daily flight of the horses of the Sun from the White Island to the White Island (Alexander Aetolus, p. 465 Rose, quoted in Athenaeus 7.296 ff.). Glaucus was also said to have been the father of the Cumaean Sibyl (Vergil, *Aeneid* 6.36), an Apolline prophetess, like the Delphic

1. Hofmann, *Road to Eleusis*.

Pythoness, who was abducted and cursed by the god, like another Cassandra or Daphne (Ovid, *Metamorphoses* 14.130 ff.).

Ergot, however, would tend to be associated primarily with an agrarian, grain-growing people, and hence with the Lycian version of Apollo. At the Eleusinian Mystery, it had such a connotation, for it represented the domestication of the wilder fungi, just as wine, too, is a fungal cultivation yielding an entheogenic potion. At the Greater Mystery, it was the culmination of an initiation that had begun with a ceremony involving the hunt for a wild fungus or its surrogates at the Lesser Mystery, and symbolically it reconciled the Indo-European shamanic heritage with what were originally pre-Hellenic agrarian rites. Thus, it is interesting that amongst the several mythical figures who bore the name of Glaucus, there was one who was a brother of the Minotaur on Crete. He too was prophetic, and was resuscitated by a magical herb after he drowned in a vat of honey (Apollodorus 1.96 ff.). Another Glaucus was actually a Lycian in the war at Troy.

The fungus of the Hyperborean homeland, in contrast, would have come, at least so it was supposed, from the wooded slopes of the Altai Mountains, where conifers and birch abound, an environment, therefore, where *Amanita muscaria* is commonly found. Presumably, it would have fruited in the autumn and been preserved, as is usual for *Amanita*, by drying so that it could be conveyed over the long journey, wrapped in straw, to arrive on Delos in late spring along with the other offerings of first fruits. Is there anything, we must now ask, in the Apolline traditions that might suggest that this was the identity of the secret plant?

The one-eyed Arimaspeans, who, as we have seen, were either just another name for the Hyperboreans or, as a separate people, were the first intermediaries in the transmission of the subterranean gold that was mined by the griffins, are a personification of one of the attributes of Soma as the 'single eye'. So too, therefore, are the Cyclopes, whose murder as primitive surrogate occasioned Apollo's expiatory sojourn amongst the people of his 'northern' homeland. There were two versions of these Cyclopes, and the Anatolian ones probably arose from a separate dissemination of the metaphor through Asia Minor, where the later discredited Lycian Telchines display the same attribute as their evil eye. These one-eyed creatures are a variant of another attribute of Soma as the figure with a single foot, a characteristic of a supposed race of people called the Shade-foots, who came from the Indus valley and were fancifully implicated, according to the comedian Aristophanes (*Birds* 1553 ff.), in a profane celebration of the Lesser Eleusinian Mystery. It appears that the Arimaspeans may have come from the same general region, for Herodotus's supposed Scythian etymology of their name is probably not correct, but they were really an Iranian tribe, called the Argempaioi or Argimpasoi.[1] All these fabulous creatures can be traced to fungal manifestations and testify strongly that it was some kind of mushroom, if not actually *Amanita*, that was originally the Hyperborean plant. In its Hesperidean version, the plant bears still another attribute of Soma as the 'mainstay of the sky',[2] which is the role that Atlas plays as 'pillar of heaven' in the west (Aeschylus, *Prometheus* 351), just as his Titanic brother in the east, Prometheus, when presented as a Shade-foot, impersonates the sacred plant as a 'parasol,' which is the Sanskrit word for 'mushroom.' The single-footed trait can also be seen in certain Greek heroes who, like Oedipus, have mythical roles as Apolline surrogates.[3]

It is also significant that only three mythical figures were said actually to have gone to the land of the Hyperboreans, and all three came from the region of Mycenae. These were Perseus, Heracles, and the ecstatic, fly-bitten heifer-maiden, Io, although she, unlike the other two, got only to the edge of the Hyperborean land. Melampous, who devised the rust potion, also was involved in the lore of Mycenae, and the Lycian Glaucus was a grandson of another figure, probably a doublet of Perseus,[4] who played a role in the same traditions. The ancient foundations of that city were supposedly built by the Cyclopes, and it was named, as it was claimed, after the 'mushroom' or *mykes* that Perseus picked at the site (Pausanias 2.16.3). The name of the city is a feminine plural, like Athens (Athenai) and Thebes (Thebai), perhaps indicating that, in fact, the word

1. Dowden, Deux Notes 492.

2. Wasson, *Soma* 47-48. Prometheus, Atlas's brother, is also involved with the attributes of Soma, for the divine plant is metaphorically 'fire' and is often identified with Agni, the god of fire (*Ibid.* 39 ff.). Soma is also the 'sun,' which travels repeatedly between the two tormented Titanic brothers (*Ibid.* 37-39). It is also described with the same adjective as the Sun's horses, which in Greek traditions, as we have seen, graze upon *Paspalum*, the Mediterranean transmutation of the entheogen.

3. On the botanical nature of the single-footed figure in Greek myth, see Lowell Edmunds (1981) The Cults and the Legend of Oedipus, *Harvard Studies in Classical Philology* 85, 221-238.

4. This was Bellerophon, who was sent to Lycia by king Proetus to be killed by the father of Proetus's Lycian wife. On Bellerophon as a doublet of Perseus, see Kerenyi, *Heroes* 79 ff., who points out that Bellerophon's name is a transparent epithet for the 'killer of the monster' and that only Bellerophon and Perseus rode on Perseus's magical horse Pegasus. It was Bellerophon who brought seven Lycian Cyclopes to build the fortress of Tiryns in the Mycenaean kingdom, whereas Perseus picked a mushroom at Mycenae, which was also a Cyclopean fortress.
Bellerophon, like so many other heroes, was a single-footed figure. When, like another Phaethon, he tried to ascend the heavens on his flying horse, it was driven mad by the gadfly and he fell into a thorn-bush and was thereby inflicted with his botanic stigma of lameness.

is not Indo-European, but from one of the pre-Hellenic languages. The same conclusion seems indicated by the naming of these cities in a matrilineal fashion after the patron goddesses, represented presumably by the priestesses or women of the city. It is equally significant, however, that the Indo-Europeans, in imposing their rule upon the pre-existent city, interpreted its name in terms of their own sacred plant, and probably equated the chthonic Cyclopes with their Hyperborean doubles.

Still more explicit is the depiction of Perseus's journey that we see on a fourth-century B.C. *amphora* from southern Italy.[1] The artist followed the tradition that confused the Hesperides and their golden fruit with the Hyperborean garden. He shows us Perseus in the far-off land as he beheads the Medusa, the primordial queen who is a manifestation of the Great Goddess to whom the Lycian god was consort. In displacing her from her former role, Perseus, as a son of the Olympian Zeus, founded the Indo-European dynasty at Mycenae. Clearly identified as the fruit of the Medusa's magical tree on the vase painting is the mushroom.

If the Hyperborean plant, then, was, by tradition at least, a mushroom, was it *Amanita*? Specific traits of *Amanita muscaria* are retained in the traditions of the Apolline surrogates. Thus, Orion had a bizarre begetting out of urine. It is perhaps significant that one of the properties of the *Amanita* entheogen is its ability to pass through the body without being entirely metabolized, a fact that was utilized in Siberian rites in modern times and that seems to persist amongst the Brahmans of India in the special healthful properties they accord to the drinking of urine. This property of *Amanita* may first have been observed, as Wasson has suggested, in the northern forests and tundra, where it is commonly known that reindeer exhibit a profound addiction for *Amanita muscaria* and for human urine, particularly if impregnated with the entheogen. Both, as the folk know, drive the herds of reindeer mad, and, in actual fact, the mushroom affects the animals in the same way as humans. Did this tradition persist in the association of the Hyperborean plant with the golden reindeer of Artemis, an animal that the classical Greeks could never have seen in their Mediterranean environment? So too, we should consider Mycenae's traditions of maddened heifers, both Io and the daughters of Proetus. It has not been determined whether *Amanita* affects cattle as it does reindeer, although the ani-

1. Pergamonmuseum, East Berlin, Staatliche Museen zu Berlin, Antiken-Sammlung, inv. no. F 3022. Published as plate 8 in Wasson et al., *Road to Eleusis*.

mals do eat the mushrooms.[1] In the Mediterranean lands, where *Amanita* cannot be expected to be found, cattle do, however, become profoundly inebriated upon the ergot of *Paspalum distichum*, the plant that Kronos sowed in the Islands of the Blessed and fed to the horses of the Sun.

The entheogen of *Amanita* also exerts a strong attraction for flies, hence the mushroom's common name of 'fly-agaric.' Flies are attracted by the mushroom's juice and rendered senseless and immobile, so that in European lore, the plant has been sometimes considered an effective means of controlling the insect. This characteristic of the plant may have determined the belief that the sacrificed victim at the Leucadian Rock was supposed to rid the populace of flies. Like the agaric, Apollo too was a 'flycatcher,' for he bore the epithet of Muiagros (Aelianus, *De Natura Animalium* 11.8).[2]

The color of the sacred plant in Greek traditions, moreover, appears to have fallen within the 'yellow-orange crimson-purple' part of the spectrum (Pindar, *Olympia* 6.55), a range represented botanically by the tawny juice of *Amanita* and the purple of *Claviceps purpurea* or ergot.

If it was an *Amanita* that actually arrived from the supposed Hyperboreans as their secret offering of first fruits, we can only speculate as to what would have been done with it on Delos. It may have simply been placed upon the Hyperborean grave as a commemoration of the transmuted identity of the god, something, no doubt, that would have been known by very few. It is, however, also possible that the plant figured in the functioning of the oracle on Delos, for there was one, although little is known of it and it never achieved the notoriety and esteem of the Delphic Pythoness (Homeric hymn 3.81), perhaps because on Delos, that archaic aspect of the god was so overshadowed by his Olympian presence. It would be all the more important, therefore, to have maintained some honored role for the deposed persona. It is in that context that we must understand the tradition of the secret offering.

1. Wasson, *Soma* 74-75. Metaphors of cattle are also attributes of Soma, which can be described as an 'udder' that yields the entheogenic milk and as a 'bellowing bull,' the latter being apparently also a characteristic of the mushroom that Perseus picked at Mycenae. The bull is the commonest metaphor for Soma, and this manifestation of the sacred plant may underlie the tradition that Zeus, in establishing European civilization, abducted the Anatolian Europa by appearing to her in the form of a bull that breathed upon her the inspiration of the flower he had grazed upon.

2. Farnell, 4, reference 275b, suggests that the epithet may indicate Apollo. Muiagros is also attested for an otherwise unknown Elean god (Pliny, *Natural History* 10.75) and a 'hero' in Arcadia (Pausanias 8.26.7). It is not certain that it is, in fact, an epithet of Apollo, himself, but that is only to be expected if it indicates one of the most secret aspects of his displaced primitive persona.

REFERENCES

Citations of ancient authors mentioned in the text and notes refer to the works in the original languages. The numerical references indicate the traditional subdivisions (such as book, chapter, paragraph, verse, *etc*) as established by the first printed edition. It is customary for all subsequent editions and translations to preserve the same numbering, and thus, except where otherwise indicated (as in the case of fragments of lost works), any edition or translation should contain the citation. Editions of fragments usually include a concordance for previous numberings.

NOTE ON THE ESSAYS IN THIS BOOK

Chapter 1 appears here for the first time. All the other essays have been published elsewhere, as follows:

Chapter 2, also written by me, first appeared as 'Lightning-bolt and Mushrooms: an essay in early cultural exploration', a contribution to a volume entitled, '*For Roman Jakobson: Essays on the occasion of his sixtieth birthday*', published 11 October 1956, by Mouton, in The Hague. This was my first publication in ethnomycology. It now appears in revised form.

Chapter 3, by Professor Stella Kramrisch, 'The *Mahāvīra* Vessel and the Plant *Pūtika*', was published in the *Journal of the American Oriental Society*, Vol. 95, Number 2, April-June 1975.

Chapter 4, 'The Last Meal of the Buddha', written by me, also appeared in the *Journal of the American Oriental Society*, Vol. 102, Number 4, October-December 1982.

Chapter 5, by Jonathan Ott, appeared first in the Harvard *Botanical Museum Leaflets* in the fall of 1983, Vol. 29, No. 4

The three Chapters 6, 7, and 8, by Professor Carl A. P. Ruck, all appeared first in the *Journal of Ethnopharmacology*, Lausanne, as follows:

Mushrooms and Philosophers, 4 (1981) pp 179-205

The Wild and the Cultivated: Wine in Euripides' *Bacchae*, 5 (1982) pp 231-270

The Offerings from the Hyperboreans, 8 (1983) pp 177-207

R. G. W.